The
PRACTICES
of CHRISTIAN
PREACHING

ESSENTIALS for *EFFECTIVE* *PROCLAMATION*

JARED E. ALCÁNTARA

Baker Academic
a division of Baker Publishing Group
Grand Rapids, Michigan

© 2019 by Jared E. Alcántara

Published by Baker Academic
a division of Baker Publishing Group
PO Box 6287, Grand Rapids, MI 49516-6287
www.bakeracademic.com

Paperback edition published 2024
ISBN 978-1-5409-6902-6

Printed in the United States of America

The Library of Congress has cataloged the hardcover edition as follows:
Names: Alcántara, Jared E., 1979– author.
Title: The practices of Christian preaching : essentials for effective proclamation / Jared E. Alcántara.
Description: Grand Rapids, MI : Baker Academic, a division of Baker Publishing Group, 2019. | Includes bibliographical references and index.
Identifiers: LCCN 2018059469 | ISBN 9780801098666 (cloth)
Subjects: LCSH: Preaching.
Classification: LCC BV4211.3 .A42255 2019 | DDC 251—dc23
LC record available at https://lccn.loc.gov/2018059469

To my daughters:

Maya, Liliana, and Evelyn

May the light of Christ burn brightly in you
and through you to others.

Contents

Acknowledgments   vii

Introduction   1

1. Preach Christian Sermons   11

2. Preach Convictionally   41

3. Preach Contextually   73

4. Preach Clearly   101

5. Preach Concretely   131

6. Preach Creatively   155

Conclusion   185

Bibliography   193

Index   209

Acknowledgments

Many of the concepts and frameworks in this project originated in an Introduction to Preaching class I taught in the fall of 2013 at Primitive Christian Church, a Latinx Protestant church in New York City. That is to say, the seeds took root some years ago. Thank you to the thirteen students who interacted with me on this material in its roughest and most untested version, and thank you to the many students (you know who you are) who have helped me to hone, clarify, and improve this material over time. You have taught *me* more than you realize.

Although most of the content in this book is new, some sections have been adapted from papers that I have delivered at academic meetings or articles that I have published. Some of my discussions concerning Pixar Animation Studios in my chapters on clarity and creativity have been adapted from an article that I published in *Practical Matters* in 2015, titled "Fail Better: Or, What Can Teachers of Preaching Learn from Improvisational Performers and from Pixar?" Also, some sections from my chapter on contextualization have been adapted from a paper that I presented at the Annual Meeting of the Academy of Homiletics in 2016, titled "Teaching Contextual Responsiveness in a Preaching Classroom," and another paper that I presented at the Annual Meeting of the Evangelical Homiletics Society in 2017 titled "Sermons with Local Soil: Cultivating Contextually Responsive Preachers." I am indebted to Paul Myrhe and my friends at the Wabash Center for Teaching and Learning for their willingness to fund a five-week special project that I conducted in the summer of 2016 on how to teach contextualization in a preaching classroom. Their support gave me the time and space to think, write, collaborate with other scholars, and test my ideas in homiletics classrooms during the 2016–17 school year. Finally, some sections from my chapter on creativity have been adapted from a paper that I delivered at the Annual Meeting of the Academy of Homiletics in 2018 titled "Teaching Students How to Cultivate Creative Environments."

I would be remiss if I did not express my appreciation to colleagues at two different institutions. Thank you to President David Dockery, Dean Graham Cole, and the board of regents for approving my sabbatical for school year 2017–18 when I was still teaching at Trinity Evangelical Divinity School, where I served from 2014 to 2018. My sabbatical created much-needed time and space to finish this project. Thanks also to Peter Cha, who encouraged and strengthened me as a mentor, and to Greg Scharf, my friend and colleague in homiletics when I was at Trinity, who ensured that my classes and other responsibilities were covered when I was on sabbatical. I would also like to thank Dean Todd Still and my colleagues in homiletics, Joel Gregory and Scott Gibson, who serve alongside me now at Baylor University's George W. Truett Theological Seminary, where I started teaching in 2018. I am grateful for their ongoing support, friendship, feedback, and encouragement, and I am blessed by the ongoing collegiality and friendship that I enjoy with colleagues on the faculty at Truett.

I also owe a debt of gratitude to two granting agencies whose support helped bring this project to completion. The videography for this project was supported in part by funds from the university research committee and the vice provost for research at Baylor University. Thank you to our videographer, Matthew Aughtry, who worked tirelessly to record, edit, and produce the excellent video content that supplements this book. A Spanish language edition of *The Practices of Christian Preaching* is planned for release at a later date and is to be supported in part by the Foundation for the Advancement of Christianity. Thank you to Burton Patterson, the foundation's director, who caught the vision for a multilingual resource and supported that vision.

Thank you to the entire team at Baker Academic. This book would not have been possible without your willingness to dream big at the beginning and provide support along the way! I especially want to thank Jim Kinney, Jeremy Wells, Christina Jasko, Julie Zahm, Brandy Scritchfield, and the many others who believed in this project from its inception in 2016, partnered with me to make it better, or provided much-needed help over a three-year journey. Thanks also to Pablo Jiménez and Thomas G. Long for reading drafts of this book and providing excellent feedback.

To the four excellent homileticians who collaborated with me—Jerusha Matsen Neal, Ahmi Lee, Kenyatta R. Gilbert, and Matthew D. Kim—your expertise, wisdom, insight, and investment made this resource better because of your involvement in it. I have so much respect, appreciation, and admiration for all of you. The academy and the church are better served because of your presence and ministry in both spaces.

Last but most certainly not least, I would like to thank my family, first and foremost my wife Jennifer, who, without a doubt, stands alone atop the list of those without whom this book would not be possible. Your sacrificial love, patience, cheerleading, and support helped me get through the long hours required for a multi-phase project like this one to come to fruition. I love you, respect you, and appreciate you! Thanks also to my parents—José and Susan—to my siblings, and to my extended family. I see the love and support you provide, and I do not take it for granted. I give thanks for it.

I dedicate this book to my three daughters: Maya, Liliana, and Evelyn. My prayer for you remains the same, that someday each one of you would become an *eshet chayil*—that is, a woman of valor (Ruth 3:11) whose strength of character, courageous resilience, godly leadership, and bold action bless those around you and change the world.

Introduction

What does Charlie Parker have to do with preaching? The answer might surprise you. Parker rose to fame in the jazz music world in the late 1930s and, with Dizzy Gillespie, pioneered a new sound known as bebop. According to jazz historian Thomas Larson, "Charlie Parker's legacy continues to shape jazz. It is almost impossible to escape his influence."[1] Some claim that Parker is the greatest jazz musician who ever lived. On occasion, if a jazz musician from a country outside the United States performs boundary-crossing music, an expert might refer to that person as "the Charlie Parker of [insert nation here]."

At first glance, the *differences* between Parker and preachers stand out more than the similarities. Parker hung out in jazz clubs. Preachers hang out in churches. Based on what we know from biographies, Parker would not have liked being associated with preachers; he made his distrust of organized religion widely known. Preachers have devoted their lives to Christian service. Parker struggled with alcoholism and frequent heroin use. Preachers tend toward piety. He died at the age of thirty-four and had so damaged his body that the coroner initially thought he was between fifty and sixty. Some of my preacher friends only use Christian-approved cuss words on the basketball court. You get the point. Despite the many differences, one similarity in particular brings the connection between Parker and preaching into focus, one point of convergence that can easily be overlooked. What does Charlie Parker have to do with preaching? In a word: *practice*.

Parker launched his career playing jazz in nightclubs in Kansas City at the age of sixteen or seventeen, and, at least at the very beginning, he

---

1. T. Larson, *History and Tradition of Jazz*, 127.

1

Figure I.1. Charlie Parker

majored in zeal and minored in skill. He barely kept up with the career musicians on the stage, and it was clear to everyone that he was an amateur, a
boy among men. Imagine trying your luck as a professional ballet dancer
on a Friday night at Carnegie Hall in New York City or attempting to shoot
three-pointers in an NBA Finals game and you will have some sense of what
Parker was up against at the beginning.

As the story goes, one night in the spring of 1937, Parker tried his best to
play the saxophone at a jam session in the Reno Club in Kansas City. The
guest star at the club that night was Jo Jones, a drummer for Count Basie's
Orchestra, one of the great swing bands in the United States. When Jones
heard Parker that night, he thought Parker was so bad that he stopped playing the drums mid-song and threw a cymbal at Parker's feet from across the
stage, a not-so-subtle hint that the time had come for him to make his exit.[2]
Parker felt humiliated and, at that moment, he had to make a choice—quit
playing jazz altogether or get better. If he wanted to improve, the profession-
als told him, he had to "woodshed"—a term that jazz musicians like to use
as a noun and a verb. To woodshed means to practice with such relentless-

2. See Fordham, "A Teenage Charlie Parker Has a Cymbal Thrown at Him"; T. Larson,
History and Tradition of Jazz, 127.

ness and tenacity that everything else revolves around getting better—it is a complete overhaul of one's priorities. The term traces back to the idea of locking yourself in a woodshed, practicing your instrument for hours, and not coming out until you demonstrate exponential improvement. If a jazz musician tells someone "Go in the woodshed a little bit" or "Spend some more time woodshedding," that is code language for "Put some *real* practice in if you expect to get better."[3]

We do not know if Parker locked himself in an actual woodshed—that part of the story just might be apocryphal—but we *do* know that the cymbal-throwing incident changed the trajectory of his life. Put simply, he decided to practice. Just a few months later, in the summer of 1937, he played almost nightly with the George E. Lee Band as they toured the Ozarks (a mountainous region of Arkansas, Missouri, Oklahoma, and Kansas). Whenever he was not on stage, he spent almost all of his spare time woodshedding—that is, practicing his instrument in a focused and deliberate way. He also kept at it when he returned to Kansas City at the end of that summer.

A pianist and band leader named Jay McShann recounts the first time he heard Parker's unique sound: "So I walked up to Charlie after he finished playing and I asked him, I said, 'Say man,' I said, 'where are you from?' I said, 'I thought I met most of the musicians around here.' Well, he says, 'I'm from Kansas City.' But he says, 'I've been gone for the last two or three months. Been down to the Ozarks woodshedding.'" In 1954, when a fellow saxophonist named Paul Desmond interviewed him about that time period, Parker told him, "I used to put in at least 11 to 15 hours a day. . . . I did that for over a period of three or four years."[4]

Practice. For some of us it may seem odd to think of preaching this way, as a craft that one must practice. Perhaps it feels too human centered, technique based, even formulaic. Popular sayings like "Practice makes perfect" or "You win the game during practice" make sense when someone is talking about music, dance, sports, or academics, but something in us resists the idea of practicing sermons. If we focus too much attention on the *how*, will we not lose the *what* and the *who* of the sermon? Preaching is supposed to be a spiritual gift, a "divine charism" as the theologians like to say.

Why should we practice? We will overtake a few hurdles when we remember what should drive our desire to improve. When we reflect on what preaching is and how preaching works, our motivation to practice should increase rather than decrease. Put simply, we practice because our motivation is grounded in

3. Berliner, *Thinking in Jazz*, 54.
4. Vitale, "Birth of Bird."

gospel reality—we love the God of the gospel and love to preach the gospel of God. We do not practice to curry favor with God or because of selfish ambition or because we long to be the center of attention. We grow as preachers because we have been called by God and because a task as noble as preaching should bring out the best in us.

Those who write introductory homiletics textbooks do not typically appeal to Romans 12:18 to make a case for preaching, but I suppose there is a first time for everything. The apostle Paul writes, "If it is possible, as far as it depends on you, live at peace with everyone." Note especially the first two phrases: "If it is possible" and "as far as it depends on you."

Surely preaching does not "depend" on us, does it? On the one hand, preaching does not depend on us at all. God offers preaching to us as a means of grace, a divine gift through which human words re-present the Word of God in time and space. When it comes to the effects of preaching—the outcomes—only God has the power to turn hearts of stone into hearts of flesh. Only God makes dry bones live. God depends on us about as much as a parent depends on a newborn. On the other hand, God does "depend" on us if, by that word, we mean that God entrusts to us a message and a ministry in which we have agency. When parents tell a teenager, "I am depending on you," it usually means that they believe in them and that they trust them, but that they also expect them do their part when it comes to what is expected of them. Consider Paul's statement once more. Even though God alone has the power to bring about total and lasting peace among people and between communities, nevertheless, Paul writes, "If it is possible, as far as it depends on you . . ." For reasons that God only knows, God grants a surprising amount of agency to those who preach. Put simply, God wills to preach through preachers. William H. Willimon writes, "What amazes faithful preachers is not that we have managed to come up with words about God but rather that God has come up with words for us."[5] How strange that God would transform sinful preachers into news anchors for the gospel of Christ.

But are preachers really supposed to woodshed like Charlie Parker did? Just as in other areas of our lives, we get better at preaching when we practice. If you want to know how much practice matters to proficiency, just ask a high-school Spanish teacher how much language students will lose after graduation if they do not continue speaking it and improving at it. The truth is, we lose proficiency in *anything* we do not practice; our proficiency at the

---

5. Willimon, *How Odd of God*, 8–9. Philip Yancey writes, "In an awesome act of self-denial, God entrusted his reputation to ordinary people." *Disappointment with God*, 162.

task weakens over time in much the same way that a muscle weakens without exercise. Practice may not make us perfect preachers, but it can make us better preachers.

The central claim of this book is that *preachers who cultivate life-giving preaching habits through deliberate practice will enhance their proficiency, grow in their commitment, and flourish in their homiletical ministry.* In the chapters that follow I will recommend five practices in particular, which I will outline shortly. But in a book focused so heavily on practice(s), I should offer a few caveats before proceeding.

First, I use the phrase "deliberate practice" intentionally, as deliberate practice means something different than normal practice, and I also want to signal to readers that I am *not* adding my voice to contemporary conversations on Christian practices in theology. According to K. Anders Ericsson, one of the leading researchers on practice and performance, a person must practice *in a certain way* in order to improve. Most of us make the mistake of assuming that "someone who has been driving for twenty years must be better than someone who has been driving for five."[6] Not necessarily. According to Ericsson and his colleague Robert Pool, "Research has shown that, generally speaking, once a person reaches that level of 'acceptable' performance and automaticity, the additional years of 'practice' don't lead to improvement. If anything, the doctor or the teacher or the driver who's been at it for twenty years is likely to be a bit worse than the one who's been doing it for only five, and the reason is that these automated abilities gradually deteriorate in the absence of deliberate efforts to improve."[7]

So if you have preached two times, it does not mean that you cannot preach, and if you have preached for twenty years, it does not mean that you can. Preachers must practice in *a certain way* in order to improve, regardless of how many sermons they have preached. "Generally the solution is not 'try harder' but rather 'try differently.'"[8] To engage in *deliberate* practice, Ericsson states, one must ascribe to at least four commitments, whether the task is driving, medicine, dancing, or preaching. One needs well-defined and specific goals, focused attention, a consistent feedback loop, and a willingness to get out of one's comfort zone.[9] This project prioritizes these commitments, but it does so in a more tacit manner through embedding them in book chapters, video discussions, sermon excerpts, and learning activities. I have structured this

---

6. Ericsson and Pool, *Peak*, 13.
7. Ericsson and Pool, *Peak*, 13.
8. Ericsson and Pool, *Peak*, 19.
9. Ericsson and Pool, *Peak*, 15–22. For more on deliberate practice, see also Ericsson, "Influence of Experience," 685–705; Ericsson, *Road to Excellence*.

project in such a way as to give you as many opportunities as I can to "try differently'" rather than "try harder."

Second, this book's approach to deliberate practice places it outside of the typical approaches that one finds in introduction to preaching books. Instead of following the standard formula of presenting readers with a method-centered, single author, monocultural, monolingual, text-based approach, it sets forth a practice-centered, intentionally collaborative, strategically diverse, consciously multilingual (English and Spanish versions), technologically interactive approach. Because I have organized the book's chapters around practices, one will not find the same organization of material that one usually finds in a typical book on preaching. I have not written separate chapters on reading Scripture for preaching, form, genre, structure, preparation, or delivery. No doubt all of these subjects matter and should receive adequate attention when one is learning how to preach. There are already many excellent homiletics books that follow the typical format. Perhaps I will publish another book someday that structures its content according to these categories. Perhaps not. I have woven some (but not all) of these themes into this book but also want to emphasize to the reader that I have adopted a different organizational framework. This strategy attempts to engage the teaching and learning needs that are emerging in diverse twenty-first-century preaching classrooms, and it also represents a logical outworking of the dispositional convictions and pedagogical recommendations that I laid out in my first book, *Crossover Preaching.*[10]

Students who read this book will have opportunities to learn about each of the five practices that I recommend, to see and hear audio and video clips of sermons, to engage with the video contributions of the collaboration team, and to take advantage of individual and group learning activities in each chapter through the companion website: **www.PracticesofChristianPreaching.com**.

Third and finally, *what* we preach matters, not just *how* we preach. As St. Augustine reminds us, "There is a danger of forgetting what one has to say while working out a clever way to say it."[11] Those who preach are called to engage in the practice of *Christian* preaching. Just as a builder cannot build a house without making sure that solid foundations are laid beforehand, so also a preacher cannot build a strong and abiding preaching ministry without building it the right way, for the right reasons, and with the right foundations.

In chapter 1, I explain why we should preach *Christian* sermons rather than the many pseudo-gospels that we are sometimes tempted to preach. Then, in

---

10. See Alcántara, *Crossover Preaching.*
11. Book IV, 11–12 in Augustine, *On Christian Teaching,* 103.

chapters 2–6, I recommend five deliberate practices designed to help preachers cultivate life-giving habits that enhance proficiency, grow commitment, and lead to homiletical flourishing. The practices that I will propose are *conviction, contextualization, clarity, concreteness,* and *creativity.* All five begin with the same letter in English and in Spanish which I hope will make them easier to learn and remember. The shorthand I use for them is the Five Cs. Think of these practices not so much as constitutive of a method you must master but as healthy habits you can implement over time. They invite you to pursue a "growth mindset" over a "fixed mindset" when it comes to your development as a preacher.[12] Here is a brief summary of each practice.

Preach Convictionally: Since God sees fit to preach through preachers, we foreground conviction inside and outside of the pulpit. We watch out for complacency and indifference in ministry and pursue life-giving habits that promote health and prevent homiletical burnout.

Preach Contextually: We preach to a particular group of people at a particular point in time. We consider what it sounds like to preach to the community where we are, to embrace the uniqueness of the place where God has called us to be, and to resist the dangers of undercontextualizing and overcontextualizing.

Preach Clearly: As the old saying goes, "A mist in the pulpit is a fog in the pew." If we do not have clarity on what we want to say and how we want to say it, how can we expect others to understand us? We practice clarity through concise exegesis, accessible language, a clear main idea, and commitment to brevity.

Preach Concretely: Many of us preach in abstract generalities rather than with concrete specificity. Our sermons remain at thirty-five thousand feet and never make their way to sea level. As preachers, we practice concreteness through focusing on specific details in the biblical text and through working hard on illustrating and applying in our sermons.

---

12. The terminology of "fixed mindset" and "growth mindset" comes from Stanford University psychology professor Carol S. Dweck and her pioneering work on mindset theory. Dweck writes: "For thirty years, my research has shown that *the view you adopt for yourself* profoundly affects the way you lead your life. . . . Believing that your qualities are carved in stone—the *fixed mindset*—creates an urgency to prove yourself over and over." *Mindset*, 6; emphasis in original. By contrast, she argues, a "*growth mindset* is based on the belief that your basic qualities are things you can cultivate through your efforts, your strategies, and help from others. Although people differ in every which way—in their initial talents and aptitudes, interests, or temperaments—everyone can change and grow through application and experience." *Mindset*, 7. Dweck's understanding of "growth mindset" comports well with the underlying approach, structure, and pedagogical assumptions laid out in this book.

**The Practices
of Christian Preaching**

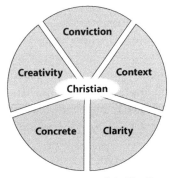

Figure I.2. Overview of the Five Cs

Preach Creatively: Preachers confront numerous roadblocks in ministry that stifle the creative process; some are environmental, others structural, and still others self-imposed. We grow in the practice of creativity when we remove specific obstacles that prevent it and pursue practices that catalyze creative thinking, processing, and production.

Consult figure I.2 for a visual way of thinking about the Five Cs.

For each of the Five Cs, readers are encouraged to access learning activities on our companion website. Some of the activities invite you to reflect through writing, others direct you to discussions between expert teachers in homiletics, still others connect you with audio and video clips of sermons. The various questions, audio and video clips, and collaborative discussions will help you to cultivate the practices that I propose in this book. Whenever you encounter a writer, a multimedia clip, or a perspective that feels unfamiliar or perhaps uncomfortable, resist the urge to shut down or be dismissive. Push through the discomfort that you experience with the encounter: whether that is the author I cite, the preacher you hear/watch, or the perspective you hear from someone whose background and preaching experiences are markedly different than your own. Disorientation can be a positive experience if it is used as a catalyst for learning and growth, leading to reorientation as a result. Try to keep an open mind, especially when you encounter divergence from your own experience.

Preaching really does have the power to change people's lives and, dare I say, to change the world. If you believe this is true of preaching, why would you not want to get better at it? If God has entrusted you with such an audacious and ennobling task, why would you not want to give your very best to it? For if it is possible, as far as it depends on you, engage in the deliberate practice of Christian preaching, and perhaps you and even those who listen to you will notice that you play clearer, better music. The gospel that you preach is worthy of the hours that you spend in the woodshed preparing to preach it.

1

Preach Christian Sermons

Church X has the sterile feel of an operating theater. . . . The sermon—on justice to one's fellows—has so squeezed out any mention of God or Jesus, maybe to sound modern, there's no sense of history. The pastor asks for peace and gives thanks for plenty, but the homily might come from *Reader's Digest*.

—Mary Karr, *Lit: A Memoir*

A church that doesn't provoke any crises, a gospel that doesn't unsettle, a word of God that doesn't get under anyone's skin, a word of God that doesn't touch the real sin of the society in which it is being proclaimed—what gospel is that?

—Oscar Romero, *The Violence of Love*

About nine miles from where I grew up in New Jersey, a beautiful colonial town called Hopewell greets you like a lost time capsule that has just been discovered. The town, established by colonists in 1691, has curved roads, rolling hills, classic homes, and a historic downtown that seem like they belong in a fairy tale rather than real life. Drive north on Broad Street, the historic main road, and you will see an old colonial cemetery on your right. Directly adjacent to the cemetery stands a regal, red-brick building. Its location and architecture suggest that it probably used to be a church. You park your car, get out, and notice a little white sign by the door that reads "Hopewell Old School Baptist Meeting House." It turns out that people used

Figures 1.1. and 1.2. Exterior Views of Hopewell Church

to meet here—to worship here. You head home that night determined to learn more about the beautiful red-brick church on Broad Street, so you decide to conduct some research in local libraries. You also enlist the help of Google, your trusty research assistant.

You discover that the church opened its doors for the first time in 1715 with fifteen charter members. Then, in 1727, it established the first Baptist school in the colonies for "the education of youths for the ministry."[1] By 1747 the congregation had grown to sixty-five. Several revivals swept through the Northeast during the next few decades and in a twelve-month span in 1764 the church added 123 converts to its growing congregation. It added 105 more in 1775–76. A new pastor came in 1796, and by the time he finished his term ten years later, he had baptized 151 more people. By all accounts, it seemed like the people who worshiped there lived like Great-Commission Christians. It looked as though nothing could go wrong for the Hopewell Old School Baptist Meeting House. What happened next took place not overnight but over time. It did not hinge on one particular decision.

In the early 1800s, the church's leaders embraced some of the latest doctrinal teachings, which in this case were heterodox rather than orthodox. They also lost their passion for people to know and be found by Christ by ignoring the mandate to make disciples, to be God's witnesses in the world. Experts might use the phrase "mission drift" to describe what took place at the red-brick church in Hopewell.[2] In 1835, the church split from

1. Griffiths, *History of Baptists in New Jersey*, 68.
2. Greer and Horst, *Mission Drift*.

the Baptist Conference of New Jersey because it (and other churches) decided to embrace a false teaching called antinomianism. Decades later, in 1904, when just a handful of laypeople remained in attendance on Sunday mornings, Thomas Sharp Griffiths, a Baptist historian, wrote these words in his *History of Baptists in New Jersey*: "It is the prayer of Baptists that the venerable First Hopewell Church will return to her 'first love' again. . . . A glorious past, is to her a robe of white, except as it has been soiled by associations and which darkens her future. When again, she incorporates the last commission of our Lord into her activities, we will rejoice together in her 'walking with God.'"[3]

Not long after Griffiths made these comments, the church held its final worship service and shuttered its doors. Today the building serves as a historic landmark and is designated for civic purposes. Local leaders open it once a year for a flag ceremony.

Stories like this one sadden us as ministers, as well they should. They also remind us of how easy it is for churches to lose their way. Again, it does not happen overnight but over time. A church can drift without standing in clear opposition to the gospel. Presumably, the writer of Hebrews warned his readers not to "drift away" because they *were* faithful believers, not because they had wandered far from the faith (Heb. 2:1). As preachers, if we are not careful, we will also drift not because we are swimming against the tide but because we are swimming with it. Anyone who has gone swimming in an ocean with a strong current knows how easy it is to look over at the beach and notice that you are fifty to one hundred feet north or south from where you entered the water. Often without even realizing it we lose touch with the gospel as our fixed point of reference and thereby neglect our responsibility to proclaim it.

In this chapter, we consider why it is so important to preach *Christian* sermons. As I stated previously, if we miss the call to preach Christianly, then we miss out on our primary task as gospel witnesses. The Five Cs hinge on the basic conviction that preaching Christianly is at the center of everything we do. I have placed the word "Christian" at the center of the accompanying figure in order to communicate that everything else we do grows out of preaching Christianly.

First, we will define and describe the gospel that we preach. Then we will discuss the pseudo-gospels that we are (sometimes) tempted to preach. Then, in the final section, we will consider various proposals concerning our call to preach Christian sermons.

3. Griffiths, *History of Baptists in New Jersey*, 72.

**The Practices
of Christian Preaching**

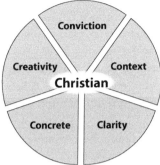

Figure 1.3. The Five Cs: Christian

The Gospel That We Preach

Preachers without the gospel are like reservoirs without water. They do not serve their intended purpose. We claim to have a grasp of the gospel, and we believe the gospel. But for various reasons we forget to preach it. Our problem is not a new one. According to Emil Brunner, "At every period in the history of the Church, the greatest sin of the church, and the one which causes the greatest distress, is that *she withholds the Gospel from the world and herself.*"[4] Perhaps if Brunner had mentioned only the world and not the church, then that would make more sense to us. But what if he is right? What if the world does not hear a compelling vision of the gospel outside the church's walls because we do not preach a compelling version of it inside the church's walls?

Before proceeding any further, perhaps we should ask a few basic questions: *What is the gospel? What language should we use to describe it? Why is it good news?* Even if we tried to posit in-depth responses to these questions, we would only skim the surface. For the purposes of this chapter, I will provide a basic definition of the gospel, and I will highlight five distinguishing marks that add depth and texture to that definition.

Defining the Gospel

Succinct definitions of the gospel abound. Gardner C. Taylor defines the gospel as follows: "God is out to get back what belongs to him."[5] Notice that God is the one who does the seeking. David James Randolph defines the

---

4. Brunner, *Divine Imperative*, 565 (emphasis added).
5. G. Taylor, "Sweet Torture of Sunday Morning (Interview)," 20.

gospel this way: "Love which is desirable for life is available in Jesus Christ."[6] In this definition, spiritual life and vitality find their source in Jesus Christ. In *Church Dogmatics*, Karl Barth emphasizes a Christocentric announcement: "Jesus Christ, very God and very man, has come as its [the world's] Savior and will come again. This is the announcement of the kingdom of God. This is the Gospel."[7] Here the focus is on Christ's work, his promises, and the kingdom he brings.[8] Back in 2017, I heard Thomas G. Long present a paper on the preaching of Jesus at a homiletics symposium in which he summarized Jesus's message of good news as, "You don't have to live this way anymore."[9]

In defining the gospel, Christians often appeal to well-known texts of Scripture. Some like to quote John 3:16: "God so loved the world that he gave his one and only Son, that whoever believes in him shall not perish but have eternal life." Others appeal to Romans 5:8: "But God demonstrates his own love for us in this: While we were still sinners, Christ died for us." Some highlight Christ as a sin offering on our behalf by quoting from 2 Corinthians 5:21: "God made him who had no sin to be sin for us, so that in him we might become the righteousness of God." Still others appeal to lesser-known texts like 2 Timothy 2:8: "Remember Jesus Christ, raised from the dead, descended from David. This is my gospel." Each of these passages of Scripture and many other well-known texts focus the attention on the person and work of Jesus Christ, a theme we will return to in a moment.

I define the gospel as *an announcement and a call from God through Jesus Christ that welcomes us into covenant relationship*. It is an *announcement* of the good news that the triune God is reconciling the world to himself through Christ—his life, death, and resurrection—instead of counting our

6. Randolph, *Renewal of Preaching*, 29.
7. Barth, *Church Dogmatics*, III, 4, *Doctrine of Creation*, 506.
8. Reeves writes,
   We naturally gravitate, it seems, to anything but Jesus—and Christians almost as much as anyone. Whether it's "the Christian worldview," "grace," "the Bible," or "the gospel," as if they were things in themselves that could save us. Even "the cross" can get abstracted from Jesus, as if the wood had some power of its own. Other things, wonderful things, vital concepts, beautiful discoveries so easily edge Jesus aside. Precious theological concepts meant to describe *him* and *his* work get treated as things in their own right. He becomes just another brick in the wall. But the center, the cornerstone, the jewel in the crown of Christianity is not an idea, a system or a thing; it is not even "the gospel" as such. It is Jesus Christ. He is not a mere topic, a subject we can pick out from a menu of options. Without him, our gospel, our system—however grace-filled or Bible-based—simply is not Christian. (*Rejoicing in Christ*, 10)
9. I attended Long's presentation, "The Preaching of Jesus," at the National Symposium on Preaching, Truett Theological Seminary, Waco, TX, September 11–12, 2017.

sins against us (2 Cor. 5:16–21; Col. 1:19–20); and it is a *call* to individuals, systems, and the whole world to acknowledge and follow Jesus by responding to God's grace through faith (Rom. 1:5; 5:2; Eph. 2:6–9) and by re-presenting Christlikeness through love (Ps. 89:1; John 13:34–35; Rom. 12:10; 13:8; 1 Cor. 13:13; Gal. 5:6; 1 Pet. 2:9–11).

The gospel is newsworthy because it offers new life for those dead in their trespasses and sins (Eph. 2:1–10), freedom for those held in captivity (Isa. 58:6–7; Luke 4:18–19), and the promise of a new reality for a world bound to powers of an age that is passing away (John 3:17; Rom. 12:1–2; Eph. 6:12). It repairs the broken relationship between God and humanity through divinely initiated reconciliation—that is, through God exchanging enmity for covenantal relationship through Christ's death on the cross, resurrection victory at Easter, and promise of new life.[10] The enmity that God exchanges for relationship at the vertical level also functions as a model for reconciliation at the horizontal level in and through the life of the church as guided by the Holy Spirit. Those who have been reconciled to God through Christ become reconcilers for God in Christ. As a community saved by grace and grounded in hope, the church proclaims to the world the good news of vertical and horizontal reconciliation (2 Cor. 5:18–20). Because of Christ, relationships characterized by enmity and estrangement have the capacity to be transformed into relationships characterized by intimacy and love (Jer. 31:31–34). The church functions as an outpost of heaven (Phil. 3:20), performing God's vision for the world in the present and signposting a future vision in which all things are made new (Isa. 40:3–5; 65:17–25; Matt. 5:13–16; 6:9–10; Rev. 21:5).

> *I define the gospel as an announcement and a call from God through Jesus Christ that welcomes us into covenantal relationship.*

In addition to announcing, the gospel calls for a response. In Christ, Lesslie Newbigin writes, "something has altered the total human situation and must therefore call into question every human culture."[11] Through Christ, God calls humankind *out of* sin, death, and destruction *into* repentance, faith,

---

10. In using the language of exchange to define reconciliation, I am indebted to the work of New Testament scholar Stanley E. Porter, who has written an extensive study on *katallasso*, the primary word (and its cognates) used for "reconcile" in the New Testament. Porter argues that reconciliation conveys the idea of exchange at both the literal and figurative levels. He writes, "*Katallasso* seems to have been used by Greek writers with two major senses, that of exchange of goods or things (although *antikatallasso* was widely used in this kind of context, especially in later writers), and that of eliminating hostility and creating friendship (i.e. exchanging enmity for friendship)." Katallasso *in Ancient Greek Literature*, 13.

11. Newbigin, *Foolishness to the Greeks*, 3.

and transformation. Although we wrestle and struggle and fall and fail, we do so grounded in a gospel of grace and mercy that summons us out of our penchant for self-destruction. God graciously pulls us away from our subjection because of sin toward life in the Spirit because of righteousness (Rom. 8:10–11). Life in the Spirit looks like Christ followers embodying the vision of God in the world through their character, conduct, and action. That is to say, it looks like faith gone public. To be children of God means that we are partners in the mission of God in the world and that we reorient our lives around that mission. Those whom God has encountered through Christ in the Spirit cannot continue in complacency or indifference, living as if nothing radical had "altered the total human situation," but instead are *compelled* into mission, into a new way of living, being, and acting in the world.

The gospel does not leave room for neutrality. C. S. Lewis writes, "Christianity is a statement which, if false, is of no importance, and if true, of infinite importance. The one thing it cannot be is moderately important."[12] Those who hear the gospel promise heed its directive to live Christlike lives of surrender, discipleship, and mission. They (we) believe in a gospel that looses people from the shackles of their allegiance to and affection for an age that is passing away, one that sets them free to reframe their allegiance and restore their affection for a God who has incontrovertibly inaugurated an age that has come, is come, and will come: the kingdom of heaven. Preachers have the privilege of announcing the good news that the kingdom of God has been established and will one day be realized in all of its fullness, and they also have the solemn responsibility to remind all who will listen—"You don't have to live this way anymore."[13]

Describing the Gospel

Now that we have outlined a basic definition of the gospel, we will consider several of its distinguishing marks. I will propose five marks in particular that will offer readers more nuance, texture, and depth to the definition provided. Preachers preach a gospel that is transformative, offensive, hopeful, prophetic, and eschatological (see fig. 1.4).

12. Lewis, *God in the Dock*, 102. The Baptist preacher George W. Truett puts it this way: "We must openly take sides with Christ, and follow with prompt and unfaltering obedience, wherever he leads. . . . Not to take sides with Christ is to take sides against Him." From the sermon "Taking Sides," in *Follow Me*, 184–85.
13. Not coincidentally, Jesus and Paul "proclaim[ed] the good news of the kingdom" (Matt. 4:23; see also Matt. 9:35; Luke 4:43; 8:1; 9:2, 6; Acts 29:27). As preachers, we announce what they announced—namely, the good news of kingdom inbreaking through Christ.

A Transformative Gospel

We preach a transformative gospel. It has the power to change individuals, families, friendships, communities, and even nations. As preachers, we know this to be the case because we too have been gripped by what Thomas Chalmers calls "the expulsive power of a new affection."[14] Theologically speaking, transformation takes place in justification, sanctification, and glorification. At its simplest, justification means that Christ—through his life, death, and resurrection—has reversed our verdict from "guilty" to "innocent" before God by declaring us righteous. Sanctification means steady growth in day-to-day Christlikeness over time. Glorification represents the consummation of our salvation, when our earthly bodies are resurrected.

The Gospel is
- Transformative
- Offensive
- Hopeful
- Prophetic
- Eschatological

Figure 1.4. Gospel Overview

Practically speaking, transformation occurs when disciples learn from and follow in the way of Jesus even if doing so leads them in a direction they would rather not go (John 21:18). Jesus said "Follow me" to Peter at the beginning of his journey in discipleship (Mark 1:17), and he said "Follow me" to Peter at the end (John 21:22). A disciple listens to and heeds the call of God, "Follow me," more than just the first time these words are uttered. One steadily moves out of self-centeredness and isolation toward other-centeredness and engagement in order to be transformed and transformative. To follow in the way of Jesus is to follow him wherever he wills to take us even if it means bearing "the disgrace he bore" (Heb. 13:13). The Japanese theologian Kosuke Koyama writes, "The periphery is the place of discipleship. If we follow Jesus we will come to the periphery with him. The periphery is the place of the cross. It is the place where we are asked to save others and not ourselves."[15]

An Offensive Gospel

We preach an offensive gospel. Perhaps you know the *New Yorker* cartoon that portrays a wealthy couple leaving church after exchanging pleasantries with the Sunday morning preacher. As they exit, the wife in her fur coat and clad in jewelry says to her husband wearing a top hat, "It can't be easy for him not to offend us."[16] There really is no way around the offensive dimensions

14. Chalmers, *Sermons and Discourses*, 2:271–78.
15. Koyama, *Mount Fuji and Mount Sinai*, 251–52.
16. *New Yorker* cartoon cited in Gomes, *Scandalous Gospel of Jesus*, 18–19.

of the gospel. According to 1 Corinthians 1:23, in preaching Christ crucified, we preach a message that is "a stumbling block to Jews and foolishness to Gentiles." Those who take that message seriously will struggle with both its divine summons and its real implications. The gospel scandalizes our sensibilities by exposing our idols, interrogating our priorities, and calling into question our alliances. More than all of these, it confronts us in our sin and rebellion, the root cause of our persistent idolatry, misplaced desire, and false allegiance.

Peter J. Gomes argues that sin is essential to understanding fallen humanity. He describes sin as "a fact of who we are, a part, if you will, of our essential DNA. . . . There is something about being human that, despite our best efforts, makes it easy for us to persist in sin, and it is to this persistent fact that the Jewish and Christian scriptures give testimony."[17] Sin does not just corrupt the lives of individuals and communities; it also pervades systems and structures (Eph. 6:12). Perhaps more than any other doctrine, the doctrine of sin has the full weight of substantive empirical proof to support its espousal; it is part of our "essential DNA" as fallen creatures this side of eternity.

The gospel offends because it forces us to tell the truth about the brokenness that exists in the world and in ourselves, that it is not just outside but also inside of us. Although we would prefer *not* to tell the truth about ourselves to ourselves, we will not fully know ourselves and our requisite need for God's grace without seeing ourselves through truth telling. Sin prevents us from seeing ourselves, and it prevents us from *wanting* to see ourselves. In a sense, the gospel offends us because we do not wish to offend ourselves.

A HOPEFUL GOSPEL

We preach a hopeful gospel. In Christ, God chooses love over hate, adoption over rejection, reconciliation over enmity. The psalmist declares that God is "compassionate and gracious, slow to anger, abounding in love" (Ps. 103:8). God does not "treat us as our sins deserve" or count them against us (Ps. 103:10). God effects our deliverance through a person—Jesus Christ—the one whose death sets us free from death and whose resurrection sets us free for life with such force and significance that we can declare, "Death thou shalt die."[18]

---

17. Gomes, *Scandalous Gospel of Jesus*, 131. Barth offers a description of what sin is and does when he writes, "In all its forms sin is man's perverted dealing with the stern goodness and righteous mercy of God addressed to him in Jesus Christ. It is their denial and rejection, their misunderstanding and misuse. It is man's direct or indirect enmity against the promise of God which as such is also His demand." *Church Dogmatics*, IV, 3.1, *Doctrine of Reconciliation*, 369–70.

18. From the sonnet "Death, Be Not Proud" in Donne and Carey, *Selected Poetry*, 202.

Hope resounds in a cross and in an empty tomb. Jesus's willingness to go to a cross bears witness to God's willingness to suffer for humanity as a supreme mark of self-giving love. As predicted in Isaiah 53, the Messiah comes into the world as one "despised and rejected by mankind, a man of suffering, and familiar with pain" (Isa. 53:3; cf. also John 1:10–11). God enters into human suffering through self-donation (Phil. 2:9-11).

Dietrich Bonhoeffer understood that God's willing abdication of rights and willful solidarity with a broken world pierced humanity's darkness with a bright light that could not be extinguished. Thus, Bonhoeffer wrote these words on the wall of his prison cell shortly before his own execution at the hands of Nazi soldiers: "Only a suffering God can help."[19]

God's willingness to enter into and identify with humanity's plight through the cross demonstrates God's supreme and abiding commitment to delivering it from despair and wooing it back into covenantal relationship (Hosea 2:14–15). Yet, Christians believe that the cross does not represent the final scene of a much larger story. Easter demonstrates God's triumph over death, destruction, and evil (1 John 3:8). Resurrection hope springs forth from God's vindication over death—both now and in the future. In the resurrection, God proclaims that not even death can defeat the divine purposes for the world. What God has accomplished at Easter previews what God will accomplish at the advent of the new heavens and the new earth.

A Prophetic Gospel

We preach a prophetic gospel.[20] The Old Testament prophets announced hope in the promises of God, but they also told the truth about realities in the world. Their truth telling took on various forms: they warned the nation of divine judgment for its disobedience; they lamented injustice in the land; they stood in solidarity with the oppressed in the society; and they spoke sharply against complacency and indifference. Christian preachers do not have the same vocation as Old Testament prophets, but we do have a responsibility to perform truth telling as they did—and, for that matter, as Jesus did.

Preachers engage in both prophetic indictment and prophetic reimagining. Prophetic indictment can be compared to the painful task of exorcising disease. Cathleen Kaveny argues that prophetic indictment functions as a form of "moral chemotherapy," a way by which one treats what is unhealthy

---

19. Bonhoeffer, *Letters and Papers from Prison*, 361. Bonhoeffer wrote these words on his prison cell wall in the same concentration camp in Germany where he was eventually killed by Nazi soldiers for opposing Hitler.

20. For more on prophetic gospel preaching, see Tisdale, *Prophetic Preaching*.

in the society for the greater good of health and healing.[21] Prophetic reimagining can be compared to the reframing that one finds in psychotherapy as a path toward healing.[22] A preacher reframes a future story that breaks into the present story through the promises God has made to us and to the world in which we live in the divine story.

Our preaching might strive to tell the truth about individuals and their estrangement from God. It might tell the truth about the brokenness that exists in marriages and families. It might even tell the truth about sinfulness in the church or in the broader community. But does our preaching tell the truth about realities in the world? Does it indict and reimagine?

We live in a world fractured by violence, poverty, prejudice, and war. The gospel speaks to these and many other realities as well. It speaks to justice issues like inequality, systemic poverty, institutionalized racism, mass incarceration, and separated migrant families or invisible migrant workers. One does not have to be an angry preacher to be prophetic. A preacher who is *always* angry has lost sight of the gospel as good news. One simply has to be a preacher who tells the truth about the way things really are in Jesus Christ. Every preacher is called to be prophetic.

> Go to www.Practices ofChristianPreaching .com to hear what preacher William Augustus Jones says about the modern preacher as both a priest *and* a prophet.

An Eschatological Gospel

We preach an eschatological gospel. By "eschatological" I mean that God's kingdom has already broken in at present and will one day be realized. Although we preach about God's faithfulness in the past and invite people to trust God in the present, preachers also imagine the *future* that God has promised to us and to the world. When Christians think about the future, many of them think about eternal life with God. For good reasons, they hold on to promises like the one found in John 5:24 when Jesus says, "Very truly I tell you, whoever hears my word and believes him who sent me has eternal

---

21. Kaveny writes,

    Prophetic rhetoric is, by its very nature, an extraordinary form of moral discourse; its purpose is not to replace moral deliberation but to return it to health. I have just suggested that we view the language of prophetic indictment as a type of moral chemotherapy. It takes aim at morally cancerous assumptions or perspectives that threaten to destroy the possibility of reliable practical reasoning within a particular community at a particular time. Like chemotherapy, prophetic rhetoric of indictment is inherently destructive, but in service of an ultimately constructive purpose: The goal of prophetic rhetoric is the reestablishment of a healthy, functioning political context for moral deliberation and decision. (*Prophecy without Contempt*, 315–16)

    22. Brueggemann claims that the preacher offers people "another scripting of reality." *Practice of Prophetic Imagination*, 29.

life and will not be judged but has crossed over from death to life" (cf. also John 3:16; 6:40, 47, 68; 10:28–30). But God's future stretches far beyond its relevance to us as individuals. God initiates an eschatological future in and through Christ, and God promises an eschatological future for the world—that is, a new heaven and a new earth with "'no more death' or mourning or crying or pain, for the old order of things has passed away" (Rev. 21:4).

The church proclaims and performs God's future in the present. It proclaims what God has accomplished at the cross, the resurrection, and the eschaton (inaugurated but not yet realized in its fullness), and it performs God's will and ways to the world around it through enacting God's vision for the world. It functions as a divine preview, if you will, offering a foretaste to the public of what eternal life with God looks like.

The five words we have studied—transformative, offensive, hopeful, prophetic, and eschatological—describe various marks of the gospel so as to provide much-needed texture and depth to our definition. Although much more could be said about the gospel than time and space permit, these five words help us appreciate its complex simplicity in a way that a stand-alone definition does not present. They also help us distinguish the gospel that we should preach from the pseudo-gospels that we are sometimes tempted to preach.

The Pseudo-Gospels That We Are (Sometimes) Tempted to Preach

In my classes, sometimes I remind students: "The gas of the gospel drives the car of obedience." This idea comes from a conviction that preachers should not ask listeners to go where they want them to go without first giving them fuel to help them get there. It also arises from a belief that we preach the text in order to preach the gospel. Usually I say this phrase whenever I hear a sermon that sounds too moralistic or legalistic; the student preacher presses for good behavior without the foundation that undergirds it or emphasizes external rule-following motivated by guilt instead of inside-out transformation motivated by gratitude.

We can also use the same imagery to make a different but related point. We have an idea of what happens when we do not put any fuel in the tank. But what happens when we put the wrong fuel in the tank? In the best of cases, we do minor damage and, in the worst of cases, we do major damage. A vehicle with no fuel is useless. A vehicle with the wrong fuel is dangerous. If we do not exercise care and caution when we preach, we will damage the people to whom we preach even if that is not our intent.

So what pseudo-gospels do we preach? Although there are many, let me propose five pseudo-gospels that appear often enough to form a pattern in preaching classes and in a lot of popular preaching today.[23] Perhaps you can identify all five of these based on the preaching you have heard from others. Consider which of the five you are most at risk of in your own preaching.

The Gospel of Moralistic Therapeutic Deism

According to the pseudo-gospel of Moralistic Therapeutic Deism, Christianity consists of three main beliefs: being a good person makes us right with God (moralistic); God's main job is to make us happy and to help us feel good about ourselves (therapeutic); and there is *a* God up there somewhere whom we can go to in a crisis (deism), as opposed to the triune God—Father, Son, and Holy Spirit—who calls us into discipleship. I borrow the phrase "Moralistic Therapeutic Deism" from the well-known sociologist Christian Smith and his fellow researcher Melissa Lindquist Denton. In 2005, Smith and Denton published their research findings from the thousands of interviews and surveys they (and others) conducted with the National Survey of Youth and Religion (NSYR). In *Soul Searching: The Religious and Spiritual Lives of American Teenagers,* they describe their main finding from the research:

> We can say here that we have come with some confidence to believe that a signifi-
> cant part of Christianity in the United States is actually only tenuously Christian
> in any sense that is seriously connected to the actual historical Christian tradi-
> tion, but has rather substantially morphed into Christianity's misbegotten step
> cousin . . . *Christian Moralistic Therapeutic Deism.* . . . It is not so much that
> US Christianity is being secularized. Rather, more subtly, Christianity is either
> degenerating into a pathetic version of itself or, more significantly, Christianity
> is actively being colonized and displaced by a quite different religious faith.[24]

In *Almost Christian,* Kenda Creasy Dean makes a similar point when she describes interviewing a significant number of teenagers who called themselves Christian, came from Christian homes, and worshiped in Christian congregations, "yet who had no readily accessible faith vocabulary, few recognizable faith practices, and little ability to reflect on their lives religiously."[25] In their

---

23. Ross Douthat, a religion columnist for the *New York Times,* describes the pervasiveness of pseudo-gospels in the US context when he writes, "America's problem isn't too much religion, or too little of it. It's *bad* religion: the slow-motion collapse of traditional Christianity and the rise of a variety of pseudo-Christianities in its place." *Bad Religion,* 3 (emphasis in original).
24. C. Smith, with Denton, *Soul Searching,* 171 (emphasis added).
25. Dean, *Almost Christian,* 16.

worldview, Dean writes, "God is more object than subject, an Idea but not a companion."[26]

Lest we rush to judgment on the next generation, the problem cuts much deeper than trite or trivial explanations will allow. Where do teenagers hear a pseudo-gospel of Moralistic Therapeutic Deism? Where do they learn about a God that wants them to be nice, feel good, and believe in a higher power? The research reveals that they learn primarily from those who lead and mentor them spiritually—that is, Christian parents and Christian leaders. Smith and Denton claim that their research findings are less an indictment of teens and more an indictment of the parents and local congregations that shape them spiritually. In the passing on of the faith, Dean observes, the problem is *not* that the older generation "teaches young people badly," it is that the older generation does an "exceedingly good job of teaching youth what we really believe: namely, that Christianity is not a big deal, that God requires little, and the church is a helpful social institution filled with nice people focused primarily on 'folks like us.'"[27] To borrow a metaphor from Jesus: bad trees produce bad fruit (Matt. 7:17).

Smith and Denton's key phrase, Moralistic Therapeutic Deism, gives us pause and helps us interrogate our natural proclivities in preaching. The majority of respondents to the surveys believed that "Central to living a good and happy life is being a good, moral person. That means being nice, kind, pleasant, respectful, responsible, at work on self-improvement, taking care of one's health, and doing one's best to be successful."[28] Although being a nice person is not inherently bad and usually enriches rather than diminishes life and society, many of the survey respondents made niceness so central to their faith that other core doctrines were diminished or even erased. Niceness was the primary means for pleasing God and for going to heaven when one dies, and it became one of the summarizing terms for the essence of one's faith.

As preachers, do we tell people about a God who wants us to be nice to one another? Do we sometimes, even if we do not intend it, tell people that doing X, Y, and Z will win them favor with God and help them get to heaven? While the world could certainly use more Christians who are nice, especially on social media, Jesus did not come into the world primarily to make us nice. One does not need God to be nice. The gospel is neither a master class in etiquette nor a vision for works-based righteousness. Lewis observes, "A world of nice people, content in their own niceness, looking no further, turned away

---

26. Dean, *Almost Christian*, 11.
27. Dean, *Almost Christian*, 12.
28. C. Smith, with Denton, *Soul Searching*, 163.

from God, would be just as desperately in need of salvation as a miserable world and might even be more difficult to save."[29]

As for faith being therapeutic, many of the survey respondents thought about religion in positive terms because it "helps to achieve a primary goal in life: to feel good and happy about oneself and about one's life." Instead of more traditional categories—such as repentance from sin, gratitude for divine grace, endurance through suffering, or participation in mission—they used terms like "feeling good, happy, secure, at peace."[30] In a sense, God functions as a means to the end of individual and relational well-being. Such a perspective often leads to insularity and isolation from the needs of others and the world. People do not have to expose themselves to anything that makes them unhappy or uncomfortable. If the main goal is happiness, then a preacher cannot say much at all about sin, offer a prophetic word, or do much of anything at all to make people uncomfortable.

Finally, many respondents believed in a God who is real, who created the universe, and who is available during times of crisis, but who is not invested in the everyday patterns of existence. They did *not* believe in a God who is "personally involved in one's affairs—especially affairs in which one would prefer not to have God involved. Most of the time, the God of this faith keeps a safe distance."[31] A God like that does not really demand or expect anything from us but is still available in moments of desperation. Describing this phenomenon, Smith and Denton write, "In short, God is something like a combination of a Divine Butler and Cosmic Therapist: he is always on call, takes care of any problems that arise, because his job is to solve our problems and make us feel good."[32] Dean compares this distortion of Christianity to opening a bank account before leaving for college. Christian faith is "nice to have . . . something you want before you go to college in case you need to draw from it sometime."[33] Faith that functions this way has little to no bearing on how one lives life in the present. Moreover, it falters during times of crisis because the account is too low and gets overdrawn. More importantly, it bears no resemblance to the vision that Jesus casts for life with God. Does our preaching invite listeners to make God peripheral rather than central to their lives so that God becomes a sort of divine reserve in the event of an emergency? Do our sermons placate or pacify our listeners, or do they challenge and convict them?

29. Lewis, *Mere Christianity*, 216.
30. C. Smith, with Denton, *Soul Searching*, 164.
31. C. Smith, with Denton, *Soul Searching*, 164.
32. C. Smith, with Denton, *Soul Searching*, 165.
33. Dean, *Almost Christian*, 15.

Again, many of us do not realize that we are in danger of preaching "Christianity's misbegotten step cousin."[34] The world could use more nice Christians in it than it has right now. But true gospel preaching requires an abiding commitment to truth telling and an incisive interrogation of the categories that Smith and Denton name in their study.

The Gospel Dressed in a Flag or Banner

In the pseudo-gospel of dressing the gospel in a flag or banner, the Christian message allies itself too closely with our national or political ideology. In making this claim, I do *not* mean to suggest that Christians should opt out of politics, that they should refrain from voting according to their conscience, that they should shy away from holding positions that they believe are consistent with Christian ethics, or that they should shrink back from the practice of civil disobedience in the face of unjust laws.[35] God expects us not only to pray for our leaders but also to exercise civic responsibility, pursue justice, and hold leaders and systems accountable. Christians everywhere should strive to be agents of the message and ministry of reconciliation in every domain, including the political one. As C. René Padilla puts it, "Mission only does justice to biblical teaching and to the concrete situation when it is *integral*. In other words, when it is crossing boundaries . . . with the purpose of transforming human life in all of its dimensions."[36]

34. C. Smith, with Denton, *Soul Searching*, 171.

35. In *Church Dogmatics*, Karl Barth claims that churches that choose to remain neutral in the face of injustice are embracing a distilled, watered-down version of the gospel of Christ. He writes, "The timeless or supra-temporal Gospel which is neutral and avoids contemporary events is certainly not the pure Gospel, and if its testimony is designed to be evangelical in an abstract sense it is not only not prophetic but is actually false prophecy. For if anything is false prophecy, it is the proclamation of a community which for safety's sake tries to withdraw into an inner line and to devote itself to neutrality." *Church Dogmatics*, III, 4, *Doctrine of Creation*, 512.

36. Here is the quote in English in its context: "Mission only does justice to biblical teaching and to the concrete situation when it is *integral*. In other words, when it is *crossing boundaries* (not only geographic but cultural, racial, economic, social, political, etc.) *with the purpose of transforming human life in all of its dimensions, according to the purposes of God, and for the empowering of men and women in order that they might enjoy the abundant life that God has made possible by means of Jesus Christ in the power of the Spirit.*" All translations from Spanish to English in this book are my own. Here is the same quote in Spanish: "La misión sólo hace justicia a la enseñanza bíblica, y a la situación concreta cuando es *integral*. En otras palabras, cuando es un *cruce de fronteras* (no solo geográficas sino culturales, raciales, económicas, sociales, políticas, etc.) *con el propósito de transformar la vida humana en todas sus dimensiones, segun el propósito de Dios, y de empoderar a hombres y mujeres para que disfruten la vida plena que Dios ha hecho posible por medio de Jesucristo en el poder del Espíritu.*" Padilla, "Hacia una Definición de la Misión Integral [Toward a Definition of Integral Mission]," 31 (emphasis in original).

Instead, let me propose that preachers lose their prophetic voice when they conflate the gospel message with national exceptionalism, a party platform, or a particular political candidate. They also give people false hope that all will be well as long as a nation, a government, or a particular person is in power. Not much has changed since the people of God pleaded with the prophet Samuel: "Appoint a king to lead us, such as all the other nations have" (1 Sam. 8:5). After Samuel told them that their actions were tantamount to a rejection of God as king, they doubled down on their request: "We want a king over us. Then we will be like all the other nations, with a king to lead us and to go out before us and fight our battles" (1 Sam. 8:19–20). Insert the name of your country, your political party, or your favorite politician in place of the word "king" and you will notice some startling parallels.

The stakes are higher than we think. As Gardner C. Taylor observes, "Whenever corrupt religion and crooked government collude, Jesus Christ is crucified all over again."[37] If preachers resort to unhealthy nationalistic diatribes (which should not be confused with national pride, patriotism, or good citizenship), not only do they lose their credibility but they also lose their capacity to stand over against those in power when they do wrong. Consider this: if the prophet Nathan had been sipping the royal wine every night in King David's house, he never would have been able to say, "You are the man!" when the time came for him to say it (2 Sam. 12:7). If John the Baptist had been enjoying the royal food every night in King Herod's palace, he never would have been able to stand up to him in the face of his corruption (Mark 6:14–29).

If we are honest, we will conclude that a significant portion of our national and political values do not line up that well with the values of the kingdom of God.[38] Gregory A. Boyd recommends that we exercise respect toward nations and governments, but that we also "practice a healthy suspicion" toward them. He writes,

> We can never assume that any particular nation—including our own—is always, or even usually, aligned with God. We may be thankful whenever our government wields the sword in ways that are just and that punish wrongdoers. But we must also always remember that fallen principalities and powers (Eph. 2:2;

37. Personal recollection by Reginald High, a personal friend of Taylor in the last few years of his life. Email correspondence, March 16, 2012.
38. Richard T. Hughes writes, "According to the Bible, the kingdom of God and the nations of the earth embody radically different values and reflect radically different orders of reality. . . . The kingdom of God is universal and those who promote that kingdom care deeply for every human being in every corner of the globe, regardless of race or nationality. But earthly nations—even so-called 'Christian' nations—embrace values that are inevitably nationalistic and tribal, caring especially for the welfare of those within their borders." *Christian America*, 3.

6:12) strongly influence our government, and every government, however relatively good that government may otherwise be.

To accept this teaching means that, while believers should strive to be good citizens, praying and working for peace and justice, they must always practice a healthy suspicion toward the "power over," sword-wielding government they are subject to.[39]

Nearly every election cycle reinforces the reality that many of us still want a "king," someone who will "lead us and to go out before us and fight our battles." Some of us go so far as to treat our leaders like messiah figures: people who will save and deliver us from the real world that we want to reject so we can thrive in the imagined world that they promise to bring us. When left unchecked and under-scrutinized, misplaced hope in *any* human leader, party, government, or nation transforms us into idolaters.

The Gospel of Prosperity

According to the pseudo-gospel of prosperity, life with Jesus means health, wealth, and prosperity for those who follow him. Some call it the prosperity gospel or "name it and claim it" theology: name what you believe God wants you to have and claim it in advance. Prosperity-theology researcher Kate Bowler notes that the prosperity gospel is also a close cousin to American-Dream mythology, a sort of baptized version of it.[40] Prosperity preachers proclaim that God wants believers to be as healthy, rich, and successful as possible. Sickness means a lack of faith that God is able to heal you and sometimes is interpreted as a sign of God's judgment. Poverty means that you have not prayed sufficiently for God to transform your economic limitation into blessing. Failure means that you cannot name the success and anointing that is already yours in Jesus Christ.

Harvard sociologist Jonathan L. Walton argues that prosperity theology is undergirded by two main anthropological assumptions: first, that every person has the capacity to be healthy and rich through faith, and second, that every

---

39. Boyd, *Myth of a Christian Nation*, 22.

40. Kate Bowler writes,
    The prosperity gospel was constituted by the deification and ritualization of the American Dream; upward mobility, accumulation, hard work, and moral fiber. The two shared an unshakably high anthropology, studded with traits that inspire action, urgency, a sense of chosenness, and a desire to shoulder it alone. . . . The movement's culture of god-men and conquerors rang true to a nation that embraced the mythology of righteous individuals bending circumstances to their vision of the good life. The prosperity movement did not simply give Americans a gospel worthy of a nation of self-made men. It affirmed the basic economic structures on which individual enterprise stood. (*Blessed*, 226)

person has the built-in potential to reach a higher plane of mental existence through Christ. In the case of the former, increases in faith through positive thinking result in increases in health and wealth since the two are "directly proportional." Healthy bodies and material riches are not just the "fruits of the higher life but they are synonymous with the higher life." Those who remain "locked in the world's system of poverty and illness" have not fully understood and lived into their Christian identity—sickness and poverty are signs of little faith.[41] In the case of the latter, prosperity theology supports the belief that people possess a godlike level of authority and power through thinking and believing, one that allows them to disrupt and even break the laws of nature.

At the risk of oversimplification, if you have bad eyesight, think and believe your way to good eyesight. If one of your parents is sick and dying in the hospital, think and believe your way to full recovery. At this higher level of thinking and being, "laws of nature no longer apply to the believer."[42] As a belief system, it mixes American mythology, nineteenth-century New Thought psychology, and an over-realized eschatology in which all things are possible for a believer in and through Jesus's name. Thinking begets existence. Imagination begets blessing. Vision begets reality.

For good reasons, many preachers react instinctively against the prosperity gospel because of how inconsistent it is with what Scripture teaches and with daily lived experience. God is not our golden retriever, ready to fetch for us whatever we desire. Prosperity teaching fails to address the problem of evil, illness and healing, and the complexities of wealth and poverty, to name just a few problems among many. Preachers *should* react with suspicion to any message that overpromises and under-delivers, especially on such sensitive topics as wellness and wealth. Even so, we should ask ourselves: *How much is our own preaching impacted by a subversive prosperity mind-set, and how much has that mind-set impacted those who listen to us preach?*

Take poverty as an example. Regardless of our socioeconomic status and the socioeconomic status of our community, what do our listeners believe about the poor, and how do they relate to the poor? Does our preaching help people understand what God thinks about the poor and about poverty? Does it help them develop a Christian framework for wealth and poverty? Do we address the poor directly when we preach, or do we assume their invisibility? Too many preachers in the West associate blessing with material wealth, possessions, and upward mobility, even if inadvertently.

41. Walton, *Watch This!*, 95.
42. Walton refers to this level of thinking and believing as "metaphysical physicality," the belief that one can be physically present in the lower level of the carnal world while operating at a higher level of metaphysical existence. *Watch This!*, 95.

Consider also the issues of health and wellness. A startling number of those who listen to sermons believe that, if everything in life is going well, then God must be pleased with them, and if everything in life is turned upside down, then God must be upset or disappointed with them. Some of them conclude that God must be angry with them on account of their sinfulness, shortcomings, and past mistakes. As preachers, we might not espouse this belief, but do we say anything in our sermons to challenge it? One of our roles as pastors is to help people unlearn bad theologies, which, of course, includes bad theologies concerning health and sickness.

The Gospel of Discipleship without Grace

According to the pseudo-gospel of discipleship without grace, God offers constraint and contrition without offering freedom and acceptance. Some refer to this as outside-in religion in contrast to inside-out transformation, the idea being that one must get the externals (outside) cleaned up and in good working condition in order to get the internals (inside) cleaned up and in good working condition (cf. Luke 11:39–41). In this framework, one's justification depends on one's sanctification.[43] Preachers communicate this pseudo-gospel in one of two ways—legalism or moralism—each one of which expresses itself differently.

Legalistic preachers emphasize obedience to the commandments down to the letter, external holiness before other people, and escape from the evil influences of the society at large. One's life revolves around and is governed by a list of rules and a code of conduct. Adherents fear that God will be upset with them, that their leaders will be upset with them, and that any inconsistency or hypocrisy in their life will be exposed.

I am an ordained Baptist minister, and we have a popular tongue-in-cheek saying: "Baptists don't drink . . . in front of each other." Remember that humor often serves as a satirical commentary on reality. Notice the focus on external behavior along with the fear of being found out by others. Legalism usually produces one of two outcomes: Christians who are demoralized by their inability to measure up to their own standards, or Christians who are mean to other people who do not measure up to the standards they have set for them. Both outcomes harm the adherents and the people around them.

---

43. Richard Lovelace argues that a significant number of Christians understand justification in an abstract sense but "in their day-to-day existence *they rely on their sanctification for justification*, the Augustinian manner, drawing their assurance of acceptance with God from their sincerity, their past experience of conversion, their recent religious performance or the relative infrequency of their conscious, willful disobedience." *Dynamics of the Spiritual Life*, 101 (emphasis added).

Moralistic preachers emphasize goodness as the ground rather than the fruit of gospel living. The great homiletician Fred Craddock says that a lot of moralistic preachers suffer from a severe case of "'must and ought and should' and 'must and ought and should.'"[44] Just as with legalism, one's justification depends on one's sanctification, but in this instance the focus is on human goodness as opposed to legalism's emphasis on rule following. In moralistic preaching, the imperative controls the sermon without much reference to the indicative, albeit a softer version of the imperative than is found in legalistic preaching.

To be clear, moralistic preaching should not be confused with preaching that exhorts listeners toward gospel obedience. The issue at hand is morality *apart* from the gospel. In his classic *On the Preparation and Delivery of Sermons*, John Broadus challenges us to remember the motivation for obedience:

> No one among us will question that we ought constantly to exhort believers to show their faith by their works, and to be holy in all their deportment, seeing that theirs is a holy God. But there is in many quarters a reluctance, for the reason just mentioned, to preach much upon particular questions of moral duty. A preacher of the gospel has certainly no business preaching morality apart from the gospel. He may present other than strictly evangelical motives, but these must be manifestly subordinate to the great motive of grateful love to Christ, and consecration to his service.[45]

In his classic *The Homiletical Plot*, Eugene L. Lowry makes a similar observation about motives. Whatever we command, Lowry writes, should be "predicated on a *new situation* being created by the gospel—a new freedom to make choices we could never before make."[46]

On the matter of moralistic preaching, Bryan Chapell recommends that we watch out for the "Deadly Be's"—messages that "exhort believers to strive to 'be' something in order to be loved by God." He nicknames them *sola bootstrapa* sermons because their implicit message is "Pick yourself up by your own bootstraps."[47] In calling them deadly, he does not mean to exclude moral exhortation from the task of preaching. In his own words, "'Be' messages are not wrong in themselves; they are wrong messages by themselves. People cannot do or be what God requires without the past, present, and future work of Christ."[48]

---

44. Craddock, "Storytelling Workshop," audio available to members of www.preaching today.com.
45. Broadus, *Treatise on the Preparation and Delivery of Sermons*, 98.
46. Lowry, *Homiletical Plot*, 87.
47. Chapell, *Christ-Centered Preaching*, 289.
48. Chapell, *Christ-Centered Preaching*, 294.

Chapell lists three categories of "Be" sermons: Be Like, Be Good, and Be Disciplined. Again, these practices are not negative in and of themselves. They become negatives on account of the motivation for doing them. Instead of serving as grateful responses to God, they center on human effort designed to please or placate God:

- "Be Like" messages exhort listeners to be like their biblical heroes. For instance, be like David and slay giants, be like Esther and stand up for justice, or be like Paul and evangelize. Although biblical writers sometimes lift up biblical characters as worthy of emulation, they typically avoid it. The Bible usually shows us the "human frailties of its most significant characters so that we will not expect to find, within fallen humanity, any whose model behavior merits acceptance."[49]
- "Be Good" messages focus on behavior modification through subtraction or addition as the path to pleasing God. Subtract various bad behaviors and cultural taboos that the community has determined are displeasing to God, even if they are not "sins." Add various good behaviors that the community has determined are worthy of emulation, even if they might be nonessentials. Be good. If one tries hard to be good and performs the right behaviors, then God will be pleased.
- "Be Disciplined" messages emphasize spiritual disciplines and practices as the vehicle for bringing the believer acceptance before God. It might sound like "Read the Bible daily. Pray more than you do now. Come to church on time. Evangelize the lost."

All three types of messages foreground moral exhortation and background divine initiative and promise. Even if the preacher sends these messages unintentionally, all three "imply that we are able to change our fallen condition on our own strength."[50]

Legalism and moralism share important similarities even though they make appeals to different human tendencies, like two branches on the same tree. At their most basic level, both focus an inordinate amount of weight on human performance as the means to grace. For the legalistic or moralistic Christian, gospel obedience does not arise in gratitude to divine initiative; it arises through the anxious desire to curry divine favor, a sort of quid pro quo arrangement. Of course, the problems with such a view are numerous, especially since the gospel turns into a "circular exchange between human

49. Chapell, *Christ-Centered Preaching*, 290.
50. Chapell, *Christ-Centered Preaching*, 293.

beings and God," to use J. Louis Martyn's phrase.[51] As Martin Luther puts it in *The Bondage of the Will*, a person "cannot be thoroughly humbled till he realizes that his salvation is utterly beyond his own powers, counsels, efforts, will and works, and depends absolutely on the will, counsel, pleasure and work of Another—God alone."[52]

The Gospel of Grace without Discipleship

According to the pseudo-gospel of grace without discipleship, God offers freedom and acceptance without expecting constraint and contrition. The Nigerian homiletician Femi B. Adeleye uses the language of deliverance without repentance.[53] I refer to it as grace without discipleship, a message that goes back at least as far as antinomian controversies in the early church. In its modern iteration, listeners hear that they are loved, accepted, and free with little to no urging from their preacher to pursue repentance and holiness, to practice reconciliation, or to partner in God's mission in the world. Perhaps it sounds hyperbolic, but if a doctor tells a patient who has just come out of open-heart surgery, "You have a free pass on diet and exercise for the rest of your life now that I have repaired your heart," then the message might sound like good news to a patient who does not want to change, but the news itself is not an accurate portrayal of reality, and it is certainly not what is best for the patient's future health.

Theologians and non-theologians alike have observed how pervasive, popular, and appealing such a message continues to be in modern preaching.[54] For the sake of brevity, I will mention just three theologians who provided critiques

---

51. According to Martyn, Paul had to confront the Galatians precisely because they had fallen into a distorted understanding of the gospel as a this-for-that exchange. To show how vehement he was in his opposition to this view, Martyn writes, "In the theology of the apostle there has never been, is not, and never will be a salvific circular exchange between human beings and God; for there is nothing human beings can do that will place God in their debt (a fact that is in itself genuinely liberating!)." "Apocalyptic Gospel in Galatians," 250.

52. Luther, *Bondage of the Will*, 100.

53. Adeleye argues that preachers have allowed themselves to preach a "strange gospel" that produces "strange Christians." Concerning repentance, he writes,

> One of the greatest losses in the church today is the emphasis on repentance. We have replaced a gospel that emphasized contrition and repentance with one that indulges our "self-esteem" or offers us deliverance services when our urgent need is to repent. How have some of us come to believe that the remedy for outward expression of a fallen sinful nature is a dose of deliverance service rather than repentance? Even those who have yet to encounter Christ in a personal way are herded to the altar of deliverance as if their sinful nature only needs a little trimming for their inward good to be released. (*Preachers of a Different Gospel*, 8)

54. For an example of a sociological survey of this trend in American congregations, see Witten, *All Is Forgiven*.

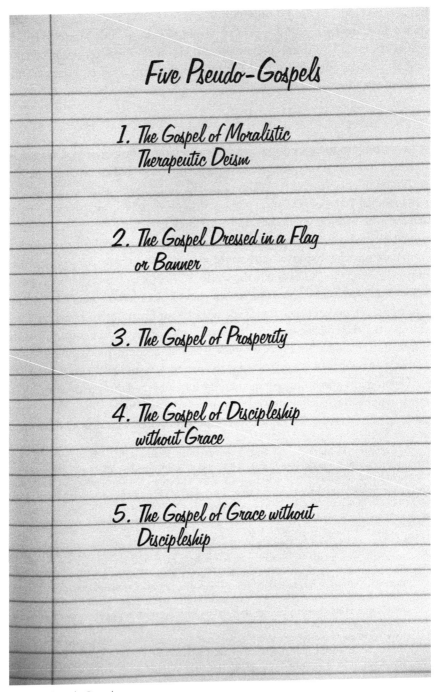

Figure 1.5. Pseudo-Gospels

decades ago but whose insights might sound familiar and even prescient to modern ears. In his critique of American twentieth-century liberal mainline Protestantism, H. Richard Niebuhr summarizes the distortion of the Christian message in this succinct phrase: "A God without wrath who brought men without sin into a kingdom without judgment through the ministrations of a Christ without a cross."[55] A pseudo-gospel of grace without discipleship proposes that God is no longer judge, humanity is no longer sinful, and the sacrifice of Christ on the cross is no longer needed. Such a belief system distorts God's divine character and human nature to such an extent that discipleship is no longer necessary.

In *The Cost of Discipleship*, Dietrich Bonhoeffer uses the language of "cheap grace" versus "costly grace" to describe the domestication of the gospel in the modern pulpit: "Cheap grace is the preaching of forgiveness without requiring repentance, baptism without church discipline, Communion without confession, absolution without contrition. Cheap grace is grace without discipleship, grace without the Cross, grace without Jesus Christ, living and incarnate."[56] Bonhoeffer refers to cheap grace as the "enemy" of Christian mission because it de-couples divine self-donation from Christian discipleship. In a church characterized by cheap grace, the world receives "a cheap covering for its sins; no contrition is required, still less any real desire to be delivered from sin."[57]

Finally, C. S. Lewis argues that many Christians are more interested in a relationship with a heavenly grandfather than a heavenly Father. That is to say, they want a God who looks on everything they say and do with a "wry smile," and answers, "What does it matter so long as they are contented?" Lewis writes, "We want, in fact, not so much a Father in heaven as a grandfather in heaven—a senile benevolence who, as they say, 'liked to see young people enjoy themselves.'"[58]

Although all three theologians made these points more than sixty years ago, how much more do their insights ring true now as compared to then?

Christian Preaching: Five Proposals

After a sermon, most preachers hope that people have encountered God, experienced the gospel, learned something new, and grown in some way.

55. Niebuhr, *Kingdom of God in America*, 193.
56. Bonhoeffer, *Cost of Discipleship*, 38.
57. Bonhoeffer, *Cost of Discipleship*, 37.
58. Lewis, *Problem of Pain*, 31–32.

But how do we make our sermons recognizably Christian? What does that look like? Thomas G. Long is right when he writes, "What is often lacking from our proclamation of the 'good news' is a deep sense of the gospel itself as 'news.'"[59] Hopefully we as preachers strive to make our sermons gospel centered, which means the good news comes through to our listeners in some way, shape, or form. They hear news of what God has done, is doing, and will do in their lives and in the world. Preachers should not want people to walk away from their sermons with *no* news at all; neither should they want them to leave the sermon with the wrong news.

> *"What is often lacking from our proclamation of the 'good news' is a deep sense of the gospel itself as 'news.'"*
> —Thomas G. Long

In this final section, I will make five brief proposals that help us to engage these to re-center on our task. You will also have more opportunities to engage this subject through the learning activities connected to this chapter.

Proposal 1: Preach the Text in Order to Preach the Gospel

I love commentaries. I get a lot out of them, and I feel like I learn a lot when I read them. But remember that commentaries have different audiences and different aims than sermons. Also remember that, without discernment, one can so yield to the commentator's authority that the commentary takes over a sermon. As homiletician Joel C. Gregory likes to remind us, "Commentaries are guides, not gods."[60] Although we benefit from reading commentaries, we do not benefit those who listen to us by sounding like them. It also does not benefit us if we return to the same commentaries over and over again; it limits our perspective and hinders our growth.

Especially if you are in seminary, avoid the common tendency to preach a sermon that sounds like it is a running commentary on the text. People might learn a lot about the text in its context, they might acquire new information or new understanding, but they will not hear the proclamation of the good news. If you preach the text without preaching the gospel, then you have failed at both tasks. No doubt we *need* good explanations from the pulpit in order to gain new understanding. But, in the end, explanation serves the larger purpose of proclamation. Preachers proclaim the gospel *as* they explain the gospel. Explanation without proclamation is like a violin without strings. If you take away the strings, then you take away the music. Without the strings,

59. Long, "No News Is Bad News," 149.
60. As heard in person on several occasions in sermons or classroom settings.

you miss out on all that a violin is and does. After enough time passes, you no longer know what it sounds like.

Proposal 2: Have a Redemptive Focus in Every Sermon

Homileticians like to engage in debates over what a Christian sermon should look like or sound like, and most of our debates are no doubt profitable to the homiletical task. Some argue that every sermon should lift up the cross and resurrection in some way. Others argue that every sermon should facilitate trust in and obedience to Christ. Still others argue that every sermon should help listeners to be godly regardless of whether or not the preacher fixes the spotlight solely on Christ.

Instead of being dogmatic about a particular approach, let me argue that preachers should strive to have a *redemptive focus* in every sermon.[61] What is the good news of the text or texts you plan to preach? In what way does the gospel reveal itself? How might you make your sermon sound redemptive rather than punitive in content and in tone even if you believe it lends itself to a prophetic tone? Sometimes the focus comes through clearly and is obvious to us, and other times it is more difficult to detect. We will return to this theme in proposal 5.

Proposal 3: Maintain a Healthy Tension between Lament and Hope

When we preach lament without hope, we offer people an incomplete picture of God's plan for human history. But when we preach hope without lament, we offer people an inaccurate picture of life this side of eternity.[62] As preachers, we hold to a healthy tension between hope and lament. Perhaps the greater danger in a chapter on preaching good news is that we would succumb to the danger of preaching hope without lament.

Preaching good news does *not* look like ignoring the front page of the newspaper, shutting ourselves off to real problems in a congregation, or offering glib or trite answers to pain and suffering in the world. Most listeners can see right through hollow visions of hope detached from realistic portrayals of hardship. Good news does not have to sound like shallow bromides. Sometimes good news will sound like hope-filled lament in the midst of sorrow.

61. For further thoughts on redemptive preaching, see Alcántara, *Learning from a Legend*, 42–43.

62. Soong-Chan Rah writes: "To only have a theology of celebration at the cost of the theology of suffering is incomplete. The intersection of the two threads provides the opportunity to engage in the fullness of the gospel message. Lament and praise must go hand in hand." *Prophetic Lament*, 23.

Proposal 4: Help People Remember What They Have Forgotten

As human beings, we have a remarkable capacity to forget what we should remember.[63] The Cuban homiletician Cecilio Arrastía argues that Christian preaching strives to "restore memory" to people who have forgotten who they are in Christ. He compares preaching's vital task to the moment when the prodigal son returns home "after recovering his memory." Arrastía writes, "When he 'returned to himself,' he arose and decided to return to the place which he should have never abandoned. To preach is to try to restore memory—*anamnesis* [remembrance] not *amnesia*—to the congregation that hears, that they might arise and return."[64]

Preaching summons us to remember who God is and who we are so that we might also arise and return. In a sense, the regular task of the preacher is to remind people on a regular basis that they need to be raised again *again*. Do we as preachers help Christian laypeople remember that they are loved in Christ, saved by Christ, united to Christ, and made alive through Christ? Do we encourage all people to hear that God is calling them out of their complacency, self-deceit, and self-absorption into authentic and abiding discipleship so that they might arise and return home?

Proposal 5: Consider the Narrative Context of the Text

Perhaps the good news leaps off the page when you read and study the Scripture passage(s). Some passages lend themselves quite well to being good-news sermons. But inspiration does not come as fast or as easy with every single text, especially when it comes to difficult and troubling passages. While we strive to do justice to the text, we also strive to do justice to the larger narrative arc of Scripture. To ask how a passage fits into the larger story does not mean that we make whatever wild assertions happen to enter our minds. Rather, we zoom out so that we can see how the passage fits in the broader context of Scripture. Think of the Bible as a large story with smaller stories scattered throughout its pages. It has at least four major acts: (1) creation, (2) rebellion, (3) redemption, and (4) restoration. The redemption that occurs in act 3 takes place in response to the rebellion that happens in act 2. The restoration in act 4 functions as a new-creation return to the beauty of the

---

63. For more on preaching and memory, see Arthurs, *Preaching as Reminding*.

64. In Spanish: "El hijo pródigo del relato de Cristo regresa sólo despues de recobrar su memoria, cuando «volviendo en si», se levanta y decide regresar al hogar que nunca debió abandonar. Al predicar se trata de devolver la memoria—*anamnesis* y no *amnesia*—al pueblo que oye, para que se levante y regrese. Y esto se logra contando la historia «de Cristo y de su amor»." Arrastía, *Teoría y Práctica de la Predicación*, 26.

creation in act 1. Connections abound. As preachers, we locate passages of the Bible somewhere between these four major acts, but we also read them as redeemed people living on this side of act 3 and not yet to act 4. That is to say, we locate our text by fitting it into the larger story God is telling.

Conclusion

During his time as pastor at Holy Trinity Lutheran Church in New York, Paul Scherer blessed thousands of people through his preaching and teaching ministry. He preached at Holy Trinity, he preached in various pulpits around the country and the world, and he preached as a familiar voice on national radio broadcasts. In the early years of his retirement, Scherer agreed to be a part-time adjunct homiletics professor at Princeton Theological Seminary. We do not know much about what happened in Scherer's preaching classes, but at least one story survives.

The story goes that Scherer was sitting in Miller Chapel listening to students preach. Back then, all the students preached in the chapel rather than in a classroom. A young seminarian named Charles L. Bartow stood up to preach, and he did not disappoint. He delivered a sermon that impressed and inspired his classmates. Bartow was a gifted preacher and an able student with a contract offer to teach at the graduate level after graduation. Years later, Bartow would become an influential homiletician and make important contributions in the field. But when the time came for Bartow to listen to the critiques of the sermon, Scherer said, "That sermon was sub-Christian." Apparently, Scherer did not struggle with mincing words. After the class concluded, Bartow's friends reassured him outside on the chapel steps that Dr. Scherer was out of line and that he had probably lost a few steps in his old age. At first, Bartow believed they were right. But the comment ate away at him to the point that he finally realized a few months later that Scherer was right. He called Scherer on the phone, who then spent several hours talking him through how to preach a recognizably Christian sermon.[65]

None of us want to hear a critique like that from someone we respect, that we have preached a sermon that impresses and inspires but sounds more sub-Christian than Christian. Who among us really wants another person to tell them that they have missed the mark on the one thing that Christian preachers are called to do: preach the gospel? Sometimes our defenses go up: "Who is he or she to say *that* about my sermon?" Other times, our

---

65. Story recounted in a phone conversation with Charles L. Bartow on March 16, 2018.

insecurities undo us: "I guess I must not be the right kind of preacher." But Bartow saw the whole ordeal as a God-ordained, transformative moment, one that redeemed his ministry even though it was painful at first. Scherer offered him the same reminder that every Christian preacher needs. Before you give people anything else, give them the gospel.

Learning activities and sermon samples for this chapter are located at www .PracticesofChristian Preaching.com.

2

Preach Convictionally

If you are a theologian, you will pray truly and if you pray truly,
you will be a theologian.

—Evagrius Ponticus, "Praktikos 60"

The hard work of preaching is actually the internal spiritual work.
In fact, the most difficult sermon you may ever preach is the one
you preach with your life.

—Luke A. Powery, in Brown and Powery, *Ways of the Word*

The year 2011 marked the fiftieth anniversary of the Freedom Rides, a
nonviolent movement designed to desegregate interstate transportation throughout the South. Led primarily by young adults, people
from different races, ethnicities, and genders boarded segregated buses in
order to desegregate them. A forty-one-year-old named James Farmer Jr. led
the movement; he was a friend of Martin Luther King Jr. and the cofounder
of the Committee of Racial Equality (CORE), the group that sponsored the
Freedom Rides.[1] Many of those who protested endured violence, intimidation
by police, physical beatings, and jail time.

Farmer died of diabetes complications in 1999, so he did not live to see the
fiftieth-anniversary milestone. But on September 17, 1985, he spoke about the
Riders in an interview with National Public Radio, which was then rebroadcast

1. The Committee of Racial Equality was later renamed the Congress of Racial Equality
but still kept the CORE acronym.

Figure 2.1. Mug Shots of Freedom Riders Arrested in Jackson, Mississippi

in 2011 on the occasion of the anniversary. In that interview, Farmer told a story about a couple of Riders who were arrested and thrown in jail in Jackson, Mississippi. The jails in Jackson and in other major cities were filling up as a result of the protests. In order to intimidate the group in Jackson, the prison guards came up with different ways to make them uncomfortable without resorting to physical violence.

They wanted to avoid negative press, so they used psychological maltreatment. But the Riders stayed united and often sang songs about freedom from their jail cells. The one comfort they could count on was the thin, straw mattress in their cells. "Everything else was cold, hard, stale, and steel," Farmer said. To make the singing stop, the prison guards decided to take away their mattresses—the last resource for comfort they had. It worked for a little while—they stopped singing.

But the mood changed in an instant when a young Bible student gave a speech to the Riders. As Farmer puts it, the young man "reminded everybody what they were doing, that here they're trying to take your soul away, you see. It's not the mattress. It's your soul." Suddenly, one of the Riders shouted: "Guards! Guards! Guards!" Thinking it was an emergency, one of the guards ran to the cell, and the man yelled loud enough for everyone else to hear:

"Come get my mattress! I'll keep my soul!" The whole place erupted, and the singing broke out once more.[2]

Stories like this one remind us that conviction is powerful and transformative in the life of a person and in the life of a community. Conviction turns a Bible student into a preacher and a prison cell into a revival meeting. No doubt courage and resilience also compel us to stand up in the face of a dangerous predicament. But I would argue that courage and resilience come from a deeper spring—conviction—which I define as *a commitment to a cause greater than oneself for the sake of a mission greater than one's life*.[3] Our calling as preachers requires that we believe what we say, not just that we say what we believe. We make claims about what we believe with our words, but we also make claims about whether we believe it with our lives. As George W. Truett reminds us, "It is conviction that convinces. The pulpit is no place for a religious stammerer. . . . It is conviction that convinces everywhere."[4] Imagine what would happen in churches and fellowships if preachers stepped into pulpits with just a fraction of the conviction that those Freedom Riders displayed. Is it too much to say that it could change the world?

The subject of this chapter is conviction; it is the first C of the Five Cs that we will study in chapters 2–6. In order to explore conviction further in this chapter, we will lift up various exemplars of conviction in Scripture and in church history, we will consider the homiletical convictions that ground conviction, and we will explore the practices that hinder and sustain conviction over time.

Exemplars of Conviction

A unique challenge lies before anyone who points to exemplars of conviction in Scripture and in church history. Not only is the list too long but it is also inevitable that the person compiling it will be selective. *We belong to a great tradition of preachers, people who modeled Christian conviction in life and ministry*. Like us, they were imperfect and fallible people, but their stories also inspire us in the work that God has called us to do. In a sense, any person

2. For a complete transcript of the Farmer interview, see "James Farmer Jr., Freedom Ride Organizer on Non-Violent Resistance."

3. In defining it this way, I delineate between *maintaining various convictions* and *having conviction*. The former has to do with what we believe, and the latter has to do with how we live. The two are interrelated, of course, but I will foreground *conviction* over *convictions*. Later in this chapter, I will lift up the various convictions that sustain conviction.

4. Truett, *President's Address: 6th Baptist World Congress* [audio recording], cited in Durso, *Thy Will Be Done*, 240.

The Practices
of Christian Preaching

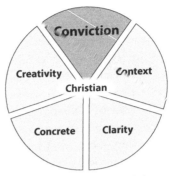

Figure 2.2. The Five Cs: Conviction

who answers God's call to preach signs up for a convictional life. By saying yes, they give themselves to a cause greater than themselves. But conviction in a preacher is a lot like water in a cistern. Unless it is replenished, it runs low. Perhaps studying exemplars of conviction will help us to replenish it in ourselves.

Models of Conviction in Scripture

Scripture provides us with many inspiring accounts of convictional preachers. To behold the ultimate convictional preacher, we need look no further than Jesus, who "resolutely set out for Jerusalem" even though he knew it would cost him his life (Luke 9:51). Besides the most obvious example, a whole host of Old Testament and New Testament preachers modeled conviction in their preaching. Consider the story of Nathan, who rebuked King David for his affair with Bathsheba (2 Sam. 12). Or consider Elijah, who confronted the prophets of Baal on Mount Carmel (1 Kings 18:16–46). Consider the story of Amos, who refused to be bullied by Amaziah the priest (Amos 7:10–17), or Jeremiah, who suffered under Pashhur the priest and persevered (Jer. 20). Queen Esther may not have been a preacher in the traditional sense, but her decision to risk her life, side with her people, and exclaim, "If I perish, I perish," preaches to this day to oppressed communities around the world (Esther 4:16).[5]

5. Old Testament commentator Karen H. Jobes points out that Esther embraces her power as a queen "only after she decides to align herself with God's covenant people. She is no longer a trophy wife, a queen in name only, but by putting on her royal robes in defense of her people she takes up the power of her position." *Esther*, 167.

In the New Testament, John the Baptist preached words of repentance and salvation to the powerless and confronted the powerful with words of judgment (Matt. 3:1–12; Luke 3:1–20; John 1:19–34). Think also of the Samaritan woman in John 4. After encountering Jesus, she went back and told everyone in the village about his message, and "many of the Samaritans from that town believed in him because of the woman's testimony" (John 4:39). Remember also that the earliest resurrection preachers were women. They encountered Jesus as a risen Savior before everyone else, and they were the first ones to spread the word to the Eleven that he was alive (Luke 24:10–12). Subsequent to the resurrection and ascension, Jesus's disciples took his message all over the Mediterranean world, and most of them paid for it with their lives.

The apostle Paul's life serves as a case study in conviction. Paul believed that his life belonged to God, that he was a vessel to advance the mission of God in the world. The task of testifying to God's grace made Paul's life meaningful, purposeful, and convictional (Acts 20:24). Within days of his dramatic encounter with Christ on the Damascus road, Paul preached "in the synagogues that Jesus is the Son of God" (Acts 9:20). On one of Paul's missionary journeys, shortly after he and Barnabas preached in the city of Lystra, some opponents from Antioch won the crowd over, had Paul stoned, and dragged him out of the city. They beat him badly enough that people thought he was dead. "But after the disciples had gathered around him, he got up and went back into the city" (Acts 14:20).

Paul's convictional commitment to Christ also revealed itself throughout his letters to the churches. For the sake of brevity, I will mention just a few examples among many that could be given:

- Romans 8:38–39: "For *I am convinced* that neither death nor life, neither angels nor demons, neither the present nor the future, nor any powers, neither height nor depth, nor anything else in all creation, will be able to separate us from the love of God that is in Christ Jesus our Lord."
- Romans 14:14: "*I am convinced,* being *fully persuaded* in the Lord Jesus, that nothing is unclean."
- 2 Corinthians 5:14–15: "For Christ's love compels us, because *we are convinced* that one died for all, and therefore all died. And he died for all, that those who live should *no longer live for themselves* but for him who died for them and was raised again."
- Philippians 1:20–21: "I eagerly expect and hope that I will in no way be ashamed, but will have *sufficient courage* so that now as always Christ

will be exalted in my body, whether by life or by death. For to me, *to live is Christ and to die is gain*."

- Philippians 3:7–8: "But whatever were gains to me I now consider loss for the sake of Christ. What is more, *I consider everything a loss* because of the *surpassing worth of knowing* Christ Jesus my Lord, for whose sake I have lost all things. *I consider them garbage, that I may gain Christ*."

- 2 Timothy 1:11–12: "And of this gospel I was appointed a herald and an apostle and a teacher. That is why I am suffering as I am. Yet this is no cause for shame, because *I know* whom I have believed, and am *convinced* that he is able to guard what I have entrusted to him until that day."

Just to clarify, conviction in Paul's letters does not mean the absence of struggle or the removal of doubt. To the Corinthians, he says, "We were under great pressure, far beyond our ability to endure, so that we despaired of life itself. Indeed, we felt we had received the sentence of death" (2 Cor. 1:8–9). Paul reaches a nadir in ministry more than once *because* of what he believes and how he lives his life. Conviction should not be conflated with naive escapism.

If anything, Paul's conviction deepens when he endures trial and goes through conflict. Challenges compel him to confront hardship rather than shrink from it. Thus he tells the Philippians with a clear conscience that he has "lost all things" for Christ because he has gained the one thing that matters most in the light of eternity (*sub specie aeternitatis*): "the surpassing worth of knowing Christ Jesus my Lord" (Phil. 3:8). To the Corinthians he can say, we are "known, yet regarded as unknown; dying, and yet we live on; beaten, and yet not killed; sorrowful, yet always rejoicing; poor, yet making many rich; having nothing, and yet possessing everything" (2 Cor. 6:9–10).

Perhaps it is not surprising, then, that the assurance and God-centeredness in Paul's writings also come through in the speeches and writings of *other* key leaders in the early church. When the rulers of the Sanhedrin forbid Peter and John from preaching in Jesus's name, the apostles tell them, "Which is right in God's eyes: to listen to you, or to him? You be the judges! As for us, *we cannot help* speaking about what we have seen and heard" (Acts 4:19–20). After affirming that Jesus is the Son of God and the great high priest who empathizes with our weakness, the writer of Hebrews exclaims, "Let us then approach God's throne of grace with *confidence*, so that we may receive mercy and find grace to help us in our time of need" (Heb. 4:16). 1 John 5:14 reads, "This is the *confidence* we have in approaching God: that if we ask anything according to his will, he hears us." For the earliest apostles and Christian leaders, nothing could compare to the confidence that came from knowing Christ, from being found by him and united to him, from serving as "co-workers" with him in the message and ministry of reconciliation (2 Cor. 5:16–6:2).

Models of Conviction in the Christian Tradition

Examples of conviction also abound in the Christian tradition. Any attempt at a survey must be selective. Consider some of the major figures of the second half of the twentieth century, preachers whose lives were marked by conviction, names that might still be familiar to us. In the United States, preachers like Martin Luther King Jr., Billy Graham, and Gardner C. Taylor come to mind; names that still mean a great deal to a lot of people.[6] For those who are older, perhaps you saw them in person, heard them preach, or got to meet them.

A self-proclaimed "drum major for justice," King called on an entire nation to repent of its "original sin" of racism in order to transform itself into a country of freedom, equality, righteousness, and generosity.[7] His influence continues to be felt decades after his assassination. Graham, who was converted at an evangelistic meeting in 1934 at the age of sixteen, spent his life reaching as many people as possible with the gospel of Christ, which, in his case, was an estimated 215 million people in 185 countries on six continents, a figure that does not include the millions more reached on radio and television.[8] A charismatic entrepreneur with impeccable character, he preached a simple gospel message of hope and forgiveness rooted in a firm belief in the Scriptures as the inspired Word of God. Taylor, who was described by his peers and protégés with titles such as the "dean of the nation's black preachers" and "the prince of the American pulpit," held a master class in preaching for forty-two years from his pulpit at Concord Baptist Church of Christ in Brooklyn, New York, and in countless pulpits in dozens of countries on six continents.[9] An untiring advocate of racial and educational justice, he possessed a rare

6. This is to say almost nothing about the US preachers who were revered in the two to three generations before the second half of the twentieth century on account of their influence and impact, people like Howard Thurman, Florence Spearing Randolph, Dwight L. Moody, William Seymour, and Charles Finney, to name just a few.
7. For a description of racism as "America's original sin," see Wallis, *America's Original Sin*. For King's sermon, see King, "Drum Major Instinct," in *Knock at Midnight*, 165–86.
8. One reputable source of the data on the numbers of people reached by Graham and the number of countries visited is Goodstein, "Billy Graham, 99, Dies."
9. For the title "dean of the nation's black preachers," see "American Preaching: A Dying Art?" For the title "prince of the American pulpit," see Mitchell, "African American Preaching," 372.

combination of pulpit eloquence, pastoral wisdom, prophetic incisiveness, and contextual responsiveness born out of an enduring belief that preaching was the spring from which all other ministry should flow.

These three late twentieth-century preachers represent only a small subset of the preachers all over the world who have made conscious decisions to commit themselves to a cause greater than themselves for the sake of a mission greater than their lives. Indeed, how great is the company of preachers. Leaders in southeast Asia like Kyung-Chik Han in South Korea and Toyohiko Kagawa in Japan come to mind.[10] F. W. Boreham had a vibrant preaching and writing ministry in New Zealand, Tasmania, and Australia, mainly among Baptists.[11] In Africa, we find countless preachers whose lives were/are marked by conviction, people like Janani Luwum in Uganda, Conrad Mbewe in Zambia, and Desmond Tutu in South Africa, to name just a few.[12] In Latin America, consider the unique and diverse contributions of evangelists like Luis Palau in Argentina, scholar-poets like Cecilio Arrastía in Cuba, and activists like Oscar Romero in El Salvador.[13] In modern Europe, Joan Alexandru's preaching impacted thousands during the revolution in Romania.

We can also look to the courageous female preachers of the nineteenth and early twentieth centuries, women who faced countless obstacles, insults, attacks, and adversity but who nevertheless persisted in preaching. Jarena Lee serves as a model of courage and resilience. Many look to her as a pioneer not just for black women preachers but for *all* women preachers. She successfully lobbied Richard Allen to allow her (and other women) the right to preach in the African Methodist Episcopal (AME) church. She developed a fruitful itinerant ministry in churches and meetinghouses throughout New Jersey, New York, Pennsylvania, Maryland, and Ohio, sometimes traveling by foot

10. Kagawa's conviction comes through powerfully in his book *Meditations on the Cross*: "It is not enough to have ideals. We must translate them into action. . . . Theology is all right, but there is no strength in a theology which does not become apparent in practice" (167). For more on Kyung-Chik Han and Toyohiko Kagawa's preaching ministries, see Old, *Reading and Preaching of the Scriptures*, 7:566–86, 635–40.

11. For Boreham's autobiography, see Boreham, *Pathway to Roses*.

12. For more on the preaching of Janani Luwum and Conrad Mbewe, see Old, *Reading and Preaching of the Scriptures*, 7:196–98, 229–36. For more on Desmond Tutu's preaching, see his book of sermons, *Hope and Suffering*.

13. Referring to Arrastía's impact on Latin America, Costa Rican theologian Plutarco Bonilla states, "Su nombre es, en América Latina, sinónimo de predicación, y de predicación altura." In English: "His name is, in Latin America, synonymous with preaching, and preaching of great heights." "Cecilio Arrastía," 11. Oscar Romero made the following claim about the church's inaction in response to government and military oppression in the final sermon he delivered before being gunned down by assassins at his church in El Salvador: "The Church . . . cannot remain silent before such abomination." For an excerpt from Romero's final sermon, see Douglass, *Nonviolent Coming of God*, 46.

for miles to reach her destination. She broke with societal norms by preaching to mixed-gender audiences. In 1836, she wrote the first major autobiography by a black woman, *The Life and Religious Experience of Jarena Lee, A Colored Lady*.[14] Moreover, she paved the way for women who followed her in the AME Church, such as Zilpha Elaw, Julia A. J. Foote, Sojourner Truth, Mary McLeod Bethune, and Florence Spearing Randolph. She accomplished almost all of this *after* her husband died unexpectedly and tragically, leaving her a widowed mother of two young children, materially poor and in poor health.

Sarah Righter Major launched her preaching ministry from Germantown, Pennsylvania, in the early nineteenth century, becoming the first woman preacher in the Church of the Brethren.[15] Some churches close to her Germantown congregation welcomed her into their pulpits, but many refused to welcome her. In 1844, she and her husband relocated to Ohio, where they continued on the preaching circuit, became early advocates for racial equality as abolitionists, and transformed their home into a stop on the Underground Railroad.[16]

These are just two examples of convictional women preachers. A growing number of historians have attempted to recover stories like these but have struggled to gain access to primary sources and non-pejorative secondhand accounts.[17] According to historian Catherine Brekus, many of these preachers were "too conservative to be remembered by women's rights activists, but too radical to be remembered by evangelicals."[18] Feminists ignored them because

14. In *Sisters of the Spirit*, William Andrews describes the impact of Jarena Lee's publication: "[It] launched black women's autobiography in America with an argument for women's spiritual authority that plainly challenged traditional female roles as defined in both the free and the slave states, among whites as well as blacks. . . . Lee's autobiography offers us the earliest and most detailed firsthand information we have about the traditional roles of women in organized black religious life in the United States and about the ways in which resistance to those roles began to manifest itself" (2). See also Lee, *Life and Religious Experience of Jarena Lee*.

15. Righter Major was a protégé of the evangelist Harriet Livermore, a prominent early nineteenth-century female preacher. Livermore had an influential itinerant ministry in the first half of her adult life, preaching to the president, congressional leaders, and other members of the public in the Capitol in 1827 in Washington, DC. According to historian Catherine Brekus, Livermore considered Righter Major a "spiritual daughter." For more on the mentor-protégé relationship, see Brekus, *Strangers and Pilgrims*, 223–24.

16. For more on Sarah Righter Major, see Frye, *Uncommon Woman*. See also Brekus, *Strangers and Pilgrims*, 203, 223–24, 264, 302.

17. For some historical accounts of women preachers, see Higginbotham, *Righteous Discontent*; Collier-Thomas, *Daughters of Thunder*; Haywood, *Prophesying Daughters*; Zink-Sawyer, *From Preachers to Suffragists*; R. Larson, *Daughters of Light*.

18. Brekus, *Strangers and Pilgrims*, 7. Commenting on the gap in the historical record for women preachers in the late eighteenth and early nineteenth centuries, Brekus writes, "Female preachers have been virtually forgotten by modern-day historians. Despite the remarkable number of books and articles published about women and religion during the last twenty-five years,

of their religious conservatism, and conservatives wrote them out of their histories because of their progressivism.[19]

Think of the many other figures throughout church history who have preached with conviction, none of them flawless but all of them committed to proclaiming the gospel of Christ even at great cost. The preacher John Knox confronted Mary Queen of Scots in Scotland. Martin Luther stood for his beliefs at the Diet of Worms and faced death threats the rest of his life. In December 1511, the Dominican friar Antonio Montesinos preached courageously against the evils of slavery in the Spanish colonies from his pulpit in Hispaniola, what is now the Dominican Republic and Haiti. John Wycliffe spoke out against ecclesiastical abuses in England in the fourteenth century, and Jan Hus followed in his footsteps in the Czech Republic in the fifteenth century. In France, Bernard of Clairvaux initiated the reform of Benedictine monasticism in the first half of the twelfth century. Also in France but much earlier, the sixth-century church leader Radegund changed lives through her itinerant ministry and ascetic lifestyle, establishing a convent, building a hospital, serving lepers, helping the poor, and engaging in peacemaking efforts for the Frankish kingdom.[20] In the fifth century, John Chrysostom rebuked the emperor and empress from his pulpit in Constantinople, and in the second century, Irenaeus protected and defended the clergy during the Roman persecution in Lyon. These are just some of the many convictional preachers whose lives continue to preach to us today.

Resolutions That Ground Conviction

If George Truett is right when he says, "It is conviction that convinces everywhere," then perhaps the next question we should ask is, "What does that look like for a preacher today?"[21] My answer comes in two parts: resolutions and practices. We will consider the resolutions that ground conviction and the practices that either hinder or sustain conviction. I use the word "resolutions" in much the same way that Jonathan Edwards used it.[22] By resolutions I mean

there has been no social or cultural history of female preaching in early America." *Strangers and Pilgrims*, 3.

19. On the issue of conservative denominational historians, Brekus writes, "Female preachers were virtually written out of their churches' histories in the mid-nineteenth century—a silence that has been perpetuated ever since." *Strangers and Pilgrims*, 7.

20. For more on the life of Radegund, see Schulenburg, *Forgetful of Their Sex*, 18–20.

21. Truett, *President's Address*, as quoted in Durso, *Thy Will Be Done*, 240.

22. Early in his ministry, Edwards wrote down seventy resolutions—that is, commitments that he embraced in order to sustain him in everyday situations. See Edwards, *Jonathan Edwards' Resolutions*.

ideals that one believes, holds to, and strives for, regardless of circumstance. For the purposes of this chapter, I will propose the following homiletical resolutions as the ground to convictional preaching.

God Has Called Us to Preach

Our sense of call should not be overlooked. As Christian preachers, we do not need to know the answer to every question; it would be arrogant and presumptuous to claim that we have plumbed the depths of theological sophistication or practical wisdom. Despite our shortcomings, remember this: *God has called us to this work no matter what others say to us or about us.* In *The Certain Sound of the Trumpet*, Samuel D. Proctor explains that the call to preach brings with it a level of urgency that one cannot ignore; it represents a watershed moment in a person's life. Proctor writes, "One simply proceeds after it is certain that no other work, no other assignment, calls forth one's total energies and commitment like the call to preach. With that, no other guarantees are offered."[23] The "call" sustains us through dark tunnels of uncertainty, extended seasons in which we feel like the cistern of our conviction has emptied and can no longer be replenished. Because we have said yes to God, we proceed without the guarantees that we would otherwise hope for or expect. Yet a lot of preachers are able to live with a lack of guarantees for the burden to preach in response to Christ's call weighs much heavier on them than the pretense of certainty.[24] In fact, our burden sometimes feels heavy enough that any other response seems like disobedience. We can't *not* preach! We resonate with Paul's statement: "For when I preach the gospel, I cannot boast, since I am *compelled* to preach. Woe to me if I do not preach the gospel!" (1 Cor. 9:16). Remember that in the ancient world, a woe oracle functioned like a curse; therefore, Paul's meaning is, "May I be cursed if I do *not* preach the gospel." Convictional preaching means that one feels compelled to preach, that one experiences a paradoxical yearning for what James Earl Massey calls the "burdensome joy of preaching."[25]

> "One simply proceeds after it is certain that no other work, no other assignment, calls forth one's total energies and commitment like the call to preach. With that, no other guarantees are offered."
>
> —Samuel D. Proctor

---

23. Proctor, *Certain Sound of the Trumpet*, 7.

24. For more on the burden of preaching, see Massey, *Burdensome Joy of Preaching*, 13–17.

25. Massey writes: "I have long looked upon preaching, and graciously experienced it, as a burdensome joy. It is 'burdensome' because of the way the preparation and delivery aspects of

Many of us would have chosen a path other than this one had it not been for the call of God on our lives. Before God called Jarena Lee to preach she was a stay-at-home mother of two young children. Before God called Gardner C. Taylor to preach, he was preparing himself to apply to the University of Michigan Law School. James Earl Massey planned to be a professional musician before God called him to preach. Massey writes: "All of the signs along the path of my interest pointed to a career as a pianist, not as a preacher. But it was not to be so, and for reasons that point back straight to God."[26] The call to preach has a way of challenging societal conventions and interfering with our vocational plans.

Several years ago, Joseph Jeter preached a sermon in which he told a story about one of his former homiletics students. When Jeter met this student for the first time in class, she made it clear that she had no plans to be a preacher. But, as often happens with young seminarians, she experienced a directional shift and an alteration of God's call on her life. She fell in love with preaching and discovered a sense of purpose in the task. After graduation, she responded to a call from a little church in a small town in Texas and gave herself wholeheartedly to the work of pastoral ministry, especially the work of regular Sunday morning preaching. Then, without warning, tragedy struck: "A garbage truck ran a red light and broadsided her car, pinning her inside." The emergency vehicles arrived to find her unconscious. They had to use the Jaws of Life to set her free from the car. She could have easily died had the situation been slightly different. After being rushed to the hospital, she regained consciousness. As the doctor was telling her that she would need extensive surgeries, "Just before she drifted off to sleep, she smiled and said four words: '*I can still preach!*'"[27]

A preacher's burden moves beyond the trite and superficial—"I'm good at it" or "It's fun to preach"—to a deeper call for life and for ministry. We believe that God has called us to preach, that "no other work, no other assignment, calls forth [our] total energies and commitment like the call to preach."[28] As a matter of conviction, we decide to become "woe to me if I do not preach" preachers.

---

the pulpit task weigh upon the preacher's selfhood—and with so many unique demands. But preaching is also a 'joy' because of the divine purpose that makes it necessary and the redeeming eventfulness that it can effect for those who receive it with faith and openness." *Burdensome Joy of Preaching*, 13.

26. Massey, *Burdensome Joy of Preaching*, 29.

27. Graves, *Fully Alive Preacher*, 6 (emphasis added). Graves recounted hearing Jeter tell this story in a sermon delivered at the annual Academy of Homiletics meeting in the early 2000s.

28. Proctor, *Certain Sound of the Trumpet*, 7.

God Preaches through Preachers

God's decision to preach through preachers seems about as counterintuitive as a parent deciding to give dynamite to toddlers. Not only does it confound intuition; it also seems careless and unwise. Yet, for reasons God only knows, God sees fit to announce the good news of the kingdom through preachers, finite sinners that we are. In preaching, God mediates the written word through human words so that human words re-present the divine Word. God speaks *to* preachers so that God-as-Preacher will reach the world *through* preaching. In the mysterious providence of God, bones become flesh; words become fire; sound sets the context for Spirit. Thus, Christian preaching remains paradoxical; it is rash and audacious on the one hand and miraculous and gracious on the other. In preaching, God has placed "treasure in jars of clay" so that both the church and the world might see and be persuaded that "this all-surpassing power is from God and not from us" (2 Cor. 4:7).

If we believe that God sees fit to preach through preaching, it requires a willingness in us to cooperate with ("co-operate" literally means "work with") and depend on the Holy Spirit in the work of Christian proclamation. It obligates us to hold divine agency and human agency in tension, recognizing our role and responsibility to study and perform the gospel while also acknowledging with humility that only the Spirit can superintend over the sermon. Preaching without depending on the Spirit can be compared to sitting in a sailboat without relying on the wind.

The apostle Paul reminds the Thessalonians of the centrality of the Spirit's presence and work when he writes, "Our gospel came to you not simply with words but also with power, with the Holy Spirit and deep conviction" (1 Thess. 1:5). Although he mentions power, the Spirit, and conviction in conjunction in this verse, in the larger context of 1 Thessalonians the Holy Spirit takes precedence and is the source of the other two. That is to say, in Paul's theology, power and conviction are Spirit-infused activities and dispositions.[29]

Concerning God's desire to preach through preachers, John Chrysostom spoke of the "condescension of God's Word"—that is, the miracle of God con-descending (coming down) and dwelling with us. That is to say, in preaching, God speaks words in our language, communicates grace and truth to the church through Spirit-indwelt human speech.[30] Whenever we preach, writes

---

29. As Angela H. Reed observes, "Paul knows it is the Holy Spirit, not words alone, that brings divine power for conviction (1:5). The Thessalonians have their own connection to God who has given them the Holy Spirit (4:8). Though Paul is the one to offer instruction on Christlike living, it is God who accomplishes personal and communal transformation (5:24)." *Quest for Spiritual Community*, 86.

30. See Old, *Reading and Preaching of the Scriptures*, 2:187.

Dietrich Bonhoeffer, "The Word of God has really entered into the humiliation of the word of man. Man's word of preaching is the Word of God by virtue of God's voluntary association, by which he has bound himself to the word of man."[31] It should humble us when we realize that the Spirit of God is "bound . . . to the word of man," hovering over Christian proclamation—working in, through, and sometimes in spite of the preacher who speaks an audacious word from the Lord.

Preaching in cooperation with the Holy Spirit makes more sense when we remember that grace in its most basic definition is the receiving of a gift we do not deserve.[32] As Lenny Luchetti puts it, preaching "reminds us that God can and does accomplish the impossible through impossible methods. He just might decide to show up through the so-so words of a so-so preacher and transform so-so people into disciples who change the world."[33] When we hold on to the healthy tension that preaching is both divine and human, presumption and grace, sound and Spirit, it balances our fear and trembling with reverence and confidence. More importantly, it enables us to believe that God really does preach through preachers.

God Expects Us to Be Faithful Stewards of the Gospel

Homileticians use different kinds of imagery and terminology to describe what preaching is, words like "heralding," "witnessing," "confessing," "prophesying," "proclaiming," and "declaring." Most of these words help us understand what preaching is and how the biblical writers might have understood its purpose and function. Yet one underutilized metaphor for preaching is "stewarding."[34] A steward is a person who has been entrusted with someone else's most cherished possessions, such as a home, cattle, land, and even family members. The steward's job is to be a faithful guardian over that which has been entrusted. We see the metaphor of stewardship more generally when Jesus uses it in the parable of the talents (Matt. 25:14–30), the parable of the

31. Bonhoeffer, *Christ the Center*, 53. Bonhoeffer's larger point is that Christ himself comes to us when the Word is proclaimed through preaching: "The whole Christ is present in preaching, Christ humiliated and Christ exalted" (52).

32. Frederick Buechner offers this description: "Grace is something you can never get but only be given. There's no way to earn it or deserve it or bring it about any more than you can deserve the taste of raspberries and cream or earn good looks or bring about your own birth." *Wishful Thinking*, 33.

33. Luchetti, *Preaching Essentials*, 19.

34. Jason C. Meyer's work represents one example that foregrounds the language of preaching as stewarding. Meyer also emphasizes preaching as heralding, so the language of stewarding is one descriptor and not the central or sole descriptor for preaching in his work. See Meyer, *Preaching*, 21–23.

minas (Luke 19:11–27), or when he describes servants who do their duty (Luke 17:7–10). With reference to preaching, the language of stewarding and being entrusted with the gospel occurs several places, especially in Paul's Epistles:

- 1 Corinthians 4:1–2: "This, then, is how you ought to regard us: as *servants of Christ* and as those *entrusted* with the mysteries God has revealed. Now it is required that those who have been *given a trust* must prove *faithful*."
- 1 Corinthians 9:17: "If I preach voluntarily, I have a reward; if not voluntarily, I am simply *discharging the trust committed to me*."
- Galatians 2:7: "On the contrary, they recognized that I had been *entrusted with the task of preaching the gospel* to the uncircumcised, just as Peter had been to the circumcised."
- 1 Thessalonians 2:4: "On the contrary, we speak as those approved by God to be *entrusted with the gospel*. We are not trying to please people but God, who tests our hearts."
- Titus 1:3: ". . . the *preaching entrusted to me* by the command of God our Savior."

Notice the emphasis on being faithful to a trust much bigger than oneself. Paul conceives of his preaching as the faithful discharging of a trust that God has placed into his hands. As a result, he cares more about pleasing God than pleasing people since he believes that God is the one who has entrusted the task to him (1 Thess. 2:4; cf. also Gal. 1:10). When we preach, we need to remember that we are stewards, not owners. Stewards do not have an exaggerated sense of self-importance in light of their roles and responsibilities. They resist the urge to make the task before them about them.

The gospel we steward has the power to change the world; it is nothing less than the "power of God that brings salvation to everyone who believes" (Rom. 1:16). In the gospel, the kingdom of God has broken into time and space. The mystery of God has been revealed through Christ (Rom. 16:25; 1 Cor. 2:7–10; 4:1; Eph. 3:2–11; Col. 1:24–27; 4:3). In Ephesians 2:14–22, Paul asserts that, through Christ, the wall of separation has come down between peoples and races, peace has been forged, a new humanity has been created, and those who were once enemies of God and of one another have been transformed into brothers and sisters in the household of faith. This is a message that is life changing and world transforming.

What do we hold in our hands as preachers? It might frighten us to think about it but, in a sense, we hold the power of God for the salvation of everyone who believes. That sounds a lot like a toddler handling dynamite to me. To be sure, we *also* hold a message that people hear in time and space. We bring our voices, our gifts, our personalities, and our contexts to the sermon—preaching can never be disembodied. Yes, God entrusts it to us in time and space, but its dynamic power and significance ripple out through time and space. As stewards of this time-transcending message, I sometimes wonder if our fear is not so much that our preaching *cannot* do what we believe it can do but that it *can*.[35]

Faithfulness Matters More to God Than Success

Preachers need to prioritize faithfulness over success. Striving for success in preaching, at least as worldly systems define it, will sabotage our ministries and produce preachers who are proud, arrogant, insecure, and unethical. One of the ironies of preaching is that a successful preacher might mistakenly conclude that God put clay into a jar of treasure instead of putting treasure into a jar of clay. I find it curious that Jesus never used the language of success when talking about ministry and refused to make it a desired outcome for his disciples. Rather, Jesus spoke most often using the language of faithfulness and fruitfulness. Have you been faithful with the talents that I've entrusted to you? Are you remaining connected to the vine? (Matt. 25:14–28; John 15:1–8).

About fifteen years ago, when I was an associate pastor, I attended a church-leadership conference with other members of the staff at our church. I remember very little about the theme, the speakers, the participants, or the action steps that our team took after the conference. In fact, I remember only one statement that one pastor made in passing. When talking about pastoring, he said, "Jesus did not say to Peter, 'You will build my church.' He said, 'I will build my church.'" What a liberating word! At that moment, I felt a peace and rest that I had not felt before in ministry. Although the speaker did not say the next part of the verse, it would serve us well to re-familiarize ourselves with it. Jesus said, "I will build my church, and the gates of Hades will not overcome it" (Matt. 16:18). What would it look like for you to be set free from performance-based obsession with outcomes?

Let God take care of the outcomes of your preaching. I believe that statement theologically, but sometimes I struggle to believe it practically. To Nicodemus, Jesus said of the Spirit, "The wind blows wherever it pleases" (John 3:8), yet something in me wants to believe that I can control the wind and perhaps even wield it.

Go to www.PracticesofChristianPreaching.com to view a video of Pastor Ken Shigematsu as he challenges us to remember how God sees us not as performers who need to be efficient but as treasured children of God.

35. James Forbes observes, "Many of us fear being grasped by an invisible presence we cannot control." *Holy Spirit and Preaching*, 23.

Something in me concludes that it is up to me to make hearts of stone into hearts of flesh. Such a perspective produces one of two dispositions: arrogance or anxiety. Arrogance arises from overreliance on and security in our gifts and puffed up feelings of self-importance. We occupy the central place, the place that God alone should occupy. I can venture a guess that God is probably not interested in filling the world with more preachers who try to be like God. Anxiety arises when we transform our love for people into an unhealthy attachment to them and to their expectations of us. Those who hear us become our ultimate judges, rather than God, and we ride the wave of emotion under the constant burden of whether they are pleased with us. We ask, "Are they happy with me and my preaching?" instead of, "Have I been faithful with the talents entrusted to me?" When I preach, it brings me great relief to remember that Jesus said "I will build my church" instead of "You will build my church." When I am discouraged, it also helps when I remember the next part: "and the gates of Hades will not overcome it."

Preaching That Lives Comes from Living That Preaches

To borrow Old Testament imagery, God would rather that we rend our hearts than rend our garments (Joel 2:13). As ministers, we know instinctively that God cares about the condition of our hearts. Jesus reminded his disciples, "The things that come out of a person's mouth come from the heart" (Matt. 15:18). We think about and talk about the people, subjects, and things that captivate us. In *You Are What You Love: The Spiritual Power of Habit*, James K. A. Smith claims, "The heart is the existential chamber of our *love*, and it is our loves that orient us toward some ultimate end or *telos*."[36] The delight of our hearts manifests itself less in public venues like worship and more in private moments when we are alone or in everyday interactions with family, friends, and strangers.

Preaching that lives comes from living that preaches.

Our character matters to God.[37] As the old-time preachers like to say, "Charisma without character is catastrophe." One can show oneself to be

36. In the same paragraph, Smith argues that the heart holds our attention and draws our affection much more than the intellect. After describing love as the "ultimate end or *telos*," he writes, "It's not just that I 'know' some end or 'believe' in some *telos*. More than that, I *long* for some end. I *want* something, and want it ultimately. It is my desires that define me. In short, you are what you love." *You Are What You Love*, 9 (emphasis in original).

37. N. T. Wright claims, "Character—the transforming, shaping, and marking of a life and its habits—will generate the sort of behavior that rules might have pointed toward but which a 'rule-keeping' *mentality* can never achieve. And it will produce the sort of life which will in

an exceptionally charismatic pastor and preacher but still lack the character attributes required to sustain a fruitful ministry. In a short teaching on true and false disciples in Matthew 7:21–23, Jesus offers a chilling warning. To some leaders of great gifts, people who prophesy in God's name and cast out demons and perform miracles, God will say: "I never knew you. Away from me, you evildoers!"[38] Perhaps our only response this side of eternity should be: *Kyrie eleison. Christe eleison.* Lord, have mercy. Christ, have mercy. May it never be that we do great things for God without ever walking with God.

Our example matters to God and to our congregation. People study whether the credibility of our living authenticates the credibility of our preaching. They wonder: Do we strive to be the gospel people that we call them to be? Before saying goodbye to the Ephesian elders in Acts 20, Paul reminded them, "You know *how I lived* the whole time I was with you, from the first day I came into the province of Asia" (Acts 20:18). To the Thessalonians, he writes, "Because we loved you so much, we were delighted to share with you not only the gospel of God *but our lives* as well" (1 Thess. 2:8). The sermon extended beyond the confines of the gathered assembly. In his classic book *The Reformed Pastor*, Richard Baxter writes, "All that a minister does is a kind of preaching; and if you live a covetous or a careless life, you preach these sins to your people by your practice."[39]

A lot of homileticians get nervous whenever conversations turn to issues of holiness and character, which is why a lot of homiletics textbooks avoid these issues altogether. For theological reasons, many authors dread that people will think they have overemphasized human agency and neglected divine agency, that holiness has somehow become a work. For practical reasons, we worry that our attempt to lift up a vision of holiness and to emphasize its centrality in preaching will be met with resistance and perhaps hostility on account of people coming from different denominations, religious expressions, and theological orientations that rightly emphasize different spiritual practices and disciplines. For personal reasons, we may suffer from what

---

fact be true to itself—though the 'self' to which it will at last be true is the redeemed self, the transformed self, not the merely 'discovered' self of popular thought. . . . In the last analysis, what matters after you believe is neither rules nor spontaneous self-discovery, but character." *After You Believe,* 7.

38. Jonathan Edwards interprets this biblical text and others by distinguishing between the "extraordinary gifts of the Spirit" and the "graces of the Spirit." He argues that it is possible for Christians to seem as though they possess extraordinary gifts but, because they have not experienced the graces of the Spirit, their falsehood will be exposed at the judgment. See Edwards's sermon, "The Extraordinary Gifts of the Spirit Are Inferior to the Graces of the Spirit," in Edwards, *Works of Jonathan Edwards,* 2:279–312.

39. Baxter, *Reformed Pastor,* 84.

psychologist Pauline Rose Clance refers to as the "impostor phenomenon," more popularly called the "impostor syndrome."[40] We worry that we will be exposed as unholy frauds. With all our drama, who are we to say anything to anyone about living a holy life? But those who write introductory books on preaching do people a disservice when they assume holiness rather than emphasize its importance.

Despite our limitations and failures, the way we live our lives and share our lives matters to God, and it should matter to us as ministers of the gospel. The nineteenth-century Church of Scotland minister Robert Murray McCheyne offered the following counsel to a young minister on the occasion of his ordination: "Study universal holiness of life. Your whole usefulness depends on this. Your sermon on Sabbath lasts but an hour or two; your life preaches all the week."[41] Pastor Robert Lewis Gilbert used to tell ministers-in-training at his church in Waco, Texas, "Seventy-five percent of your sermon is the life that you live."[42] Let it be said of us what was said of Barnabas in Acts 11:24: "He was a good man, full of the Holy Spirit and faith, and a great number of people were brought to the Lord."

The Practices of Conviction

So how do we become convictional preachers? Perhaps this image comes to mind because I struggle with my weight, but think of these proposals as one might think of counsel from someone who has just returned from visiting a dietician or nutritionist. I cannot in good conscience call myself an expert, and I am most certainly not a master teacher in this area. But I *can* share a few things that other people have taught me about the difference between healthy and unhealthy choices. If I might stretch the analogy further, let me offer a simpler and perhaps more intuitive claim: *some habits will make you healthy, and other habits will make you sick.*

I enter this discussion with some reticence on account of worrying that I will sound "preachy" in a book on preaching. Also, I do not mean to imply

---

40. See Clance, *Impostor Phenomenon*.

41. McCheyne, "Sermon XI: Positions and Duty of a Minister," at the ordination of P. L. Miller, Wallacetown, Dundee, 1840, in McCheyne, *Works of Rev. Robert Murray McCheyne*, 68.

42. Pastor Robert Lewis Gilbert (1941–92) was the father of homiletician Kenyatta L. Gilbert, who, in his first book, writes, "Taking a page from Grandpa Benny's folk wisdom, my father, also a working preacher, would say to the ministers-in-training that served our church: 'Seventy-five percent of your sermon is the life you live.'" *Journey and Promise of African American Preaching*, 1–2. Robert Gilbert was the first African American graduate of Baylor University and the pastor of the Carver Park Baptist Church in Waco, Texas, from 1978–89.

that there are context-free, hard-and-fast rules that should be followed in every situation by every person without exception, unless we are talking about the sort of major issues that would disqualify a person from Christian ministry. Most of what I will describe in this section comes from what I have seen others embody in their lives and ministries, and what I am still working on and growing toward in my own life.

In the first part, we will consider unhealthy habits for preachers to avoid—what I call negative habits to resist. These are the habits that make us sick. Then we will examine good habits for preachers to cultivate—what I refer to as practices to pursue. These are the habits that make us healthy.

Negative Habits to Resist

Although we could no doubt have a fruitful discussion on the general struggles that all Christians face, it would serve our purposes better to discuss the specific struggles that preachers face.

WORKAHOLISM

Many of us measure our value before God based on whether we have overspent ourselves on behalf of others. To be sure, some pastors have a different proclivity; they struggle with laziness and lethargy. But most of the pastors I meet struggle with the opposite problem. They work too hard and log too many hours; they are exhausted and soul weary. Pastoral ministry is a lot like trying to clean a house with young children in it. The moment you think it's clean, it's messy again, and you have either stepped on or in something that wasn't there a few minutes ago. It seems like there are always more people who need counseling, more emails or phone calls coming in than going out, and more crises than can be dealt with in a single week by a single person. The temptation is to let these come at us with such force that we sacrifice our families, physical health, soul health—everything—to keep up with the people we feel called to love and serve. Add to this our love for preaching, and we can be swallowed up by our vocation. The danger of becoming workaholics is probably more subversive among ministers because we use God talk to authorize it. Perhaps we should call it what it is instead of rationalizing it away. As the old saying goes, even if you put lipstick on a pig, it is still a pig.

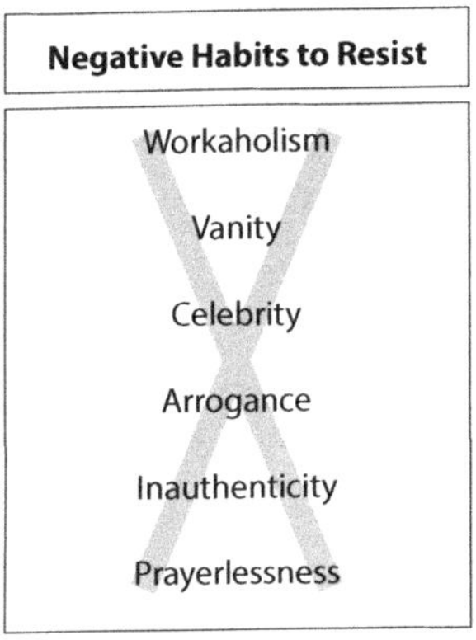

Negative Habits to Resist
Workaholism
Vanity
Celebrity
Arrogance
Inauthenticity
Prayerlessness

Figure 2.3. Negative Habits

VANITY

Vanity can be defined as "excessive pride in one's appearance or accomplishments; conceit."[43] Vanity creeps into our preaching ministry when we convince ourselves that God is fortunate to have us and that our faith communities are blessed to have us as their leader. Vanity leads us to believe that all of the success the church has is based on our performance, and all of the challenges the church faces are based on someone else's failures. People who struggle with vanity think they are too important to do menial tasks. They often measure their preaching based on their superiority to other preachers. This temptation can be especially strong among those for whom preaching comes easily. It is easy to get a big head if people keep telling you how great you are. Problems will inevitably arise when you believe them.

CELEBRITY

This temptation bears a close family resemblance to vanity, but it is a slightly different problem. When Oprah Winfrey was younger, she told a close personal friend, "I want to be an actress," and her friend responded, "You don't want to be an actress. You want to be a star."[44] Many preachers struggle with the same temptation, especially in a celebrity-obsessed culture. The British Anglican bishop Charles Gore saw this danger coming around the turn of the twentieth century when he said, "The disease of modern preaching is its search after popularity."[45] Sometimes I wonder if the advent of social media has made this struggle especially pervasive. If we lack humility and dispense with accountability, we can easily fall into this trap. No church should be a cult of personality around the preacher. We must be wary of pushing Jesus out of the central place because of a desire to occupy that place by ourselves.

ARROGANCE

In many local church settings, preachers function as the theologian in residence, the biblical-exegetical expert. If we do not exercise caution, we will use our position and knowledge to make people feel inferior. In addition to intellectual arrogance, we also risk spiritual arrogance. Pride can creep into our souls in such a way that we find ourselves growing impatient with those

43. *American Heritage Dictionary*, 1,902.
44. The story about Oprah Winfrey wanting to be a star was recounted secondhand by a pastor interviewee in Burns, Chapman, and Guthrie, *Resilient Ministry*, 76.
45. The Bishop Gore quotation appears in Stewart, *Heralds of God*, 29.

whom we perceive as not on the same level as us spiritually.[46] An overestimation of our intellectual and spiritual capabilities does not comport well with a Christian theology of power—how we use power and for what purposes (Mark 10:38–45). Our status as a spiritual authority does not exist as a weapon to inflict harm on people (Ezek. 34:1–10).[47]

INAUTHENTICITY

Most people can sense inauthenticity from a mile away. We do everyone a disservice, ourselves included, if we major on impression management, image preservation, and false performance of the self.[48] "At the core of the false self," David G. Benner writes, "is a desire to preserve an image of our self and a way of relating to the world. This is our personal style—how we think of ourselves and how we want others to see us and think of us."[49] As preachers, part of our job is to close the gap between the persona that we perform and the person that we are. In so doing, we embrace our true selves rather than the false selves that we project. God loves us deeply in Christ, an indicative reality designed to set us free from exhausting ourselves in false performance and to liberate us toward a better version of the person God longs for us to be. In rejecting the false self, Benner writes, we experience paradox: "If we find our true self we find God, and if we find God, we find our most authentic self."[50] As John Calvin states in the opening lines of *The Institutes*, "Nearly all the wisdom we possess, that is to say, true and sound wisdom, consists of two parts: the knowledge of God and of ourselves."[51]

PRAYERLESSNESS

To be honest, I really struggle with this temptation as a preacher. Some people have a natural ability to pray deeply for extended periods of time. Often, my sinful nature leads me to feel annoyed rather than inspired by them. I have not yet learned how to experience God with such depth and endurance. I forget to pray. I forget to ask God to meet with me as I study the

46. For more on the dangers of egotism in pastoral ministry, see Reid and Hogan, *Six Deadly Sins of Preaching*, 29–40.
47. Ian Pitt-Watson reminds us, "Sometimes our failure as preachers is only our failure as pastors in disguise." *Preaching*, 59.
48. For more on the dangers of inauthenticity in pastoral ministry, see Reid and Hogan, *Six Deadly Sins of Preaching*, 17–28.
49. Benner, *The Gift of Being Yourself*, 76.
50. Benner, *The Gift of Being Yourself*, 15. For more on distinguishing between the false self and the true self, see also Mulholland, *Deeper Journey*, 22–25, 46–51.
51. Calvin, *Institutes of Christian Religion*, 1:35.

Scriptures. I get distracted and, as a result, miss out on communicating with and listening to the Triune God.

Unfortunately, prayer does not receive enough attention in the majority of homiletics classrooms or textbooks. Describing the virtual absence of teaching on prayer in homiletics classrooms, Luke A. Powery writes, "Prayer is not viewed as a priority, at least compared to biblical exegesis, a theology of the word, or dialogue about sermon form. . . . Prayer is placed on the homiletical back burner even though, ironically, it is the spiritual practice that fuels the fire of preaching."[52] For many of us, myself included, the temptation to forget about God, to ignore communion with God, is subtle enough that we fail to see its deleterious effects. Prayerlessness limits fruitfulness. It impedes our ministry and wearies our souls. Powery's commentary on prayer as the fuel that fires preaching brings to mind the words of the nineteenth-century preacher George MacGregor, who once said, "I would rather train ten [people] to pray than a hundred [people] to preach."[53]

Practices to Pursue

Resistance to negative habits will take us only part of the way toward becoming more convictional as preachers. A young seminarian once asked the renowned Old Testament scholar Brevard Childs how to become a more competent exegete, and Childs answered, "If you want to do better exegesis, become a deeper person."[54] Preachers benefit when they become deeper people, when they remove destructive tendencies *and* when they replace them with life-giving ones. We have discussed which habits make us sick. Now we will consider which habits make us healthy. I will make three proposals and present them as dialectics.

52. Powery, "Preaching and Prayer," in S. Brown and Powery, *Ways of the Word*, 54.

53. MacGregor died young. This quote was attributed to him in a personal recollection by G. Campbell Morgan, another highly respected preacher of the late nineteenth and early twentieth centuries. Morgan writes,

In the last conversation I had with my beloved and glorified friend, George MacGregor, we had been talking of the condition of the church, of the condition of the world, of the need there was for some new power with which to deal with men, and suddenly rising from the chair in which he had been sitting, and pacing the room with that earnestness that characterized him, he said, "Morgan, I would rather train ten men to pray than a hundred men to preach." At the moment, perhaps, I thought the expression superlative; I have become convinced that he was right. ("Possibility of Prayer," 381)

54. O. Wesley Allen Jr. reports that Childs said this to a student (cited in Graves, *Fully Alive Preacher*, 7). Echoing Childs's sentiments, Gordon D. Fee argues that the aim of exegesis is "to produce in our lives and the lives of others true Spirituality, in which God's people live in fellowship with the eternal and living God, and thus in keeping with God's own purposes in the world." *Listening to the Spirit*, 6.

ALONENESS AND COMMUNITY

Convictional preachers maintain a healthy tension between silence and solitude on the one hand and community and accountability on the other. One does not have to choose between aloneness and community; both are needed in the life of a preacher. Which of these poles do you naturally gravitate to, and why do you gravitate in that direction? How might you develop a healthier tension than what you have now?

It starts with what psychologist D. W. Winnicott refers to as "the capacity to be alone."[55] Our life with God deepens when we turn silence and solitude into an intentional practice, even if in small doses. Silence reminds us to listen for God's voice in a world where chatter and noise drown it out with alarming frequency and intensity.[56] Solitude forces us to confront our spiritual, emotional, and physical health in detachment from those around us so that God can deal with us as we are.[57] In *Life Together*, Dietrich Bonhoeffer writes, "*Let him who cannot be alone beware of community. He will only do harm to himself and to the community. . . . You cannot escape from yourself; for God has singled you out. If you refuse to be alone you are rejecting Christ's call to you, and you can have no part in the community of those who are called.*"[58]

We live in a hyper-connected society—one that is rich in information and poor in wisdom, strong in efficiency and weak in engagement, quick to speak and slow to listen. Silence and solitude allow us the space to recalibrate our souls and to disconnect from speaking, a practice that preachers presumably need more than many others since we speak in public with such regularity.

Preachers also need community much more than they think they do. We live in an age beset by an epidemic of loneliness.[59] Recently, Great Britain ap-

55. Trained in child psychology, Winnicott describes the capacity to be alone as "one of the most important signs of maturity in emotional development." "Capacity to Be Alone," 416. See also the work of practical theologian Jaco J. Hamman, who writes, "To become a pastor is to be alone with yourself in the presence of others and God." *Becoming a Pastor*, 88. Drawing on Winnicott's work, Hamman devotes an entire chapter to aloneness: "Capacity to Be Alone," in *Becoming a Pastor*, 88–116.

56. Dallas Willard writes, "Many people have *never* experienced silence and do not even know that they do *not* know what it is. Our households and offices are filled with the whirring, buzzing, murmuring, chattering, and whining of the multiple contraptions that are supposed to make life easier. Their noise comforts us in some curious way. In fact, we find complete silence shocking because it leaves the impression that nothing is happening. In a go-go world such as ours, what could be worse than that!" *Spirit of the Disciplines*, 163 (emphasis in original).

57. Willard writes, "In solitude we find the psychic distance, the perspective from which we can see, in the light of eternity, the created things that trap, worry, and oppress us." *Spirit of the Disciplines*, 161.

58. Bonhoeffer, *Life Together*, 77 (emphasis in original).

59. For research on loneliness in the field of social neuroscience, see Cacioppo and Patrick, *Loneliness*.

pointed its first-ever minister for loneliness because researchers in that country discovered that more than nine million people reported that they often or always felt lonely.[60] Comparing recent data with past data, they concluded that the numbers of those experiencing loneliness and isolation had skyrocketed, especially in populations of the sick and elderly.

Preachers cannot exempt themselves from the same feelings of loneliness, even though they interact with people on a regular basis. One can preach *to* a community but never actually be *in* community. The problem cuts both ways. Sometimes members of a congregation look at their pastor only "in terms of their role rather than as human beings who need others."[61] Other times, pastors struggle with self-disclosure because they feel restricted by their role, on account of confidentiality reasons, or because they would rather protect themselves from knowing and being known by others. Just as we need to develop the capacity to be alone, so also we need to develop the capacity to be in authentic community. Bonhoeffer makes a similar point after his comments on silence and solitude: "The reverse is also true: *Let him who is not in community beware of being alone.* Into the community you were called, the call was not meant for you alone; in the community of the called you bear your cross, you struggle, you pray. You are not alone, even in death, and on the Last Day you will be only one member of the great congregation of Jesus Christ. If you scorn the fellowship of the brethren, you reject the call of Jesus Christ, and thus your solitude can only be hurtful to you."[62]

For the sake of your spiritual, emotional, and physical health, maintain relationships characterized by deep community. Have good friendships with people who share common interests, and even closer friends before whom there are no secrets. Some preachers find community in their own congregations— say, with their elders or deacons. Others pursue meaningful relationships outside, often with other pastors because they need spaces to talk openly about unique challenges and frustrations that ministers face.

ACTIVITY AND RECEPTIVITY

In her book *Kindling Desire for God*, Kay L. Northcutt advises preachers to pursue practices of activity and practices of receptivity in order to form themselves spiritually so that they in turn can form others spiritually. *Active* practices, she claims, engage us with exteriority—that is, with the world around us. Some active practices engage us with the life of the church: corporate worship,

60. See Yeginsu, "U.K. Appoints a Minister for Loneliness."
61. Burns, Chapman, and Guthrie, *Resilient Ministry*, 20.
62. Bonhoeffer, *Life Together*, 77 (emphasis in original).

prayer meetings, committees, programs, and special occasions. Other active practices engage us with life outside the church: "visiting the sick, clothing the naked, feeding the hungry, and working for justice."[63] *Receptive* practices engage us with interiority—that is, soul tending and contemplation. I have already mentioned two receptive practices: silence and solitude. According to Northcutt, other practices might include reading Scripture devotionally, meditation, *lectio divina*, silent prayer, spoken prayer, journaling, and prayer walks.

Let me make two more recommendations for receptive practices that do not show up in Northcutt's book. Care for our physical bodies can be a receptive practice. Our interior life is destined to suffer if we do not pay adequate attention to the connections between our souls, bodies, and minds. We need times to sleep, to exercise, and to maintain a healthy relationship to food. How much physical energy will we be able to expend preaching if we do not have any physical energy outside of preaching? If we do not take care of our physical bodies, how effective can we be in the long term caring for the body of Christ?

Fasting can also be a receptive practice. It compels us to pray during times of hunger, and it refocuses our attention on God as the source of everything that we have. I remember a former student who was born and raised in Kenya and came to the United States to attend seminary. He told me that almost all the pastors he knows from his denomination in Kenya choose to fast at least once per week. They fasted not just because they believed it brought them closer to God; they also did it as a spiritual-homiletical practice. They fasted as part of the sermon preparation process in order to help them center their thoughts, focus their hearts, and listen for God's voice.

If we fail to engage in active practices, we risk becoming distant, aloof, and detached from the world around us. But if we fail to engage in receptive practices, we risk becoming distant from ourselves, offering living water to others while we die of thirst. If we begin with ourselves and never touch the lives of others, we lose the community around us. But if we begin with the community around us and never engage ourselves, we lose our souls. As J. Kent Edwards reminds us, "Deep sermons cannot be preached by shallow people. Profound sermons only come from people who enjoy a profound relationship with God. Like it or not, the condition of our personal relationship with God will control our public ministry for God."[64]

We work *in* the world around us, and we work *on* our inner lives. Preaching requires both. We draw from the well of receptive practices in order to empower the church (and ourselves) to pursue active practices.

63. Northcutt, *Kindling Desire for God*, 104.
64. J. K. Edwards, *Deep Preaching*, 43.

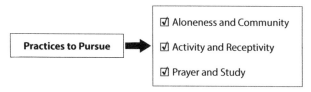

Figure 2.4. Healthy Habits

PRAYER AND STUDY

Convictional preachers maintain a healthy balance of prayer and study. Of course, these two virtues do not run on parallel tracks; they should intersect. The medieval monastics used to say, "To work is to pray" (*Operare est orare*). One can pray through work and work through prayer. However, many preachers have a proclivity toward one habit over the other. We pray without studying or we study without praying. A convictional preacher pursues prayer not just in public but also in private—alone, with close friends, or with family members.[65] I need to hear this just as much as anyone else. Paul exhorts the Colossians: "Devote yourselves to prayer, being watchful and thankful" (Col. 4:2). To the Ephesians, he writes, "And pray in the Spirit on all occasions with all kinds of prayers and requests. With this in mind, be alert and always keep on praying for all the Lord's people" (Eph. 6:18). The New Testament scholar Gordon D. Fee claims,

> To be a good exegete, and consequently a good theologian, one must know the fullness of the Spirit; and that includes a life of prayer ("praying in the Spirit," Paul calls it) and obedience.
>
> A great danger lurks here, you understand, especially for those who have been called of God to serve the church in pastoral and teaching roles. The danger is to become a professional (in the pejorative sense of that word): to analyze texts and to talk *about* God, but slowly to let the fire of passion *for* God run low, so that one does not spend much time talking *with* God.[66]

How much do we prioritize prayer outside of preaching? How have we integrated prayer into our preparation and delivery of the sermon? How much of our time do we devote to prayer in the sermon preparation process? Have we bifurcated the exegetical-homiletical task from the spiritual task of soul preparation?

---

65. R. A. Torrey writes, "The one who wishes to succeed in the Christian life must lead a life of prayer. Much of the failure in Christian living today, and in Christian work, results from neglect of prayer." *How to Succeed in the Christian Life*, 73.

66. Fee, *Listening to the Spirit*, 7 (emphasis in original).

When we look to the church fathers, we find such a heightened level of attention to prayer that it might seem odd if the same emphasis were to appear in modern homiletics textbooks. Remember the words of Evagrius Ponticus from the beginning of the chapter: "If you are a theologian, you will pray truly and if you pray truly, you will be a theologian."[67] Most of the church fathers and mothers did not separate prayer from theology or theology from prayer. Basil of Caesarea believed that prayer "finds the soul stirred by yearning towards God, fresher and more vigorous"; it allows those who pray to "hold God ever in memory" as a "shrine established within us."[68] Basil's monastic community gathered seven to eight times a day to pray and sing the psalms.[69] Tertullian describes the transformative power of prayer in a believer's life. It serves as a protector and defender, a wall and a weapon:

> [Prayer] knows nothing save how to recall the souls of the departed from the very path of death, to transform the weak, to restore the sick, to purge the possessed, to open prison-bars, to loose the bonds of the innocent. Likewise it washes away faults, repels temptations, extinguishes persecutions, consoles the faint-spirited, cheers the high-spirited, escorts travellers, appeases waves, makes robbers stand aghast, nourishes the poor, governs the rich, upraises the fallen, arrests the falling, confirms the standing. Prayer is the wall of faith: her arms and missiles against the foe who keeps watch over us on all sides. And, so never walk we unarmed.[70]

Saint Augustine claimed that prayer was an indispensable prerequisite to sermon effectiveness. A preacher ought to be a "[person] of prayer before becoming a [person] of words" (*sit orator antequam dictor;* literally, be a "pray-er before being a speaker").[71] That is to say, God calls us as preachers to be pray-ers before we engage our congregations as speakers.

Study also matters to the preaching task. As Calvin Miller reminds us, "Mystics without study are only spiritual romantics who want relationship without effort."[72] How can one relate to the Scriptures seriously without engaging them through study? It would be like saying you know someone while not respecting them enough to spend time with them. Some of us do not study because we are too busy. Others of us have allowed the habits that

67. Evagrius Ponticus, "Praktikos 60," cited in Corrigan, *Evagrius and Gregory*, 163.

68. "Letter II: Basil to Gregory [of Nazianzus]," in Basil, *Saint Basil, The Letters*, 17.

69. For an account of Basil's monastic community and their habits of daily prayer, see Hildebrand, *Basil of Caesarea*, 143–44.

70. Tertullian, "On Prayer (Chapter 29)," 690–91.

71. Augustine, *On Christian Teaching*, 142.

72. Miller, *Table of Inwardness*, 83.

make us sick to deter us from the task. H. B. Charles writes, "A passion to preach without a desire to study is a desire to perform."[73]

A convictional preacher engages with the Scriptures intellectually, develops a theologically shaped mind, and does the hard work required to prepare and deliver sermons. If we are seminary trained and we have studied the original languages, it will take work to keep them up rather than to leave them behind. But keeping them up through the years will add texture, depth, and color to our exegesis and preaching. Without a doubt, it takes effort to study the Scriptures, to become a good Berean. Remember the Berean converts to Christianity? They "received the message with great eagerness and examined the Scriptures every day to see if what Paul said was true" (Acts 17:11). At a basic level, studying Scripture strengthens our knowledge and understanding so that we do not preach out of ignorance—there is no compelling reason to run from the life of the mind. At a deeper level, Scripture study gives us the strength and resilience to experience intimacy with God and to engage others in Christlike ways.

In addition to studying Scripture, we pursue active study when we work hard on our sermon from start to finish through activities such as brainstorming, note-taking, writing, revising, practicing, dialogue with others, feedback loops, and reflection. Earlier in my ministry, when I was an associate pastor, I visited a family in crisis in the hospital after they called me on a Saturday afternoon. Normally they would call the senior pastor, but he was out of town with his family. I went to the hospital that afternoon, and on my return home that evening, I arrived to a family with stomach flu. I ran several loads of laundry throughout the night, preached on Sunday morning, and visited with the same family in the hospital on Sunday afternoon. This is just one minor example of many that pastors can share of the fast-paced and unpredictable nature of ministry and one's personal or family life converging. In pastoral ministry, life tends to operate on a different timetable than the one we would choose for ourselves. Many of us face relentless demands, unrealistic expectations, and unpredictable crises. Even so, our homiletical habits do not have to deteriorate just because our ministry schedules are difficult to tame. Just as in other areas of life, we will make time for what we care about in ministry. As the great Lutheran preacher Paul Scherer used to say, "The first step toward a good sermon is hard work, the second step is more hard work, and the third step is still more."[74] To return to some themes that are found in the introduction, we will weaken at the tasks that we do not practice, and

73. Charles, *On Pastoring*, 122.
74. Scherer, *We Have This Treasure*, 142–43.

we will also weaken at those same tasks without some deliberateness and intentionality whenever we practice them.

The dialectics mentioned here—aloneness and community, activity and receptivity, prayer and study—function a lot like healthy recipes in a good cookbook: the meals are good to the taste and good for the body. A steady diet of these practices will help a preacher become stronger, healthier, and more resilient over time. More relevant to this chapter, they will help us sustain a preaching life characterized by conviction.

Conclusion

Three years after the Freedom Rides took place, and about nine thousand miles away, an activist in his early forties stood trial for speaking out against apartheid in South Africa. After the prosecution presented its case, the defense team took its turn at the rostrum. Among their other clients, they were defending the young activist, a man named Nelson Mandela. On April 20, 1964, the defense team gave Mandela a chance to speak for himself. Instead of testifying, he addressed the court from the dock and delivered arguably the most compelling speech on race and apartheid in the history of South Africa. It captivated listeners for three to four hours. Instead of summarizing the speech, I will mention only the final paragraph, especially since that paragraph more than any other illustrates my central point. Mandela said, "During my lifetime I have dedicated myself to this struggle of the African people. I have fought against white domination, and I have fought against black domination. I have cherished the ideal of a democratic and free society in which all persons live together in harmony and with equal opportunities. It is an ideal which I hope to live for and to achieve. But if needs be, it is an ideal for which I am prepared to die."[75]

When the trial was about to conclude and the time came for a verdict, the judge had the power to impose the death penalty or a sentence of life imprisonment. He chose the latter, opting to send Mandela and most of his fellow codefendants to Robben Island, where Mandela resided for the majority of his twenty-seven years as a political prisoner. Yet even with such a ruling, the judge did *not* have the power to take away the one thing that Mandela mentioned more than once in the last paragraph of his speech—the judge could *not* take away his ideals. Mandela remained convinced that the ideal of racial harmony was not only worth his life if it could be achieved; it was worth his death as well.

75. Mandela, *In His Own Words*, 42.

Figure 2.5. Nelson Mandela

Not every preacher will share the same level of courage that Mandela displayed in the Rivonia Trial of 1964. We know Mandela's name because of how exceptional he truly was. But we share at least one thing in common. We have committed ourselves to the gospel of Christ, to an "ideal" that is also a person—a person we believe is worthy of our one and only life. A commitment to a cause greater than ourselves—the cause of gospel proclamation—fuels a life of faithfulness to God's call. A preacher without conviction is like a car without gasoline. It serves *a* purpose, but it does not serve the purpose for which it was created.

Learning activities and sermon samples for this chapter are located at www.PracticesofChristianPreaching.com.

3

Preach Contextually

> To preach contextually is to connect the preached word with the deep needs of these people at this time. . . . The sermon is not a standalone piece of performance art.
>
> —Mary S. Hulst, *A Little Handbook for Preachers*

> Every sermon is stretched like a bowstring between the text of the Bible on the one hand and the problems of contemporary human life on the other. If the string is insecurely tethered to either end, the bow is useless.
>
> —Ian Pitt-Watson, *Preaching*

When I was in my early twenties, I received a beautiful Christmas card with a short Scripture verse inside: "Celebrate by sending each other gifts" (Rev. 11:10). The verse piqued my interest since I was a college student and had plans to attend seminary. At this stage in my life, I had read the book of Revelation at least once, although I was sure that I did not understand it. The book of Revelation fascinates, inspires, and engages the imagination, but it also perplexes and bewilders the uninitiated. Curiosity got the best of me, so I looked up Revelation 11:10, which reads in its entirety, "The inhabitants of the earth will gloat over them and will *celebrate by sending each other gifts*, because these two prophets had tormented those who live on the earth." The "them" in this context refers to the two witnesses sent from heaven that the Beast has come up from the Abyss to attack, overpower, and kill (cf. Rev. 11:3, 7). In other words, one of the phrases in Revelation 11:10 works well in a Christmas card if the one who gets it does not chase down the reference. Revelation 11:10 in its entirety works well if you want to curse an enemy or warn someone of impending doom. My hunch is that the person at the card company did not look up the passage, and I hope that the person who sent me the Christmas card did not look it up either. Otherwise, I need to be more selective about my friendships.

Context matters. It matters when we read Scripture, and it matters when we preach sermons. Faithful preachers study the context in which they preach as diligently as they study the context of the biblical text from which they preach. In his classic book *Preaching*, Fred Craddock writes, "Whatever may be provided a preacher by any and all resources, it is only when *local soil* has been added that the sermon will take root and flourish."[1] No one would deny that preaching addresses issues that matter to all people: life and death, sin and salvation, hope and despair. But preaching also takes place at a particular time; it has a local accent. It attends to the abstract, the transcendent, and the universal while *also* wrestling with the concrete, the immanent, and the particular. Preaching straddles the divide between the trans-contextual and the contextual, the timeless and the timely, faithfulness and fittingness. Sensitive to circumstance without being dogmatically parochial, it honors time and place without succumbing to "chronological snobbery," to use C. S. Lewis's phrase.[2]

In this chapter, we will consider various examples of contextualization in Scripture; we will discuss what context and contextualization mean with reference to preaching; and, we will describe how to make contextualization a homiletical practice. Context is the second C of the Five Cs.

Suffice it to say that "context" is almost as slippery a word as "culture." Theologians and non-theologians alike have written scores of essays and books on context and on contextualization.[3] How does one define it? What checks and balances should preachers put in place to prevent under-contextualizing on the one hand and over-contextualizing on the other? Is context fixed and static, or is it malleable and transformable? On account of globalization,

---

1. Craddock, *Preaching*, 98 (emphasis added).

2. Lewis defines chronological snobbery as "the uncritical acceptance of the intellectual climate common to our own age and the assumption that whatever has gone out of date is on that account discredited." *Surprised by Joy*, 201.

3. For examples of non-theologians interacting with issues of context, see Adamopoulos and Kashima, *Social Psychology and Cultural Context*; Hartmann and Uggen, *Contexts Reader*; de Vet, "Context and the Emerging Story." For examples of systematic theologians and homileticians who define or describe context, see Bevans, *Models of Contextual Theology*; Schreiter, *Constructing Local Theologies*; Soskice, "The Truth Looks Different from Here"; Tanner, *Theories of Culture*; Tisdale, *Preaching as Local Theology*; Nieman, *Knowing the Context*.

The Practices
of Christian Preaching

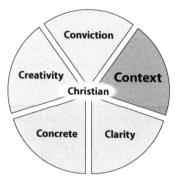

Figure 3.1. The Five Cs: Context

should we not also speak of the fragmentation or hybridization of context(s)? How do we strike a balance between the timeless and the timely when we preach? Answers to these and other questions require much more time and space than is afforded here. For the purposes of this chapter, we will strive to be more focused in our discussion.

Context and Scripture

We need look no further than the Scriptures to recognize how much context matters to Christian proclamation. Much of the Old Testament addresses a significant contextual question: *What does it look like to be the people of God in a strange land, whether in slavery, sojourn, or exile?* Israel spends a significant portion of its history *outside* the promised land and has to figure out a way to live in another culture without forsaking its distinctiveness (Lev. 18:1–3). The letter to the exiles in Jeremiah 29 (especially vv. 4–7) represents a fascinating example of a healthy respect for peculiarity and presence. When faced with the dichotomy of running from Babylon or razing it to the ground, the answer comes back: *Reside in Babylon!* God calls the nation to reject the false dichotomy of assimilation or destruction and calls them instead to contextualize through engaging with their neighbors while in exile. As Eldin Villafañe puts it, God calls Israel to pursue "critical engagement" with Babylon.[4] What does that look like? According to Jeremiah 29, critical engagement

---

4. Villafañe writes, "Against the false prophets who might call for 'assimilation,' 'revolution,' or 'escapism,' Jeremiah called for 'critical engagement'—for presence." *Seek the Peace of the City*, 2.

looks like this: build homes, plant vineyards, raise families, and pray for and seek the shalom of the city where God has placed you (vv. 4–7).

We also see contextualized proclamation in the four Gospels, the primary witnesses to Jesus's life and ministry. The Gospels represent four different interpretive communities facing unique life situations, challenges, and needs. Janet Martin Soskice offers a helpful image to describe the unique differences between the four communities of the Gospels: "Like so many facets of a gemstone these particularities are the means by which we apprehend, even if we cannot comprehend, the glory of God and God's creative and redemptive act."[5] Put differently, the diverse witnesses to Jesus *enlarge* rather than diminish our vision of who Christ is and what he came to do. The most beautiful gemstones reveal their beauty through multiple angles of vision.

The book of Acts also offers an intriguing case study in contextualization. I will mention just one well-known example. The apostle Paul quotes from the Old Testament when preaching to a predominantly Jewish audience (though some non-Jewish "God-fearers" attended) in the synagogue in Pisidian Antioch (Acts 13:13–52).[6] Yet when he preaches at Mars Hill (Acts 17:16–33) before the Stoic and Epicurean philosophers, he references their religiosity, observes their altar with the inscription, "TO AN UNKNOWN GOD" (Acts 17:22–23), and quotes from their poets (Acts 17:27–28) before calling for salvation.[7] In both instances, Paul identifies with his listeners, finds common ground, and speaks contextually without compromising his commitment to the gospel.[8]

---

5. In the same paragraph, Soskice writes, "We have not one gospel but four. The Bible discloses God to us through human history and from different perspectives, and these perspectives we must believe are not in default of one plain and uncontroversial text or set of propositions, but indeed required by the complexity of that which is revealed, God Godself." "The Truth Looks Different from Here," 58.

6. Dean Flemming writes, "The audience, the setting, the address and the content of Paul's sermon affirm with one voice that this is *not* a case of cross-cultural communication of the gospel. Paul speaks as a Diaspora Jew to fellow Diaspora Jews within the framework of the Jewish Scriptures and the worship of the God of Israel." *Contextualization in the New Testament*, 58 (emphasis in original).

7. In his discussion of Acts 17, Flemming writes, "Paul thus begins where his audience is and builds on as much common territory as possible. Rather than demeaning their belief system or condemning their religiosity, he recognizes there is something genuine in their religious aspirations and felt needs, and he uses them as steppingstones for communicating the gospel." *Contextualization in the New Testament*, 76.

8. According to Flemming, one of the central lessons we can take from Paul's speeches in Acts is a two-pronged approach: "identificational" and "transformational." He writes, "These speeches model for us a magnificent balance between, on the one hand, an *identificational* approach that proclaims the gospel in ways the audience can understand and, on the other, a *transformational* approach that resists compromising the gospel's integrity in a pluralistic

Examples like these abound throughout the Old Testament and New Testament and are too numerous to mention here.[9] But at least this much remains clear: biblical writers and preachers make context-specific decisions in both verbal and written proclamation. In *Contextualization in the New Testament*, Dean Flemming makes a convincing argument that the New Testament writers "model for us a process of doing theology in context, of engaging their cultures and offering their audiences a fresh and fitting articulation of the good news."[10] Presumably, the New Testament writers also demonstrated their commitment to contextualization for *all* by writing their letters in *Koine* ("common") Greek, the language of the people, rather than in the language of the political and philosophical elites.

Defining Context and Contextualization

Etymologically speaking, the word "context" comes from the Latin *contextus*, meaning "interwoven, connected, or united." In its original verb form, *contextere* meant "to weave or twine together."[11] People also used the word when talking about building, constructing, or compiling.[12] About two hundred years ago, scholars started using the word in environmental and cultural discussions.[13] Today, the word has much broader currency. Especially in Christian circles, one often hears people talking about "the local church context," "my/your/our context," "rural versus urban contexts," "multiethnic contexts," the

---

world. This is a challenge that every preacher or communicator of the Word must face." *Contextualization in the New Testament*, 86.

9. For instance, Grant Osborne looks at 1 Cor. 9:19–23, the passage in which Paul writes about becoming all things to all people, as a form of "evangelistic contextualization." *Hermeneutical Spiral*, 413.

10. Flemming, *Contextualization in the New Testament*, 296.

11. For instance, the rhetorician Cicero claimed, "Sheep's wool weaves together the clothing of men [*ovium villis contextis homines vestiuntur*]." Cited in Simpson, *Cassell's Latin Dictionary*, 146.

12. Several first-century-BCE writers use the word this way. Julius Caesar uses the verbal participle: "One after another all works are put together [*sic deinceps omne opus contexitur*]" (cited in Simpson, *Cassell's Latin Dictionary*, 146). The biographer Cornelius, also writing in the first century BCE, describes the continuity of "story woven together in our time [*contexta historia eorum temporum*]" (cited in Arnold, *Cornelius Nepos*, 106). That is to say, readers could compile or weave together a history based on the progression and continuity of Cicero's writings.

13. In recent history, historians of ancient Greece and Rome have spoken of "historical context" when describing the life settings of the texts and artifacts they examined. Literary theorists have spoken of "literary context" when they discussed texts in their context. Anthropologists have used "cultural context(s)" as an umbrella term for the people groups that they studied as a way to describe the community's beliefs, values, practices, and structures of meaning at both the discursive and nondiscursive levels.

"North American context," the "Latin American context," "post-Christian context," the "postmodern context," or "contextual theology."

I define context as *a community shaped by local and global identity markers, experiences, expectations, and allegiances.* On the one hand, we preach to people connected to one another at the local level; they are particular people in a particular place at a particular point in time. They speak with a local accent. No one else preaches to them on a regular basis besides us, and no one else (usually) listens to us most Sundays besides them. They belong to a local faith community and, much like members of a nuclear family, they share family resemblances. Perhaps they share an identity-marker family resemblance, such as that they are millennials or retirees, rural or urban, black or white, rich or poor. They might also share a different family resemblance such as their background, affiliation, geographical location, educational level, country of origin, or language.

I define context as a community shaped by local and global identity markers, experiences, expectations, and allegiances.

Consider also that most preaching contexts are fluid and permeable rather than static and fixed.[14] Some of this fluidity comes from rapid demographic change in the society, along with the precipitous growth of multi-ethnic churches and immigrant diaspora churches. As Gabriel Salguero observes, "Preaching challenges are heightened when you have multiple ethnicities, cultures, and generations in your congregation."[15]

On the other hand, we preach to people connected to one another at the global level. They belong to a larger human family and share commonalities: they are created in the image of God; they partake in a common sinful nature; they live and they die; they long for answers to deeper questions about meaning, purpose, and human flourishing; and they have souls and

14. Homiletician Ronald J. Allen notes, "Preaching is never generic. It always takes place in a particular context. In fact, preaching typically takes place in multiple overlapping and interacting contexts: the preacher's personal life, the preacher's household, the local congregation, the denomination, the global Christian community, the neighborhood and city, the state and nation, the globe, and the cosmos. Contexts include elements that are physical, intellectual, emotional, and behavioral. A context is not static, but changes." *Interpreting the Gospel*, 19.

15. In an interview on preaching, Gabriel Salguero explains the complexities of preaching in multiethnic, multilingual, and multigenerational contexts: "Each group has its own particularity, both in worship and in proclamation. If we are not aware of the differences, as a popular movie title suggests, things can be 'lost in translation.' In reality, the charge today is not just about preaching to multicultural congregations but preaching to the multiple identities that congregants inhabit, which include generation, class, ethnicity, political persuasion, and culture." See Salguero's interview with several other preachers in multiethnic churches in Johnston, Smith, and Tisdale, *Questions Preachers Ask*, 79.

are eternal beings.[16] Haddon W. Robinson observes, "Normal people do not lose sleep over the Jebusites, the Canaanites, or the Perizzites, or even about what Abraham, Moses, or Paul has said or done. They lie awake wondering about grocery prices, crop failures, quarrels with a spouse, diagnosis of a malignancy, a frustrating sex life, or the rat race where only rats seem to win."[17]

Listeners all over the world also have this in common: they hear our sermons in the contemporary world *right now* and not fifty years ago, one hundred years ago, or in the ancient world of the text. The world they live in vies for their allegiance, competes for their affection, challenges their resilience, and tempts them toward idolatry. But that same world also provides for their basic needs, challenges them in their self-centeredness, invites their participation, and calls them into mission. "If the sermon does not make much difference in that world," Robinson writes, "[listeners] wonder if it makes any difference at all."[18]

Perhaps an analogy will help us to think differently about a familiar term. Consider the similarities between context and the air that we breathe.[19] Most of us do not stay up at night thinking about the air, even though it is all around us. We take it for granted just as we might soil or water. Yet the air shapes our overall health, habits, and experience of the world. The air also contains various pollutants that have the potential to damage, disrupt, and even poison the ecosystem. Some pollutants impact the air in ways that we can observe, while others are so subtle and subversive that we are oblivious to them. It would be naive to conclude that the air we breathe is somehow untainted or pure, and it would also be presumptuous to assume that we could contain or summarize everything about the air in all of its complexity and nuance

16. Gardner C. Taylor understood these global connections well when he described the shift in his preaching in the mid-1950s toward the "great universal considerations, our hopes, our fears, the fact that we are born, we love, we hate, we sicken, we die, we laugh, we cry." As told in Thomas, *African American Preaching*, 100.

17. H. Robinson, *Biblical Preaching*, 10.

18. H. Robinson, *Biblical Preaching*, 10.

19. I owe the use of air imagery for context to the feminist philosopher Luce Irigaray. She argues that something so fundamental as air still remains "unthought by the philosopher." Without air, we die. We take it for granted even though we need it to survive. Irigaray uses "air" metaphorically by claiming that the context in which many modern Western philosophers conducted philosophy was the "air" that shaped their thought, an air they failed to name. She takes aim at Martin Heidegger in particular. Irigaray argues that Heidegger's phenomenology, a legacy that Ricoeur follows and with which he self-identifies, has sealed women into "envelopes, propositions, and theres" that are not only patriarchal but that also completely ignore women's ways of knowing. In Irigaray's judgment, Heidegger has forgotten to breathe the air of lived experience—what she calls the "open expanse"—because he looked inward in disengaged and disembodied introspection. See Irigaray, *Forgetting of Air in Martin Heidegger*, 26, 56–57.

with total objectivity and finality. In other words, it takes a healthy dose of humility to pause and reflect before saying with certainty, "I understand my context completely."[20]

In much the same way as air, our context shapes our health, habits, and experience of the world at both the conscious and unconscious levels. Some people have more awareness than others about how context shapes their experience because of their life circumstances or levels of intercultural competence.[21] Some navigate more than one context with flexibility and ease, whereas others struggle in contexts that are unfamiliar to them.[22] The good contextual preacher asks, What is the air like in *my* community? A nuanced and textured analysis reveals beliefs and values that shape behaviors, levels of diversity within a context, and pollutants that threaten to undermine the community's health. For instance, power issues often exist in a context; some voices are privileged, and other voices are silenced.[23]

20. Here, I am heavily indebted to systematic theologian Kathryn Tanner and her work on culture. Tanner contends for a more fluid, kinetic understanding of culture as opposed to an understanding that is static and fixed. Tanner writes, "It seems less and less plausible to presume that cultures are self-contained and clearly bounded units, internally consistent and unified wholes of beliefs and values simply transmitted to every member of their respective groups as principles of social order. What we might call a postmodern stress on interactive process and negotiation, indeterminacy, fragmentation, conflict, and porosity replaces these aspects of the modern, post-1920s understanding of culture." *Theories of Culture*, 38. I would argue for a similar way of thinking about context in homiletical discussions. In my judgment, we make a costly mistake when we neglect the fluidity, malleability, contingency, and even fragility of the contexts in which we preach.

21. I define intercultural competence as the "cultivation of knowledge, skills, and habits for effectively negotiating cultural, racial, and ecclesial difference." Alcántara, *Crossover Preaching*, 30. For more on the importance of intercultural competence in preaching, see *Crossover Preaching*, 30, 191–236.

22. For instance, some non-majority schoolchildren know how to navigate majority-culture school settings through "code switching" or "code meshing"—that is, altering grammar, syntax, and behavioral patterns. Some of the research on "code switching" and "code meshing" in education theory considers the linguistic improvisation that African American students use in predominantly white schools, public schools in particular. See Young et al., *Other People's English*. See also DeBose, "Codeswitching."

23. In *Ways of the Word*, Sally A. Brown uses the language of the "hidden view" of congregational life in order to name existing power dynamics in a church context. When preachers conduct congregational analysis, Brown argues, they must consider three vantage points: the close-up view (pp. 108–14), the wide view (pp. 114–17), and the hidden view (pp. 117–20). The close-up view examines the local congregation's symbols and stories. The wide view examines the "cultural dynamics that affect a congregation's life." The hidden view examines the power dynamics in a local church. Concerning the third view, Brown writes, "Preachers need to know who exerts control over decision-making processes and who is marginalized. . . . Tracking the flow of power in a congregation is crucial to wise pastoral leadership." "Preacher as Interpreter of Word and World," in S. Brown and Powery, *Ways of the Word*, 117. See also Tisdale, *Preaching as Local Theology*, 64–77.

Preachers with high contextual responsiveness ask themselves community-specific questions: What makes the air different where I am than it might be somewhere else? What pollutants undermine my community's health? How is the air different today in comparison to last year or five years ago?

If context is the community in which preaching takes place, then *contextualization* is the process and the act by which preachers localize a sermon to a community. Because contextualization is such a loaded word, let me provide some clarification as to what I do *not* mean by it.

What Contextualization Does Not Mean

First, by contextualization I do *not* mean that learning how to connect with one's listeners absolves preachers of the responsibility to carefully and prayerfully study the Scriptures. Before sermon writing begins, Samuel D. Proctor writes, the operative assumption should be that "there has been private prayer and reflection, faithful study of the text for the sermon, and a thorough examination of available scholarly commentaries on the text."[24] Steer clear of the temptation to leave behind engagement with Scripture and soul-nourishing prayer. As much as I enjoy (and benefit from) watching a popular TED Talk on YouTube, I am also persuaded that our pulpits are filled with too many presenters and not enough preachers. Of course we need to understand our congregational contexts better than we do now, and we need to preach in a language specific to our listeners' time and place, but these commitments do not have to come at the expense of exegetical, theological, and spiritual competency. Contextualization should not be equated with poor preparation, bad theology, careless exegesis, or a steady habit of prayerlessness. One must also do the exegetical and spiritual work. Ian Pitt-Watson reminds us, "Unless our Biblical exegesis and theology are sound we will not recognize Christ in contemporary experience even if we meet him there."[25]

Sometimes preachers use contemporary context as a trump card over against anything connected to the world of the text. Unbalanced emphasis on the contemporary world often leads to the neglect of the ancient world and the demands that the biblical text makes on listeners today. The preacher must engage in *critical* contextualization as opposed to uncritical contextualization. In the words of Paul G. Hiebert, "The gospel must be contextualized, but it must remain prophetic. It must stand in judgment of

24. Proctor, *Certain Sound of the Trumpet*, 19.
25. Pitt-Watson, *Preaching*, 70.

what is evil in all cultures as well as in all persons."[26] Aware of this tendency among pastors, the Lutheran preacher Paul Scherer used to say that a preacher should not meet someone "where he is. Too often he is in the wrong place."[27] Uncritical acceptance of everything in our contemporary context may lead to unintentional endorsement of—rather than exposure of—the idols we worship. The missiologist David Bosch writes, "Of course, the gospel can only be read from and make sense in our present context, yet to posit it as criterion means that it may, and often does, critique the context and our reading of it."[28]

John Stott uses the phrase "double listening" to describe contextualization's critical dimension.[29] In double listening, preachers listen to the world of the text and to the world of the listeners but do not necessarily listen to each world in the same way. They listen to both worlds with intentionality and sensitivity, but not in an indiscriminate or uncritical manner.[30] In doing so, they allow the divine summons of the ancient text to offer a prophetic word to the contemporary situation.

Second, by contextualization I do *not* mean simplistic, cookie-cutter adaptation. Preachers contextualize in communities that are complex and heterogeneous. In his book *Paradox and Discovery*, John Wisdom describes meeting a zookeeper who had a high success rate with breeding lions; his name was Mr. Flood. When Wisdom asked him about the secret to his success, Flood answered, "Understanding lions." When he pressed him further as to what he

26. In 1987, Hiebert wrote a now-classic essay on critical contextualization in which he rejects the imperialism often associated with undercontextualization and the syncretism often associated with over-contextualization. He opts instead for a form of contextualization that is post-relative, interdependent, and anthropologically rooted while still being uncompromising and prophetic. He writes, "A call for contextualization without a simultaneous call for preserving the gospel without compromise opens the door to syncretism. . . . The foreignness of the culture we add to the gospel offends and must be eliminated. But the gospel itself offends. It is supposed to offend, and we dare not weaken its offense." *Anthropological Reflections*, 86; the essay originally appeared as Hiebert, "Critical Contextualization."

27. Scherer, *Word God Sent*, 7. John Stott makes a similar point when he writes, "If we become exclusively preoccupied with answering the questions people are asking, we may overlook the fact that they often ask the wrong questions and need to be helped to ask the right ones. If we acquiesce uncritically in the world's own self-understanding, we may find ourselves the servants rather of fashion than of God." *Between Two Worlds*, 139.

28. Bosch, *Transforming Mission*, 430.

29. See Stott, *Contemporary Christian*, 13.

30. Stott writes, "We listen to the Word with humble reverence, anxious to understand it, and resolved to believe and obey what we come to understand. We listen to the world with critical alertness, anxious to understand it too, and resolved not necessarily to believe and obey it, but to sympathize with it and to seek grace to discover how the gospel relates to it." *Contemporary Christian*, 28. For more on Stott's understanding of "double listening," see Scharf, "'Double Listening' Revisited"; Scharf, *Let the Earth Hear His Voice*, 131.

understood about lions, he responded, "Every lion is different."[31] Remember that even if a local context seems homogeneous, you will find more diversity than you initially assumed if you peel back enough layers.

Contexts exist within a context.[32] Let me offer a personal illustration to elaborate this point. I am half Honduran. Whenever I hear definitive statements about Latinx "experience," it goes wrong more often than it goes right. Someone tells me "Happy Cinco de Mayo!" and I gently remind them that Cinco de Mayo is a Mexican holiday and that my family comes from Honduras rather than Mexico. Another person says something about tortillas being a staple at every meal in a Latina/o home without realizing that Puerto Ricans (my wife is half Puerto Rican) do not typically eat them. Do all Latina/os trace their cultural roots to Spain? Spanish speakers of Korean descent in Argentina do not; neither do Spanish speakers of Japanese descent living in Peru, nor Spanish speakers of Jewish Eastern European descent living in Argentina. Do all those who identify as Latina/o speak Spanish? No. Brazilians speak Portuguese. Mayans, Aztecs, and many peoples of African descent speak in local or tribal dialects, and they may or may not know Spanish. If they do, it might be their second or third language. Do all Latina/os in the United States know Spanish? Many second-, third-, or fourth-generation Latina/os grew up in English-speaking homes. Some learned it in school rather than at home; others understand it but do not speak it; and still others know about as much Spanish as I know Klingon or Elvish. Have all Latina/os immigrated to the United States since the huge swell in non-European immigration in the 1960s? A significant number of people have immigrated in the last sixty years, but many others have lived in the United States for up to five or more generations. If you talk to a lot of Latina/o families in the Southwest, you will discover that they have lived in the United States a lot longer than many Anglo-Americans. Their roots go back to a time when parts of the South and the Southwest were Mexican territories. Thus they never immigrated. They did not "come" to the United States. The United States came to them. Differences exist even in terminology due to the "complexity of Latino identity."[33] Some

31. Wisdom, *Paradox and Discovery*, 138.
32. In their book *One Gospel, Many Ears*, Joseph R. Jeter Jr. and Ronald J. Allen claim that at least eight factors shape the way that listeners hear and filter sermons: gender, age, personality type, patterns of mental operation, ethnicity, class, race, and theological orientation. They do *not* suggest that some of the prevailing issues around race, ethnicity, class, and gender are somehow unimportant in congregations where a lot of diversity exists in these particular domains. Rather, they complicate traditional understandings of what counts as diverse, especially in situations where pastors might prematurely conclude that they minister in a homogeneous context.
33. Juan Francisco Martínez makes the following observation regarding terminology:
On Plaza Olvera in Los Angeles one can buy tee shirts that say things like "I am Chicano, not Hispanic." On the other hand, a friend who recently arrived in the United States was

6

prefer to use the term Latina/o, others Hispanic, others Latinx, and still others prefer terms connected to their national background (e.g., Argentinian, Cuban, or Colombian). The numerous examples of diversity in Latina/o communities represent one case among many that could be used to describe contexts within a context.

Third, by contextualization I do *not* mean that every preacher should spend long hours attempting to become an expert in popular culture. In saying this, I do not intend to imply that cultural relevance is unimportant, and I most certainly do not want to sound like a curmudgeon. Preachers should have *some* knowledge of trends in music, art, film, television, literature, and sports. Too many preachers know next to nothing about what is taking place in the world around them. One can presume that our credibility goes up when people discover that we do not live under a rock somewhere. Too many pastors promote a "quarantine style" of preaching in which the goal is to protect everyone from the world "out there."[34] If Daniel and his friends had "knowledge and understanding of all kinds of literature and learning" (Dan. 1:17), then they must have known *something* about Babylonian culture. We tread on dangerous ground when we ignore movements in popular culture or when we underestimate its unyielding and subversive influence over those to whom we minister. A quarantine approach will not suffice.

That stated, we do not benefit from idolizing relevance either. Is expertise in popular culture always the best way to reach people? Not necessarily. There are many forms of relevance. We can still be relevant without knowing every

---

lamenting: "I have been an Argentinian all my life. Now I am in the United States and they tell me I am Latino. I have never been Latino and I really do not understand what that is." These two examples reflect the complexity of Latino identity. We use terms like Latino or Hispanic to describe ourselves and some of us insist on one or the other. Many among us reject both of the terms and do not understand why we are identified as Latinos or Hispanics and not by terms that identify our specific national backgrounds. (*Walk with the People*, 15)

34. I borrow the language of "quarantine style" from Lamin Sanneh's *Translating the Message*. Sanneh lists three major types of religious organizations, with the third being the preferred model: quarantine, syncretist, and reform/prophetic witness. Here is how he describes the quarantine style: "Because of timidity, anxiety, expectancy, or eschatological warrants, believers separate themselves to maintain close vigilance over their life and conduct in relative seclusion from the world. Contact with outsiders is reduced to a minimum, and the disciples undertake prayer, the breaking of bread, exhortation, and mutual aid" (44). Although some positive markers exist in this style, such as a communitarian impulse and a concern for holiness, Sanneh warns, "If quarantine turns permanent it becomes a sealed ghetto, a temporal enclave suspended in space. In this respect, although there were elements of quarantine in the primitive church, those elements were modified by the pilgrim impulse of the Christian movement." *Translating the Message*, 45.

cultural reference from TV shows, films, or music. Active investment in the lives of people is a higher and more genuine form of relevance—knowing kids' names; sitting by bedsides in the hospital; remembering anniversaries, birthdays, and the passing of loved ones. In the end, the best way for a preacher to be relevant is to be present. Perhaps the statement attributed to William Ralph Inge, the twentieth-century dean of St. Paul's Cathedral, serves as a helpful reminder: "Whoever marries the spirit of this age will find himself a widower in the next."[35] Emil Brunner offers a similar insight: "When the Church tries to be modern she always arrives too late, and the world—rightly—is only amused by her 'modernity.'"[36]

What Contextualization Does Mean

Now that I have established what I do not mean by contextualization, the question remains, What do I mean by it? Broadly speaking, I define contextualization as *the intelligible interpretation and transmission of Christian faith through concepts and means that are tailor-made and custom-fit to the needs of a particular community*. Christian leaders (e.g., pastors, missionaries, academic theologians, teachers, elders, etc.) engage in theological reflection, education, formation, or mission *in* a particular community—all theology is contextual theology. Likewise, they communicate in a manner that makes sense *for* a particular community—all theology is missional theology, or at least it should be. They interpret biblical texts, daily lived experience, and the "signs of the times" *from* a particular community and through a particular interpretive lens, *and* they deploy strategies to transmit faith intelligibly in community-oriented ways. They tailor-make and custom-fit their work to their context in much the same way that a tailor custom-fits a dress or a suit for a particular individual. Their strategies "fit" the context. They do not attend to the needs of their community as pop psychologists or cultural gurus but as anthropologists and ambassadors—as interpreters of the local culture and as those sent by God to call people to be reconciled to God and to one another (2 Cor. 5:16–21).

I define contextualized preaching as *faithful and fitting proclamation in a language that is local, intelligible, hospitable, and transformative*. Contextually responsive preachers proclaim the gospel using a local accent (locality); they speak in a language that people understand (intelligibility); they communicate in a manner that respects and dignifies them (hospitality); and

35. Attributions abound, but the original quote could not be found. For an attribution, see Bass, *Christianity after Religion*, 7.
36. Brunner, *Divine Imperative*, 566.

they call them to repentance and Christlikeness (transformation).[37] They root themselves *in* their communities, recognize local and global influences that *surround* their communities, navigate diversity *within* their communities, and seek the transformation *of* their communities into the image and likeness of Christ (Gal. 4:19).

Two words in particular—"faithful" and "fitting"—shed further light on my definition. I borrow these terms from Leonora Tubbs Tisdale, who says that the goal of contextualization should be "preaching that not only aims toward greater faithfulness to the gospel of Jesus Christ but also aims toward greater 'fittingness' (in content, form, and style) for a particular congregation."[38] Contextual preachers maintain faithfulness to a gospel that transcends context on the one hand, and they practice fittingness to "local communities of faith" on the other.[39] The preacher holds on to Christian distinctiveness while also making locally contingent decisions concerning content, form, and style.

The Goal

Figure 3.2. The Twofold Goal

When preachers hold these two commitments in tension, they do not have to forsake gospel fidelity for contemporary relevance or contemporary relevance for gospel fidelity. Fittingness does not compete with faithfulness. Preachers proclaim a message that is *both* timeless and timely. As James S. Stewart puts it, "The gospel is not for *an* age, but for all time: yet, it is precisely the *particular* age—this history's hour and no other—to which we are commissioned by God to speak."[40]

Three Elements of Good Contextualization

Good contextualization in preaching requires at least three elements: translation, balance, and love. Contextually responsive preachers *translate* the gospel into a language that people understand. I will make this claim later on in my chapter on clarity when I call for an approach to preaching that uses

---

37. Concerning the need for repentance, C. S. Lewis writes, "Fallen man is not simply an imperfect creature who needs improvement. Laying down your arms, saying you are sorry, realizing that you have been on the wrong track and getting ready to start life over again from the ground floor—that is the only way out of our 'hole.' This process of surrender—this movement full speed astern—is what Christians call repentance." *Mere Christianity*, 56.

38. Tisdale, *Preaching as Local Theology*, 33.

39. Tisdale, *Preaching as Local Theology*, 30.

40. Stewart, *Heralds of God*, 11.

accessible, relevant, and relational language as a form of translation. Even so, the task requires more from us than oral clarity. Translation requires a steadfast commitment to understanding, studying, and communicating in the local dialect of those we serve.[41]

Consider the work of the Bible translator serving as a newcomer in a host culture. He or she learns the language, but doing so requires more than the capacity to come up with word-for-word equivalents in order to publish a lexicon. The translator also asks: What are the prevailing questions in the place where I serve? What are the beliefs and values beneath the surface of the observable customs? What are the stories, metaphors, analogies, and colloquialisms? How do I make the unfamiliar familiar in a place and among a people that are different from me?

In *Preaching: A Kind of Folly*, Ian Pitt-Watson argues that most pastors preach sermons in the "language of Canaan" when the listeners we preach to are fluent in the "language of Babylon." They have some knowledge of our language, but the majority of what we say gets lost in translation. Because we have not studied *their* language and culture with sufficient time and energy, we end up offering theological answers to questions that people are not asking in a language that they do not understand.[42] While God can use any human communication to speak to people, most listeners will not benefit from sermons that sound like they are in a foreign language. I could probably gain *something* positive from watching a news program in a language that I do not know, but my time is better spent listening to an anchorperson who speaks my language and knows at least something about the place where I live. Which is easier: for the preacher to improve at speaking Babylonian, or for all the listeners to become fluent in the language of Canaan? Pitt-Watson does not mean to assert that the language of Canaan lacks value or that it is irrelevant to the task of preaching.[43] Rather, he pushes preachers to translate the language they know into the language their people know. The goal, Pitt-Watson writes, is to engage people in "the questions they are asking, using the language they are speaking."[44]

Also, contextually responsive preachers *balance* their work in order to avoid the opposite extremes of under-contextualization and over-contextualization.

41. James R. Nieman critiques simplistic understandings of context: "Contextual awareness ought not be reduced to a slogan in theological education and ministerial practice, a byword affirmed by all that therefore needs no further thought." *Knowing the Context*, 1.

42. Pitt-Watson writes, "Before people will listen to our theological answers they must be satisfied that we have understood the questions *they* are asking. Much of our preaching gives the appearance of offering painstaking answers to questions that *nobody* is asking." *Preaching*, 52 (emphasis in original).

43. Pitt-Watson, *Preaching*, 51–52.

44. Pitt-Watson, *Preaching*, 52.

The Old Testament prophets had to strike a similar balance. When Israel moved toward quarantine and isolationism (under-contextualization), the prophets reminded them of their call to be people of mission, that the God of Israel was also the God of everyone else (Amos 9:7). But when the nation moved toward idolatry and syncretism (over-contextualization), the prophets summoned them back to worship of the living God (1 Kings 18:21; Ezra 9:1–4).

The British missiologist Lesslie Newbigin describes the two extremes of under-contextualization and over-contextualization as the "Scylla" and "Charybdis" of Christian witness. Newbigin writes, "Every missionary path has to find the way between these two dangers: irrelevance and syncretism. And if one is more afraid of one danger than another, one will certainly fall into the opposite."[45] Newbigin writes specifically about cross-cultural mission, but his proposal applies to Christian preaching. When we under-contextualize, we risk losing the people *to whom* we preach. Perhaps we "dabble in great biblical concepts, but the audience feels that God belonged to the long ago and far away."[46] When we over-contextualize, we risk losing the good news *that* we preach.[47] We may find a point of contact, but we lose the point of preaching.

In my definition of contextualized preaching, I also mention hospitality and transformation because a preacher must learn to navigate the tension between them. A preacher who has good contextualization instincts identifies with listeners, respects and dignifies them by speaking their language, and addresses their questions. This is what I mean by hospitality. But the preacher also challenges listeners, calling and even pleading with them to pursue Christlikeness.

---

45. Newbigin, *Word in Season*, 67. David Allan Hubbard makes a similar claim about contextualization:

> The evangelist and mission strategist stand on a razor's edge, aware that to fall on either side has terrible consequences. Fall to the right and you end in obscurantism, so attached to your conventional ways of practicing and teaching the faith that you veil its truth and power from those who are trying to see it through very different eyes. Slip to the left and you tumble into syncretism, so vulnerable to the impact of paganism in its multiplicity of forms that you compromise the uniqueness of Christ and concoct "another gospel which is not a gospel." (foreword to Gililand and Hubbard, *Word among Us*, vii)

46. Haddon Robinson writes, "A minister may stand before a congregation and deliver exegetically accurate sermons, scholarly and organized, but dead and powerless because they ignore the life-wrenching problems and questions of his hearers. Such sermons, spoken in a stained-glass voice using a code language never heard in the marketplace, dabble in great biblical concepts, but the audience feels that God belonged to the long ago and far away. Expositors must not only answer the questions our fathers and mothers asked; they must wrestle with the questions our children ask." *Biblical Preaching*, 47–48.

47. As David Bosch writes, "In spite of the undeniably crucial nature and role of the context, then, it is not to be taken as the sole and basic authority for theological reflection." *Transforming Mission*, 431.

This is what I mean by transformation. Critical contextualization in preaching requires a commitment to identification *and* transformation.[48] The right balance helps one to steer clear of the Scylla and Charybdis.

Finally, contextually responsive preachers *love* the people who hear them with such resolve that they are willing to make sacrifices in order to reach them. Martin Lloyd-Jones notes, "The problem with some of us is that we love preaching, but we are not always careful to make sure that we love the people to whom we are actually preaching."[49] Consider Moses's jealous love for the people of Israel when he prayed, "But now, please forgive their sin—but if not, then blot me out of the book you have written" (Exod. 32:32). Remember the resolve that Esther displayed to pray, fast, and act courageously on behalf of the nation. When faced with the annihilation of her own people and the eradication of the covenant, she exclaimed, "If I perish, I perish" (Esther 4:16). Think of the depth of Paul's love when he penned these words: "For I could wish that I myself were cursed and cut off from Christ for the sake of my people, those of my own race, the people of Israel" (Rom. 9:3–4). Love for people covers a multitude of homiletical sins. Contextually responsive preachers practice the spiritual discipline of being with, praying with, and praying for people. They practice the art of loving them rather than just liking them.

> "*The amorphous bones of universal humanity take on flesh and blood, personality and character, as the preacher grapples with issues of faith and life on behalf of particular individuals represented within the congregation.*"
>
> —Leonora Tubbs Tisdale

People usually listen if they believe that their pastor cares about them. A pastor who loves people finds ways to tailor-make and custom-fit sermons to reality, to the concrete situations that people are dealing with in the here and now. Tisdale writes, "The preacher who is also pastor sits in the study with the full awareness that Susan and Dave are on the brink of divorce, that Ida has just been informed that her cancer is terminal, that Ray is the latest victim of job loss due to corporate takeover, and that five-year-old Libby shows all the signs of being physically abused. . . . The amorphous bones of universal humanity take on flesh and blood, personality and character, as the preacher grapples

48. Flemming uses the language of "identificational" and "transformational" in his description of the apostle Paul's preaching in the book of Acts in *Contextualization in the New Testament*, 86.
49. Lloyd-Jones, *Preaching and Preachers*, 92.

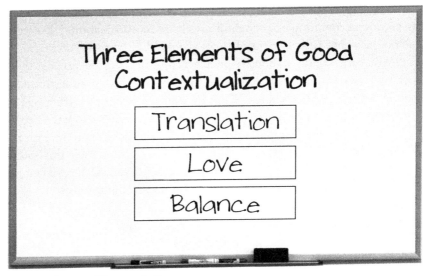

Figure 3.3. Elements of Contextualization

with issues of faith and life on behalf of particular individuals represented within the congregation."[50]

Pastors preach an embodied and specific word to people in all their specificity, not a disembodied word to all of humanity in the abstract. Although the gospel has a universal significance that we must *not* forget, it also incarnates itself as a localized word in the language and culture of time and space, a word that walks into the neighborhoods where people live and work and play.[51] Preachers who know and love people, who know and love the neighborhoods where they live, might not reach the same level of eloquence, education, or gifting as others, but their love achieves for them what Fred Craddock describes as the "irreplaceable power [of] appropriateness."[52]

---

50. Tisdale, *Preaching as Local Theology*, 11–12.

51. Newbigin writes,
Neither at the beginning, nor at any subsequent time, is there or can there be a gospel that is not embodied in a culturally conditioned form of words. The idea that one can or could at any time separate out by some process of distillation a pure gospel unadulterated by any cultural accretions is an illusion. It is, in fact, an abandonment of the gospel, for the gospel is about the word made flesh. Every statement of the gospel in words is conditioned by the culture of which those words are a part, and every style of life that claims to embody the truth of the gospel is a culturally conditioned style of life. There can never be a culture-free gospel. (*Foolishness to the Greeks*, 4)

52. Craddock writes, "Much hoopla to the contrary, the most effective preachers in this or any generation are pastors, whose names we may or may not ever know. This is not a comment on oratorical skills nor is it a broad benediction on every pulpit effort by pastors. It is rather a

Most people notice if their pastors care about them, if they love rather than tolerate them, if they remember them in prayer, if they choose solidarity over enmity. Does it mean that people will always hear and heed Jesus's call to discipleship? Not necessarily. Some people do not heed God's call for the simple reason that their hearts are hard (1 Sam. 6:6; Ps. 95:8; Zech. 7:12; Matt. 19:8; Mark 10:5). But are people *more likely* to respond to the call of God if they believe that their pastor cares about them? Yes.

The Practices of Contextualization

In the last section of this chapter, I will recommend three homiletical strategies designed to help us practice contextualization: interrogate cultural blind spots, become a congregational ethnographer, and listen to our listeners. This list is not exhaustive but suggestive. It sets us on the right road but does not take us to a final destination.

Interrogate Cultural Blind Spots

On one occasion, a group of North American theologians invited Gonzalo Arroyo, a Chilean Jesuit priest, to come to the United States and speak at one of their gatherings. He started his presentation this way: "Tell me, why is it that when you speak of *our* theology you call it 'Latin American theology,' but when you speak of *your* theology you call it 'theology'?"[53] In asking the question, Arroyo exposed a perennial problem: *our cultural blind spots often make us oblivious to how our social location shapes our theology, ministry, and way of being in the world.* To return to an analogy from earlier, those in attendance had not only forgotten about the air that they breathed but they had also forgotten about how much the air shaped their experience of the world. Remember that all theology is contextual theology. As Orlando E. Costas reminds us, theology is a "contextual reflection on the action of God in history. To pretend to be anything else is but an illusion, and a very dangerous one for the church."[54]

---

recognition of the central importance of knowing one's hearers, a fact which makes it possible to have that irreplaceable power: appropriateness." *Preaching*, 91–92.

53. Original story in R. Brown, *Gustavo Gutiérrez*, xix.

54. Costas, *Christ outside the Gate*, 3–4. Other theologians would agree. David Bosch writes, "Interpreting a text is not only a literary exercise; it is also a social, economic, and political exercise. Our entire context comes into play when we interpret a biblical text. One therefore has to concede that all theology (or sociology, political theory, etc.) is, by its very nature, contextual." *Transforming Mission*, 423.

Every preacher has cultural blind spots. The sooner we realize it, the better off we will be. We can choose to ignore this truth about ourselves, but then we will be a lot like a driver who ignores blind spots in the rearview mirror—we will become a danger to ourselves and to those around us. Some of our blind spots exist simply because we are modern readers interpreting an ancient text. Books such as Kenneth E. Bailey's *Jesus through Middle Eastern Eyes* and E. Randolph Richards and Brandon J. O'Brien's *Misreading Scripture with Western Eyes* attempt to bridge the inevitable gap that exists when modern readers try to interpret an ancient Middle Eastern text.[55]

Other cultural blind spots exist on account of our nationality, race, ethnicity, gender, and class. Sometimes these identity markers help us see things that others might not see, and other times they keep us from seeing what is plainly in front of us—they make us oblivious. For example, John S. Mbiti warns North American theologians of the dangers of forgetting how people's life experiences shape their theological reflection when he writes, "The African theologian who has experienced the agonies of having a burning appetite but nothing to eat will surely theologize differently on the theme of food from the American theologian who knows the discomfort of having a plate full of steak but no appetite."[56]

If you want to interrogate your blind spots, ask some hard questions such as the following:

- How does racial privilege impact me positively or negatively?[57]
- How does my gender impact my life and ministry or others' perceptions of me?
- Which parts of my racial/ethnic background should I celebrate, and which parts might be broken and in need of repair?
- How does my wealth or the lack thereof impact me positively or negatively?
- How does my social location (e.g., race, class, and ethnicity) lead me to privilege some perspectives and neglect others?
- How does my social location impact the way I relate to others (e.g., culturally different others or those in power) and the way others relate to me?

55. See Bailey, *Jesus through Middle Eastern Eyes*; Richards and O'Brien, *Misreading Scripture with Western Eyes*. See also Bailey, *Paul through Mediterranean Eyes*.

56. Mbiti, "Theological Impotence," 15.

57. In asking this question, one helpful resource to consult is Emerson and Smith, *Divided by Faith*. They argue that racial privilege impacts one's view of the world and how one generates solutions to society's problems.

Just because some of us are not accustomed to asking these critical cultural questions does not mean that we should avoid asking them. Matthew D. Kim observes that, sometimes in pastoral ministry, "with the busyness of life and being swayed by the 'tyranny of the urgent,' seldom do we think about who we are, where we have been, and who we are becoming as persons and preachers."[58] But if we want to reach others in preaching and thrive in ministry ourselves, we need more critical cultural self-study.[59]

Our cultural blind spots come from our cultural value system, which is often (but not always) tied to our nationality.[60] Our cultural values exist beneath the surface of our customs and practices as beliefs and interpretive frameworks, and often we do not know what they are.[61] Although they drive our attitudes and behaviors, they often disguise themselves as norms rather than culturally specific values, especially in cross-cultural contexts. In his pioneering work, Geert H. Hofstede argued that societies operate according to the following seven cultural values:[62]

- *Individualism versus collectivism*: individual identity and rights are prioritized over the group, *or* the group's identity and values are prioritized over the individual

- *Low power distance versus high power distance*: little to no interest in status differences and a more democratic approach to leadership, *or* greater investment in status differences with decisions typically made by those in authority

- *Low uncertainty avoidance versus high uncertainty avoidance*: high tolerance for unpredictability, flexibility, and improvisation, *or* low tolerance for the same

- *Cooperative versus competitive*: focus on collaboration and mutuality in work, *or* focus on individual achievement and accomplishment of tasks in work

58. Kim, *Preaching with Cultural Intelligence*, 45.
59. For a deeper analysis of critical cultural self-study and its necessity for preaching, see Alcántara, *Crossover Preaching*, 198–201, 287–90.
60. I use the word "often" with respect to nationality because "cultural clusters" will often exist in the same nation on account of its diversity, migration patterns, and demographic shifts, the United States being a prime example. For instance, we live in a largely individualistic society in the United States, but it would not be strange to find collectivistic subcultures, especially in immigrant communities coming from collectivistic societies. For more on what cultural clusters are and how they work, see Livermore, *Expand Your Borders*.
61. For a helpful resource for understanding your own culture and understanding cultural differences between you and others, see Lane, *Beginner's Guide to Crossing Cultures*.
62. See Hofstede, *Culture's Consequences*. See also Livermore, *Expand Your Borders*.

- *Short-term time versus long-term time*: focus on producing immediate results right now, *or* focus on long-term goals and benefits over quick results
- *Low context versus high context*: direct communication with greater attention to verbal discourse, *or* indirect communication with greater attention to the nonverbal
- *Being versus doing*: relationships and social commitments create blurred lines between work and life, *or* task achievement takes precedence over relationships

Some of these values matter more to pastoring than preaching. For instance, our location on the power distance spectrum will probably teach us more about our leadership style than our preaching style. However, many of these values shape our preaching. Do we tend toward individualistic application when we preach—Jesus and me—or do we talk about application for the church, the society, or the whole world? Do we communicate using direct, low-context communication in a setting where a lot of our listeners might be indirect and high context? Do we focus on calling people to do rather than to be, or to be rather than to do? These and other questions should push us to deepen our levels of cultural intelligence. As Kim reminds us, "A proper and healthy view of self can be one of the most empowering and encouraging tools one can possess in the pulpit."[63]

Become a Congregational Ethnographer

I borrow the term "congregational ethnographer" from Tisdale, who uses it to describe what contextually responsive preachers are called to do.[64] The word "ethnographer" means "one who writes about/studies culture." An ethnographer studies the community in which she or he lives, reflects on that community, and functions as both an insider and an outsider, a participant and a critic at one and the same time. As congregational ethnographers, preachers do more than study texts; they also study congregational contexts. No one can claim to have the job of an ethnographer without taking the time and making the effort to study, learn from, and listen to a community. Would you trust someone who claimed to be an expert ethnographer on your race, ethnicity, or nationality but who had not taken the time to get to know anyone from your race, ethnicity, or nationality? Why would a congregation

63. Kim, *Preaching with Cultural Intelligence*, 45.
64. Tisdale, *Preaching as Local Theology*, 18, 35, 59–61, 64–76, 91.

believe a preacher who claimed to know them but had not spent any time getting to know them?

According to Tisdale, local ethnography requires a "symbolic analysis of culture in congregational life" with a specific aim in mind: "coming to know our congregations more deeply in order that we might also preach to them in ways that are both more fitting and more transformative for who they truly are."[65] In *Preaching as Local Theology and Folk Art*, Tisdale lifts up seven symbols of local context that preachers can study in order to understand their communities better than they do now:

- *Stories and interviews.* The stories of a local community of faith have inherent power. What institutional stories do you know about your context? Who were the key stakeholders when the congregation was formed? Who are they now? If you meet in a building, who built it, and how was it built? How did the community end up at the location where it is now? Tisdale recommends doing interviews. Ask key people questions about their connection to the community.

- *Archival material.* Documents also tell us about context. Archives tell us the story of the church, as do minutes of board meetings, weddings and funerals, and other sources of wisdom.

- *Demographics.* Study how your church's demographics have changed and how the community around you has changed. For example, at the church where I used to serve as a teaching pastor in New Jersey, non-whites represented the fastest-growing demographic in new membership during the four years that I served there, from 30 percent of new membership the first year to 70 percent the final year. These trends reshaped our local congregation.

- *Architecture and visual arts.* This symbol has more to do with historic church buildings but is still relevant in other contexts. What does the space tell you about the people? Do certain groups "own" spaces? What does the building tell visitors? What does the architecture of the pulpit, platform, or altar communicate?

- *Rituals.* Learn about baptisms, communal celebrations, marriages, confirmations, funerals, and other significant events. What are the customs? Why do people perform these customs the way that they do?

- *Events and Activities.* What types of activities and events receive the most attention? Which events are the most controversial? Which events are joyful?

65. Tisdale, *Preaching as Local Theology*, 65.

- *People.* Who are the key stakeholders in the church? Who is vocal, and who is silenced? Who is considered wise in the congregation? Who fits, and who doesn't?[66]

Tisdale does not claim that these seven sources are the only symbolic sources present in a given context. Neither does she claim that every source carries equal weight in every context. In some situations, stories and interviews matter more, whereas in other situations demographic shifts matter more. Because pastoral ministry usually moves at a frenetic pace and there are not enough hours in the day, data gathering will probably be more informal, ad hoc, and occasional than in an academic setting. The goals are different. We do not learn more about a community because we want to write a master's thesis; we learn about it because we love our community and want to reach it.

As we seek to understand the people to whom we preach, it will also help us to ask interpretive questions: How is my community changing? What does it sound like to make the gospel intelligible in this space at this time? What is the wound in need of redress here? What gifts of the community do I need to celebrate? What idols do I need to expose? What pollutants do I find in the air? How can I reach more people than I might be reaching now? These and other questions help us to move beyond understanding data and stories to interpreting data and stories.

Listen to Listeners

If we want to learn more about how people process and interact with our sermons, then maybe we should ask them. It is much more accurate than wondering and speculating about what they think and feel. Their responses will presumably look a lot like a bell curve. The opposite ends of the bell curve matter less than the data in the center. Ten percent of people will overpraise us, 10 percent will criticize us unfairly, and the 80 percent in the middle will probably give us accurate and important information. It takes a healthy dose of humility to ask listeners what they think about our preaching if we know that their responses might make us feel insecure or defensive. But the feedback they provide is invaluable. Not only does feedback teach us about our preaching in general; it also teaches us how to be more contextually responsive when we ask the right questions and go about it the right way. The benefits we gain outweigh the sacrifices we make, even if the feedback we receive bruises our egos a little bit.

---

66. For an overview of the seven sources of congregational exegesis, see Tisdale, *Preaching as Local Theology*, 64–77.

Preachers use a number of different strategies to solicit feedback.[67] Some focus a lot of attention on "feed-forward." They preview sermon material in a Bible study, with a leadership team, with a worship-planning team, or with designated collaborators whom they select ahead of time. In doing so, they familiarize themselves with people's questions, reactions, ideas, and input. Both Lucy Atkinson Rose and John S. McClure argue that recruiting strategic collaborators from one's listening community (usually not another pastor or staff person) even at the earliest stages in the preparation process can make a huge difference in one's preaching.[68]

Other preachers receive feedback immediately or shortly after the sermon from people they trust. Those who preach the same sermon multiple times in the same weekend might solicit informal feedback from the pastoral team, staff members, or laypeople between worship services in order to get even the smallest bit of information on how the sermon landed with people. A more common approach involves asking listeners to write down their feedback on some kind of evaluation sheet so they can give it to the preacher afterward. Evaluations usually contain all sorts of questions, some that are related to contextualizing and others that are unrelated to it. Here are some context-related questions that you can include on a potential evaluation sheet:

- Did the sermon connect the ancient world to the contemporary world in some way? If so, how? If not, why not?
- Did the preacher make his or her language accessible to modern listeners, or did the sermon come across as too academic, aloof, or distant? If the language was accessible, what made it accessible? If it was not, what made it inaccessible?
- Were the illustrations understandable and relevant? Why, or why not?
- Did the sermon address your life personally, the lives of those around you, or issues in the contemporary world in some way? If so, how? If not, why not?
- Did the sermon seem like it was in touch with the real world? If so, how? If not, what made it out of touch with reality?

67. For several strategies on starting a healthy feedback loop with laypeople in your congregation, see Shaddix's chapter "Rising above Foyer Feedback" in Shaddix and Vines, *Progress in the Pulpit*, 167–83.

68. They use the "roundtable" imagery and approach to planning as a way to advocate for a collaborative rather than unilateral approach. For more on the roundtable approach to preaching, see Rose, *Sharing the Word*; McClure, *Roundtable Pulpit*.

- If you are in a multigenerational church: Was the sermon accessible enough that a sixth grader could get something out of it but substantive enough that a sixty-year-old could also benefit from it? If so, why? Use examples. If not, why not?

Remember: Do not ask *only* people who look like you to evaluate your preaching. Ask people who are racially or culturally different from you, people of a different gender, people of a different age. If you listen to diverse perspectives on your preaching, it will give you a better sense of your blind spots and decrease the likelihood of an echo-chamber approach to evaluation. Also, make sure to widen the circle of your evaluators beyond pastors and staff members. You can solicit feedback from pastors or paid staff from time to time, but remember that, just like you, many of them speak the language of Canaan rather than the language of Babylon. Even if you cannot pay the volunteers you select, find a different way to "pay" them through recognition, celebration, or some kind of written or verbal affirmation. Some preachers like to solicit feedback using anonymous surveys. Sometimes anonymity leads to more honest and open feedback in a way that other modes of evaluation might stifle or prevent.

A final possibility for feedback involves recruiting coaches into our lives—in particular, people who are already good at contextualization in preaching—who can mentor us. Think of Christian leaders in your sphere of influence who already preach in a language that people understand, connect with contemporary listeners, and maintain a healthy balance between faithfulness and fittingness. Recruit them into your life to listen to your sermons. Ask them what they hear when they listen to you preach. Invite them to help you get better at preaching. In particular, ask them to help you get better at connecting with people. We can also recruit coaches who mentor us from a distance. We can listen to excellent preachers who are also great at contextualizing who can mentor us from afar.

Conclusion

In this chapter, we observed how biblical writers contextualized, defined terms, discussed the commitments of contextualization, and recommended homiletical practices. A wise and able homiletician could publish a tome on contextualization—defining what it is, how it works, why it matters, what to prioritize—and it would still offer a partial rather than a complete analysis. Even if a handbook like that existed, local preachers in their local settings would still be the resident experts on their context and on contextualizing in it. That means that you know your context a lot better than I ever will. Why does contextualization matter? Perhaps a brief anecdote will provide a partial answer. The popular Kenyan theologian John S. Mbiti tells a fictional story of a young African theology student who left his village church to pursue doctoral studies at a renowned divinity school in the West. After nine and a half years away from home, he passed his oral exams and graduated with a doctorate in theology. Besides learning English, he learned several ancient and modern languages and all the classical disciplines of theology. He wrote a dissertation on an "obscure theologian of the Middle Ages."[69] Before boarding the plane home, he gladly paid the fees for excess baggage, which consisted of copies of the Bible in all of the languages that he knew and books by all the big-name theologians that he studied.

On arriving home, the young theologian discovers that almost everyone in the village has gathered to celebrate his return—musicians, dancers, relatives, old friends—people he remembers well and young children whose names he has yet to learn. Mbiti writes, "Everyone has come to eat, to rejoice, to listen to their hero . . . who has read so many theological books, who is the hope of their small but fast-growing church." Then, without warning, tragedy strikes. The young man's older sister shrieks and falls to the ground, wailing in pain. He rushes to her side and shouts, "Let's take her to the hospital!" The villagers are taken aback, and a young schoolboy replies, "Sir, the nearest hospital is fifty miles away, and there are few buses that go there." Another person shouts, "She is possessed. Hospitals will not cure her." The village chief says, "You have been studying theology overseas . . . now help your sister."[70] Not knowing what to do, he rushes to one of his favorite books, looks in the index, and finds the section on spirit possession, after which he insists that his sister is not possessed. It must be something else. As the people shout, "Help your sister! She is possessed!," he shouts back, "But Bultmann has demythologized demon possession."[71]

69. Mbiti, "Theological Impotence," 7.
70. Mbiti, "Theological Impotence," 7.
71. Mbiti, "Theological Impotence," 8. In the context of this article, Mbiti uses this story not just to make a point about the gap between the academy and the church; more in line with the message of the entire book, this story also illustrates the gap between Western Christianity and lived experiences in churches in the Global South. Later in the article, Mbiti writes,
Theologians from the new (or younger) churches have made their pilgrimages to the theological learning of older churches. We had no alternative. We have eaten theology with you; we have drunk theology with you; we have dreamed theology with you. But it has all been one-sided; it has all been, in a sense, your theology (if we can for a moment go back to the agonizing dichotomy which is real and yet false). We *know you*

Though apocryphal, Mbiti's story reminds us that we stand before real people with real questions in real situations. How much will the language of Canaan help those who speak the language of Babylon? Of course, the work of pastoral ministry requires that preachers read and study the biblical text, that they exegete and theologize. Ask almost anyone devoted to theological education (myself included) whether these things matter and we will tell you, "Absolutely, yes!" without hesitation. Even a little bit of bad theology can do an awful lot of damage. But how much of a difference will our theologies make in the lives of real people without at least a satisfactory capacity to contextualize? Our listeners live in a particular time and place. If we want to lead the sheep, we should probably take the time to get to know them first.

Learning activities and sermon samples for this chapter are located at www.PracticesofChristianPreaching.com.

theologically. *The question is, do you know us theologically? Would you like to know us theologically? Can you know us theologically?* And how can there be true theological reciprocity and mutuality, if only one side knows the other fairly well, while the other side either does not know or does not want to know the first side? ("Theological Impotence, 16–17 [emphasis added])

4

Preach Clearly

To attain simplicity in preaching is of the utmost importance to every minister who wishes to be useful to souls.

—J. C. Ryle, *Simplicity in Preaching*

The secret to being a bore is to tell everything.[1]
—Voltaire, *Oeuvres Complètes de Voltaire*

The subject of this chapter is clarity: its importance to preaching and its implementation in sermons. Clarity is the third C of the Five Cs of preaching. Clear sermons exhibit simplicity and sophistication, cogency and concision. In this chapter, I will argue that clear sermons exhibit four characteristics in particular: concise exegesis, accessible language, a clear main idea, and commitment to brevity.

But before we delve into the subject of clarity, let me share at least one story about why it can be so impactful.

The speech ran just over two minutes and totaled 272 words. Most preachers have not finished the introduction to their introduction in two minutes, let alone delivered an entire message from start to finish. What can one really say in such a short amount of time? Depending on our denominational affiliation, some of us believe that we need at least twenty, thirty, or even forty-five minutes. "After all," we say to ourselves, "my sermon should

1. In French: *Le secret d'ennuyer est celui de tout dire* (my translation).

**The Practices
of Christian Preaching**

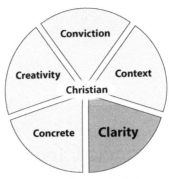

Figure 4.1. The Five Cs: Clarity

have an engaging introduction, explain the intricacies of the preaching text, offer a clear main idea, contain compelling illustrations, apply the text thoroughly enough to address the diverse needs of various listeners, and then tie things all together with a memorable conclusion." With so many plates to spin, the last thing a preacher wants to hear is, "Keep it to about one double-spaced page."

Some scholars claim that he was putting finishing touches on the speech on the train. When he and his party arrived, people extended a warm welcome, and they expressed their profound gratitude for his willingness to come so far despite the somber occasion that prompted the visit on such a cold November day. A different person was the featured speaker that day, a man named Edward Everett. According to Ted Widmer of the *New York Times*, Everett had spent his entire life preparing for this moment: "His immense erudition and his reputation as a speaker set expectations very high for the address to come."[2] As expected, Everett delivered the type of speech customary to the time: "a eulogy in the traditional style, spending two hours praising the virtues of the soldiers."[3] All in all, the speech contained roughly thirteen thousand words, and he delivered it in its entirety without notes.[4]

2. Referring to Everett's prominence, Widmer writes, "He lived deeply in the present, as governor of Massachusetts, congressman, president of Harvard, minister to the Court of St. James's, Secretary of State, and senator. But he never stopped acting as America's Oracle, channeling the spirits of the dead as America raced headlong into the future. His speeches were extraordinarily popular—on one occasion in New York, he spoke in an auditorium that seated thousands, and nevertheless, a mob stormed the barricades, desperate to be admitted." "The Other Gettysburg Address."

3. Duarte, *Resonate*, 176.

4. For the length of the speech and its contents, see Widmer, "The Other Gettysburg Address."

When Everett concluded, the next speaker took his place at the rostrum and delivered the 272-word speech that ran just over two minutes. According to Widmer, his words were "mostly one and two-syllables, delivered from Anglo-Saxon and Norman roots, the way that Americans actually spoke."[5] The date was November 9, 1863. President Abraham Lincoln started and finished the Gettysburg Address so quickly that most of the photographers did not have time to set up their equipment. Thus, no close-up photographs exist of Lincoln consecrating the National Cemetery at Gettysburg, and only about nine photographs exist of the ceremony.[6] Yet many consider the Gettysburg Address to be one of the greatest speeches delivered in US history. Even Everett agreed. The next day, he wrote Lincoln a letter praising the "eloquent simplicity and appropriateness" of the speech. "I should be glad," he wrote, "if I could flatter myself that I came as near to the central idea of the occasion, in two hours, as you did in two minutes."[7] It turns out that one *can* say a lot in one double-spaced page.

Many of us preach more like Edward Everett than like Abraham Lincoln, perhaps because we have convinced ourselves that the two-hour version will always be better than the two-minute version. But are we really better off if a longer sermon obstructs our clarity? Which is easier: to preach a forty-five-minute sermon from 2 Corinthians 5 on how God is reconciling the world through Christ or to preach a fifteen-minute sermon on the subject? What is more difficult: to trace the arc of the narrative in the book of Ruth in twenty minutes or to take an hour?

Should every sermon be two minutes long? Do not let your hearts be troubled! I am not asking you to rival Lincoln's "eloquent simplicity and appropriateness." My own inner monologue calls out: "You, sir, are no Abraham Lincoln." In a lot of churches, people will wonder what you have been doing all week if you stand up and preach for two minutes. In fact, in a lot of non-white preaching traditions, guest preachers reserve the first few minutes for thanking hosts, recognizing family, acknowledging church members, honoring mentors, and giving God praise. If a preacher jumps straight into a sermon without first going through the culturally appropriate steps, it would be like serving supper without setting the table. Even if the meal looks and tastes

---

5. This served as a sharp contrast to Everett's speech and, according to Widmer, "No one expected a major utterance from the president. This was not his role. He was not a historian. He could not read Greek, or even Latin." "The Other Gettysburg Address."

6. Only three photos from that occasion feature Lincoln at Gettysburg—one undisputed photo and two disputed. For more on the undisputed and disputed photos taken at Gettysburg, see Lidz, "Will the Real Abraham Lincoln Please Stand Up?"

7. For this quotation and Lincoln's letter of response, see Nicolay and Hay, *Complete Works of Abraham Lincoln*, 9:210–11. See also Duarte, *Resonate*, 176.

Figure 4.2. Abraham Lincoln at the dedication of the Soldiers' National Cemetery in Gettysburg, Pennsylvania. Lincoln is slightly left of center, just behind the mass of blurry people.

good, the server comes across as rude and uncouth. Usually if you preach for two minutes, you have not preached. The Gettysburg Address is a special and historic case that illustrates a point.

My larger point is *not* that every sermon should be brief—it is that every sermon should be *clear.* Saint Augustine reminds us, "The function of eloquence in teaching is not to make people like what was once offensive, or to make them do what they were loath to do, but to make clear what was hidden from them."[8] To put it differently, the old adage is right—"A mist in the pulpit is a fog in the pew." An unclear sermon is a fog whether it lasts for twenty, forty, or sixty minutes. A preacher must grasp the core of the message to be communicated and present that message in a manner that makes sense to those who listen; otherwise, the preacher's inability to communicate clearly will make it that much more difficult for listeners to comprehend what is being said.

8. Augustine, *On Christian Teaching,* 117.

As an entry point to this discussion, let me enlist the help of an unconventional dialogue partner in most conversations about preaching: the famed Italian Renaissance painter and inventor Leonardo da Vinci.

What Leonardo da Vinci Can Teach Preachers about Clarity

What can preachers learn from Leonardo? Perhaps the greatest lesson is to *avoid false dichotomies*. To improve at clarity, one does not have to choose length or depth, complexity or simplicity, breadth or concision. A preacher can be clear without being kitschy or trite. Leonardo liked to say it this way: "Simplicity is the ultimate sophistication."[9] Preachers who practice clarity in the delivery of sermons pursue sophisticated simplicity in the preparation of sermons.

> *A preacher can be clear without being kitschy or trite. Leonardo liked to say it this way: "Simplicity is the ultimate sophistication."*

The high level of sophistication in Leonardo's paintings and inventions reminds us that one does *not* have to abandon complexity in order to achieve simplicity. That is to say, simplicity in preaching should not be mistaken for simplistic preaching. Some of us make the mistake of concluding that, if a person strives for simplicity, it will somehow water down the content of the message or turn profound truths into empty slogans. Do not underestimate how challenging it is to achieve sophisticated simplicity. The US Supreme Court justice Oliver Wendell Holmes is reported to have said, "I would not give a fig for the simplicity this side of complexity, but I would give my life for the simplicity on the other side of complexity."[10]

Sophisticated simplicity strives for the simplicity that exists on the other side of complexity. Which is more difficult: to communicate abstract thoughts using abstract thoughts that make sense to those with your level of education or to communicate those same thoughts concretely to diverse listeners of various educational levels? For those who are training for Christian ministry, which is easier: to use language that sounds like it belongs in a textbook or to use language that is accessible to "common people"? If our goal is to preach a sermon that only the most highly sophisticated congregants can understand, what does it say about our priorities? Most preachers would agree that it is more challenging to communicate abstract ideas in concrete ways using

9. This quotation appears in several books, essays, and articles and is attributed to Leonardo. For one example of a citation, see Mounce, *So They Say*, 2.

10. Cited in Covey, *8th Habit*, 103.

Figure 4.3. *Mona Lisa*

language that people can understand. Sophisticated simplicity requires greater time, energy, and skill than does overly complex argumentation.

Leonardo supported his claim throughout his life and most especially in his work. He found a way to bring simplicity and sophistication together in his paintings, sketches, and inventions. Consider a painting like the *Mona Lisa* or a sketch like *The Vitruvian Man*.

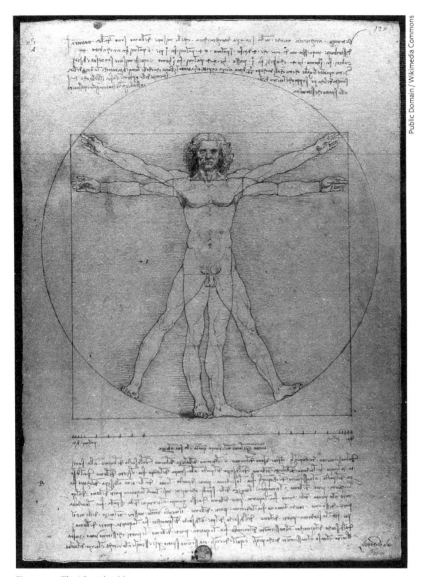

Figure 4.4. *The Vitruvian Man*

Leonardo also sketched prototypes for a hang glider and a parachute. These were just sketches and not the actual inventions, but even a superficial glance at them shows us how prescient they were for their time.

The technology did not yet exist to transform Leonardo's sketches into real-life inventions during his lifetime. Even though another man is credited with inventing the parachute—Louis Sébastien Lenormand in France during the

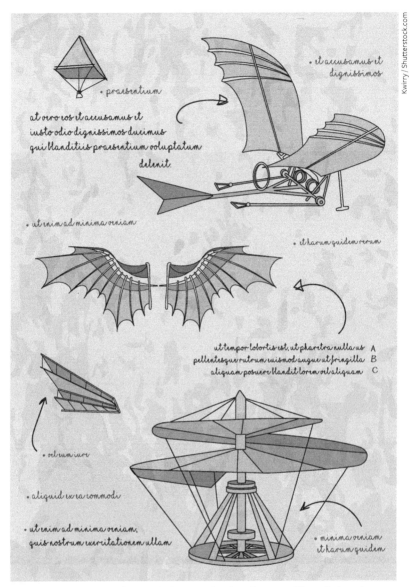

Figure 4.5. Reproductions of Leonardo da Vinci's Sketches of a Hang Glider and a Parachute

late eighteenth century—Leonardo laid the groundwork for the idea hundreds of years earlier. In 2000, a British daredevil named Adrien Nicholas designed a parachute that matched Leonardo's exact dimensions. Ignoring advice from experts that the "canvas and wood contraption would not fly," Nicholas got up in a hot air balloon and dropped himself from ten thousand feet wearing a parachute that weighed roughly 187 pounds. Sure enough, it worked remarkably well over the plains of South Africa where he conducted the test.[11]

What do the sketches and paintings have in common? Each one holds simplicity and sophistication in healthy tension. They are neither one nor the other. Leonardo believed that his work could model both.

Clarity in Scripture and in Church History

Perhaps Leonardo took his cues from the Bible. Consider that some of the most powerful ideas in Scripture are both simple and sophisticated. When God encounters a poor, pregnant, Egyptian slave woman named Hagar in the middle of the desert, and she responds in faith, the text says, "She gave this name to the LORD who spoke to her: 'You are the God who sees me'" (Gen. 16:13). God is a God who sees us in times of trial and distress. Think also of the psalms. We read these words from the pen of King David: "The LORD is my shepherd, I lack nothing" (Ps. 23:1). God leads, guides, protects, feeds, and cares for us with such dedication that we have everything we need. Consider one of Jesus's statements in the Gospels. Confronted with the death of Lazarus and the sorrow of Martha, Jesus declared, "I am the resurrection and the life. The one who believes in me will live, even though they die" (John 11:25). After Martha tells Jesus that she knows she will see her brother raised to new life in the resurrection at the last day, Jesus tells Martha that he *is* the resurrection and the life.

Of course, on several occasions, Jesus's teaching confounds the disciples rather than giving them clarity. Nonetheless, in the Scriptures we find a book with deep but understandable ideas written to common people in their common language. The biblical writers remind us that one does not have to have a professorship to be profound. Although many biblical texts exist that challenge the most skilled of commentators, in the same book we encounter writing that remains accessible to the poor, the uneducated, the simple, and the marginalized.

In Scripture we also find examples of clarity in *preaching*. Consider the dramatic scene in Nehemiah 8 when Ezra read the Book of the Law. Men and women along with all those old enough to understand gathered in Jerusalem to hear Ezra read from the Torah on a high wooden platform (some translate the Hebrew *migdal* as "pulpit") built especially for the occasion (Neh. 8:2, 4).[12]

11. Carrington, "Da Vinci's Parachute Flies."
12. Some translations render the word "platform" as "pulpit," including the American Standard Version, Revised Standard Version, and King James Version.

The Levites "instructed the people in the Law while the people were standing there. They read from the Book of the Law of God, making it clear and giving the meaning so that the people understood what was being read" (8:7–8).[13] Notice how the Levites played an important role in making the Torah accessible to the community.[14] In Nehemiah 8, we see instruction, translation, and interpretation delivered so that all the people—women and men, adults and children—have access to understanding.

In the New Testament, Jesus models sophisticated simplicity in his preaching and teaching. He uses parables as his primary mode of communication in a community immersed in a narrative world. Moreover, he employs an abundance of agrarian imagery in a mostly rural society. Jesus preached in a manner so simple that "poor laypeople were able to comprehend," but he never made his preaching so simplistic as to sound superficial.[15] The New Testament scholar Adolf Deissmann describes Jesus's preaching well:

> No long sentences, no speculative questions, everything popular, simple, concise, transparent, pithy, plastic; all this and yet He was never trivial. Although preached on the street corners it was never street corner wisdom; although clear it was never shallow; never abstract formulations, but always realistic drawings and sketches. . . . The listener not only hears but also looks and sees, and what is heard and seen remains. That is, the words remain in the minds and souls of simple men, who had never been burdened with learned ballast. But they also charm the well-educated as expressions which have not been made but have grown.[16]

Jesus made himself accessible and profound, winsome and prophetic. He spoke in a language that the "simple" could understand, yet he never talked down to them. At the same time, he convinced the well-educated that they were listening to no ordinary teacher.

In addition to examples in Scripture, church history is filled with preachers who understood the importance of clarity. Church fathers such as Basil the Great and John Chrysostom adopted a *sermo humilis* approach: a basic and

---

13. According to Old Testament scholar Mark A. Throntveit, the Levites' task was to "interpret, explain, or possibly paraphrase in Aramaic, the language of the people, what Ezra read in Hebrew, as an aid to comprehension." *Ezra-Nehemiah*, 96.

14. In Hebrew, "making it clear" (*meporash*) can be rendered as "translating," and "giving the meaning" (*vesom sekel*) can be rendered as "interpreting."

15. Martin Luther writes, "When Christ preached he proceeded quickly to a parable and spoke about sheep, shepherds, wolves, vineyards, fig trees, seeds, fields, plowing. The poor laypeople were able to comprehend these things." *Luther's Works*, 54:160.

16. Deissmann, *New Testament in Light of Modern Research*, 94.

simple style of communication, especially among the unlearned.[17] The medieval French Benedictine preacher Guibert of Nogent advocated for an approach that appealed to the uneducated. In his treatise "How to Make a Sermon," Guibert writes, "When a preacher has great fervor in his soul and his memory does not lack varied matter to be touched upon, and he also possesses power to speak eloquently and elegantly, sufficient for his needs, let him consider the weak ability of those who silently listen and that *it would be better for them to receive a few points with pleasure than a great many of which none will be retained.*"[18]

The Protestant Reformers also valued clarity. John Calvin preached in a familiar style using images, expressions, humor, and everyday language. Commenting on Calvin's preaching, T. H. L. Parker writes, "He deliberately adapts his style to the grasp of common people in the congregation. To use a term that he [Calvin] frequently employs of biblical writers, he 'accommodates' himself to the ignorance of the people."[19] Martin Luther believed that clarity was essential to the Christian sermon. The same person who translated the Bible into German (New Testament in 1522; Old Testament and Apocrypha in 1534) and engaged his opponents' critiques through highly technical theological treatises *also* bristled at the idea that his preaching belonged only to the provenance of the intellectual elites. Referring to his ministry as pastor at Wittenberg, Luther once remarked, "I don't look at the doctors and masters, of whom scarcely forty are present, but at the hundred or the thousand young people and children. It's to them that I preach, to them that I devote myself, for they, too, need to understand."[20]

One can also find numerous examples in American church history. I will mention just two. First, Sojourner Truth was "one of the most recognized women of the nineteenth century" mainly because of her advocacy for women and African Americans. Priscilla Pope-Levison argues that the *real* reason that Truth changed her name to Sojourner and moved east was for "the purpose of 'testifying of the hope that was in her.'"[21] Her true calling was as an itinerant

17. Jaclyn L. Maxwell writes, "Basil advocated the simple style, because their [preachers'] goal should be to educate listeners and not to show off their skills. He believed that homilies should be fit for their primary audience, that is, for simple and uneducated people. Similarly, John Chrysostom could complain about his congregation and call attention to their ignorance and bad manners, but also tell with pride how illiterate fishermen had triumphed over philosophers." *Christianization and Communication in Late Antiquity*, 35.

18. Guibert of Nogent, "How to Make a Sermon," 9:290. Guibert published his treatise sometime in the early twelfth century (emphasis added).

19. Parker, *Calvin's Preaching*, 148.

20. In the same paragraph, Luther states, "I adapt myself to the circumstances of the common people." *Luther's Works*, 54:236; see also 54:160, 235–36, 383–84.

21. Pope-Levison, "Sojourner Truth," 510–11.

evangelist. According to Annelise Orleck, Truth's ministry platform grew (as did her audience size) because of two main qualities that she possessed: "oratorical power and clarity."[22] In her preaching and speaking, Truth reached the educated and the uneducated, the rich and the poor, whites and African Americans, powerful elites and common people. She spoke in a language that was intelligible to people of many different backgrounds.

Second, consider also the preaching of Martin Luther King Jr. in the second half of the twentieth century. King received an excellent education, first at Morehouse College and Crozer Theological Seminary, and then at Boston University for his doctorate. Yet King made sure that his numerous academic accomplishments did not produce an intellectual elitism aligned with bourgeoisie values. He always connected the life of the mind back to the public proclamation of the church in society. Academic theology did not exist to propagate ivory-tower, out-of-touch intellectualism but rather to produce theology that made a difference in the lives of everyday people. Thus in 1954 the twenty-five-year-old King made his preaching as accessible as possible to parishioners when he took his first pastorate at Dexter Avenue Baptist Church in Montgomery, Alabama. A series of events in 1955–56 transformed King from a local preacher into a mouthpiece for the 380-day Montgomery bus boycott, which then launched him to national prominence as the most recognizable civil rights leader in US history. Blessed with a rare combination of intellectual sophistication, pulpit eloquence, everyday clarity, and improvisational adeptness, King used his gifts in much the same way that Sojourner Truth used hers: by making his preaching and speaking accessible both to common people *and* to intellectual elites. Perhaps more than any other preacher in the twentieth century, King knew how to communicate with sophisticated simplicity. Here are just a few examples that display his gift for clarity:

- "It is no longer a choice, my friends, between violence and non-violence. It is either non-violence or non-existence."[23]
- "We must use time creatively, in the knowledge that the time is always ripe to do right."[24]
- "Darkness cannot drive out darkness. Only light can do that. Hate cannot drive out hate; only love can do that."[25]

22. Orleck, *Rethinking American Women's Activism*, 8.
23. From the sermon "Remaining Awake through a Great Revolution," in King, *Knock at Midnight*, 220.
24. King, "Letter from a Birmingham Jail," 266.
25. From the sermon "Loving Your Enemies," in King, *Strength to Love*, 51.

- "We must face the shameful fact that the church is the most segregated major institution in American society, and the most segregated hour of the week is . . . eleven o'clock on Sunday morning."[26]
- "There is nothing new about poverty. What is new is that we now have the techniques and the resources to get rid of poverty. The real question is whether we have the will."[27]
- "Injustice anywhere is a threat to justice everywhere."[28]

Notice how King makes profound statements using just a few words and through basic language. These statements are both true and pithy. Even if we cannot replicate his giftedness and influence, we can still learn from his example. Everyone wins when we cultivate clarity in our preaching. Listeners hear sermons that offer them length and depth, complexity and simplicity, breadth and concision. But how do we learn to strike the balance? How do we cultivate clarity?

The Four Modes of Clarity in Preaching

In this section, we will consider how to cultivate clarity in preaching through what I call the four modes of clear preaching. The word "mode" can be used in a number of ways, but I use it here in the sense of "way" or "means," as in "modes of transportation." We need all four in order to make the journey smoother and get where we want to go. The four modes of clarity are concise exegesis, accessible language, a clear main idea, and commitment to brevity.

Practice Concise Exegesis

If you want to become a clearer preacher, become a concise exegete. In 2 Timothy 4:2, Paul gives Timothy this charge: "Preach the word; be prepared in season and out of season; correct, rebuke and encourage—with great patience and careful instruction." If Paul calls on Timothy to major in any book, he calls him to major in Scripture. Of course, the call to preach the Word requires *more* than concise exegesis. We should not confuse preaching from the Scriptures for commentary without reverence, information without

26. From the sermon "How Should a Christian View Communism?," in King, *Strength to Love*, 101–2.
27. From the sermon "Remaining Awake through a Great Revolution," in King, *Knock at Midnight*, 216.
28. King, "Letter from a Birmingham Jail," 257.

application, exposition without contextualization, or explanation without proclamation. Concise exegesis does not consist of downloading information onto people's brains. Although today's pulpit does not need more dispassionate commentators on biblical texts, neither does it need more preachers with little to no commitment to exegesis. My point is that too many preachers go to the Bible as an afterthought. As Haddon Robinson observes, "In many sermons the biblical passage read to the congregation resembles the national anthem played at a baseball game—it gets things started but is not heard again during the afternoon."[29]

Clear and careful exegesis displays respect and love for Scripture. One does not leave it behind or discard it. John Wesley described himself as a *homo unius libri*: a "man of one book."[30] What would need to change in your preaching in order for you to remain tethered to the text, to be a person of "one book"?

In the work of exegesis, Cecilio Arrastía claims, the preacher is like a master jeweler, and the text is the jewel (*como una joya*). When we exegete Scripture, we go down into "the mines of God" (*las minas de Dios*) to unearth the gemstone. On discovering it, we examine and appreciate its beauty: its colors, cuts, facets, and dimensions. Then, like a master jeweler, we hold it up at just the right angle in the light in order to study its features and explore its facets. We love the text the way that a master jeweler loves the jewel. Arrastía writes, "One cannot preach without loving the text, without enticing it until it surrenders to us its most intimate secrets. . . . To love the text is to do exegesis."[31] Orlando Costas makes a similar point when he contends that the text "should be studied with seriousness. Every preacher should try to be a good exegete. He [or she] should live with a constant concern to know the mind of God through biblical revelation."[32]

As preachers, we do not come to the text as detached observers, aloof academics, or skeptical critics. We come to it as those with a vested interest in hearing a word from the Lord. We conduct *homiletical* exegesis in order to preach to a community, as opposed to *academic* exegesis in order to write a

29. H. Robinson, *Biblical Preaching*, 5.

30. Wesley, *Wesley's Standard Sermons*, 1:32.

31. Here is the quote in Spanish: "No se puede predicar sin enamorar el texto, sin seducirlo hasta que nos entregue sus secretos más íntimos. . . . Enamorar el texto es hacer exégesis." Arrastía, *Teoría y Práctica de la Predicación*, 26–27.

32. Here is the quote in its context in Spanish: "Dada la importancia de la Biblia en la predicación y, por consiguiente, en la vida del predicador, este debe ser estudiarla con seriedad. Todo predicador debe procurar ser un buen exegeta bíblico. Debe vivir con una constante preocupación por conocer la mente de Diós a través de la revelación bíblica." Costas, *Comunicación por Medio de la Predicación*, 163.

commentary.[33] We dialogue with Scripture as a spiritual-homiletical practice with proclamation as our aim. We allow the Holy Spirit to preach the Word to us before we preach the Word to others. In our exegesis, we take the time to go down into the mine of God so that God might speak to us through the text. Do we love the text the way the psalmists loved the Torah? Hear again what the psalmist declares: "Oh, how I love your law! I meditate on it all day long" (Ps. 119:97). Psalm 119:72 reads, "The law from your mouth is more precious to me than thousands of pieces of silver and gold."

One way to respect the text as text and to achieve clarity as a result is to use tools to guide your exegesis. Exegetical tools can help you focus more attention on understanding what the Scriptures are saying and doing. Use the resources at your disposal. Utilize the historical, literary, and grammatical resources that you have at your fingertips, especially in an electronic age.[34] If you know Greek and Hebrew, do the work of translating the text(s) from the original language. Translation forces you to slow down your reading of the passage so that you notice things you would not otherwise notice. I compare it to walking down a street on which you normally drive. When you walk down the street, you slow down enough to notice things about it that you never noticed before.

The original languages are one tool among many available to you as an exegete. Take time to study the theology of the text, the historical context, the author, the audience, the occasion for writing, the larger message of the book, the genre, the literary devices, and the imagery. Read the commentaries in order to learn more background information along with unfamiliar words, places, and names. Unlike in the past, you can find a lot of these resources available for free on websites or through apps on mobile phones. Just make sure that you expose yourself to different perspectives when you study the Scriptures so that you can appreciate the many facets of the jewel.

Use Accessible Language

Use language that your listeners can understand. Just as preachers should not talk down to their listeners, so also they should not succumb to the opposite danger—talking past their listeners with academic jargon or confusing

---

33. For more on homiletical exegesis—in particular, the spiritual-exegetical practice of interpreting Scripture in preparation for preaching—see S. Brown, "Interpreting Scripture for Preaching," in S. Brown and Powery, *Ways of the Word*, 123–49.

34. Luchetti writes, "The diligent preacher will explore the use and meaning of words, the sociohistorical background, the literary context, and the genre of the biblical text." *Preaching Essentials*, 82.

argumentation. As one of my professors in seminary used to say, "Remember that they are God's sheep and not God's giraffes." Clear preachers make sure the food is in a place where the sheep can reach it. If listeners do not understand what you say because you do not speak accessibly or because your language is too abstract, who needs to move in order to resolve the problem?

To use accessible language in a sermon, a preacher does not have to cut out all of the unfamiliar words (e.g., "sanctification" or "eschatology"), refrain from rhetorical sophistication, or avoid substantive content. Most listeners do not necessarily mind hearing a new word if it is defined for them. The problem usually arises when every *fifth* word is a word that they do not know. Remember what Luther said. Although he acknowledged that the doctors and business leaders were present in the sanctuary, he made sure that the language of his sermon was accessible to young people and children. In some situations, such as in university chapels, academic subcultures, or other places where the average level of education is quite high, you can get away with more sophisticated language, but even in these contexts, preachers should use language that their listeners can understand. Just because a person preaches in an academic climate does not mean that he or she will be understood.

I still remember a meeting during my doctoral program in which I sat down with one of the members of my dissertation committee and we discussed the chapter I had submitted a few weeks earlier. He said to me, "It is clear that you have done your homework for the chapter you have submitted, and it is clear that you know what you are talking about with respect to the research, but let me be honest with you for a moment. This chapter was tedious and boring." That is a clear message, isn't it? What was he saying? "You passed the research presentation test, but you failed the clarity in communication test." In other words, I needed to pass two tests rather than one. I had not written with the sort of clear, understandable language that would make my work both relevant and interesting to my readers.

In preaching, just as in writing, a person can present a message that is both accurate and true without being cogent or intelligible. As we prepare our sermons, we should ask ourselves whether we use the right language in the right way at the right time for the right reasons for the right audience.

Preachers who use accessible language also understand the shift from written discourse to oral discourse. They can discern the difference between *preaching for the ear* and *preaching for the eye*. A famous Arabian proverb reads, "He is the best speaker who can turn the ear into an eye."[35] Often, mod-

---

35. For a reference to this Arabian proverb in a late nineteenth-century textbook, see Ryle, *Simplicity in Preaching*, 36.

ern communications theorists use this proverb to emphasize the need to be visual when we engage in public speaking so that listeners will see, feel, taste, and touch the scenes we describe and the stories we tell. Speakers enrich the experience of listeners when they transform what listeners hear into what they can see. Although this is true (and we will touch on this some in the chapter on creativity), another point can also be extrapolated from the same proverb: *if you want to turn the ear into an eye, preach for the ear rather than the eye.*

When you write a sermon for the ear, you write the way you talk, and your audience is your congregation. When you write a sermon for the eye, you write for a person who will read your work. In the case of the former, you write a sermon that sounds like it belongs to the genre of sermons: oral, aural, and prepared for a community. In the case of the latter, you write a sermon that sounds like it belongs in the genre of academic term papers—that is, an oral exegesis report prepared for an individual reader such as a professor.

Writing for the ear requires a shift in thinking. A preacher has to *un*learn a lot of the most basic rules of writing for the eye. The rules sound a lot like this: "No sentence fragments. None. Run-on sentences are an abomination and you should never use them because you'll get marked down when the teacher grades your paper. Don't use contractions. It's not a good idea to ever split infinitives. A preposition is something you should never end a sentence with. And don't begin sentences with 'and.' Never, never, never repeat yourself."[36]

These rules work well when we want to write a term paper for a class, but they often strain relevance when we want to write a sermon for a congregation. As Donald R. Sunukjian notes, "We don't follow these rules when we talk. None of them. We talk in short sentences. Fragments. Easy-to-follow phrases. We don't use big words. We don't sound literary. We sound normal. We talk so that eleven-year-olds can understand us."[37]

So how do we write sermons for the ear rather than the eye? The easy answer is to write the way we speak. Use sentence fragments. Shorten sentence length. Speak using words that people know rather than ones they don't know. Instead of, "An in-depth analysis of the pericope in the Gospel according to Mark, chapter 2, reveals an illuminating conclusion," how about, "When I was studying Mark 2, here is what I discovered"? Here are a few strategies that will facilitate preaching for the ear:

36. Jacks, *Just Say the Word!*, 2. Note that Jacks intentionally breaks these rules in this quotation in order to illustrate his point. For another helpful resource, see "Writing for the Ear," in Sunukjian, *Invitation to Biblical Preaching*, 256–67. See also Troeger and Tisdale, *Sermon Workbook*, 115–18.
37. Sunukjian, *Invitation to Biblical Preaching*, 258.

- *Remember that repetition and restatement are your friends, not your enemies.* When writing a term paper, repetition and restatement sound redundant and even distracting. However, both are expected (in moderation) when writing a sermon for the ear. If you use points in a sermon, make sure to repeat and restate them. Repeat the main idea of the sermon. Learn to say the same thing differently instead of introducing new ideas in every sentence. In speech, words disappear; they are ephemeral. They need to be repeated and restated.

- *Watch out for big words.* In a letter written in 1956, C. S. Lewis said to a young American writer, "Don't use words too big for the subject. Don't say 'infinitely' when you mean 'very'; otherwise, you'll have no word left when you want to talk about something *really* infinite."[38] In academic settings, a person tends to use big words in order to convey complex concepts. If we are honest with ourselves, some of us use big words because we like to sound smart in front of other people. Guilty as charged. If we are not careful, a sermon with a lot of big words will sound like it has been delivered *only* for those smart enough to understand it. Is that really the message we want to send to people?

- *If you know the original languages, be careful that you do not use them to create distance.* When you say, "The Greek says," or, "The Hebrew says," you may actually build hurdles rather than remove obstacles. Yes, listeners may gain new insights into the biblical text, but they may also feel disempowered from studying the Scriptures for themselves. Use original languages to build a bridge rather than a wall. Remember that the more challenging task is to use accessible language to communicate a concept that is difficult to understand. Scott Manetsch, a well-respected Reformation scholar, reminded me in a personal conversation that a preacher as reputable as John Calvin never said, "The Greek says," or "The Hebrew says," in his sermons.[39]

---

38. Lewis, *Collected Letters of C. S. Lewis*, 3:766.

39. The sixteenth-century Puritan preacher William Perkins agreed with Calvin. Perkins cautioned against using Greek and Latin instead of Greek and Hebrew, but the essential argument was the same:

> Spiritual speech is the speech which the Holy Spirit teaches (1 Cor. 2:13). It is both simple and clear, tailored to the understanding of the hearers and appropriate for expressing the majesty of the Spirit (Acts 17:2, 3; 2 Cor. 4:2–4; Gal. 3:1). For this reason, none of the specialized vocabulary of the arts, nor Greek and Latin phrases, nor odd turns of phrase should be used in the sermon. These distract the minds of those listeners who cannot see the connection between what has been said and what follows. In addition, unusual words hinder rather than help people in their efforts to understand what is being said. And they also tend to draw their minds away from the subject in hand to other things. (*"Art of Prophesying,"* 69)

Consider another way to communicate your grammatical insights—such as, "The phrase we have is, 'Be filled with the Spirit,' but the writer here actually writes, 'Walk in the Spirit,'" or perhaps "The word here is the same word that Paul's contemporaries used to talk about beauty" or "the word here was used for military battles." It might be harder for you as the preacher to prepare, but it ends up being easier for your listeners to understand.

- *Use relational language.* Remember that you have prepared your sermon for a congregation and not a biblical studies professor or literary scholar. A tendency in academic writing is to take out as much relational language as possible so as to sound more intellectual and scholarly. Not so with preaching! Make sure you use "we/us" and "me/you" language. If you want to preach for the ear, put the relational language back into your sermon. The sentence, "In Acts 2, Peter calls on the people of Israel to repent and be baptized as a response to the gospel message he proclaimed concerning Jesus Christ," can be stated relationally as, "Our response to the gospel should be clear: God calls us to repent and to be baptized."

- *Practice your sermon out loud.* Your outline or manuscript will sound more like a sermon if you speak it out ahead of time. While it helps to interrogate the manuscript or outline before you practice, it makes a big difference if you hear what your phrases and sentences actually sound like. Whenever you practice, whether listening in real time or listening to yourself on a recording, watch out for big words, peculiar expressions, or academic jargon. Not only can you make editorial changes as a result of practicing but you can also internalize your outline or manuscript in such a way that you sound more like a preacher preaching to people in a congregation than a writer writing a paper for an editor.

- *Use colloquialisms.* Colloquialisms are informal words, expressions, or slang. The goal is to sound more like we talk. In English, we might use a colloquialism like, "I wasn't born yesterday," to convey to someone that we are not foolish or naive. Someone might say, "Unless you've been living under a rock for the last few years, you've probably heard of this famous musician." "Living under a rock" is a way to communicate that a person is oblivious or out of touch. Every culture and language has different colloquialisms, so it is important to know which ones make sense in your context. How might you use everyday expressions, key phrases, or slang in order to make your sermon more accessible to people in your particular context?

To be sure, these strategies will not apply in quite the same way if you find yourself preaching an academic sermon in a university chapel or if you preach in some other critical listening community. In these contexts, colloquialisms or relational language might create distance rather than disarm listeners. The strategies recommended above will work better in communities where there is more generational and educational diversity.

Remember that if you are used to writing for the eye rather than the ear, it may take some practice and dedication to make your language more accessible to listeners. Sermons are not spoken essays; rather, as a form of oral discourse, they abide by a different set of rules.

Develop the Main Idea

Too many sermons have no clear main point or, if they do, the preacher is the only one who knows it.[40] If you could tell your listeners one thing, what would you tell them? If you could state the main point of your sermon in one sentence, what would that sentence be? If you could translate what you believe is the primary thrust of the Scripture passage(s) into a language that people can understand, what would you say?

Homileticians use different words or phrases—such as the focus, big idea, thesis statement, main idea, core, primary claim, or central theme—to refer to the main point of a sermon. In this chapter, I will refer to it as the main idea. Most homileticians agree that a sermon with a clear main idea has a better chance of reaching those who listen to it. H. Grady Davis writes, "That the best sermon is the embodiment of a single generative idea is not a rule but an accurate reporting of fact."[41] Samuel D. Proctor comments, "It may be assumed that from the text, or out of an experience related to the text, one consuming idea, one driving proposition, has possessed the mind and stirred the soul of the preacher."[42]

Granted, God can work powerfully through the fragility of an unclear sermon with an unclear point. But should God's sovereignty be an excuse for sloppy communication? The difference between a sermon with a clear main idea and a sermon without one is a lot like the difference between a layup in basketball and a full-court shot at the end of the game. Both have a chance of going in the basket, but only one has a high-percentage chance.

---

40. When Gardner C. Taylor delivered the 1976 Lyman Beecher Lectures on Preaching at Yale University, he said, "How many points should there be in a sermon? At least one!" For this story, see McMickle, "What Shall They Preach?" 103.

41. Davis, *Design for Preaching*, 36.

42. Proctor, *Certain Sound of the Trumpet*, 19. See also Ian Pitt-Watson, who writes, "It should be possible in one simple sentence, without relative clauses, to state what the subject matter of a sermon is." *Preaching*, 66.

A main idea should be both compelling and controlling in its reach: compelling in the sense that it is memorable and worth repeating, controlling in the sense that it is the core of the sermon around which other content is organized and structured. After you develop the main idea, find a way to restate it several times in a sermon. As a general rule, if you preach shorter sermons (less than twenty minutes), state and restate the main idea at least four to six times. If you preach longer sermons (over twenty minutes), aim for at least six to eight times.

Imagine a large archery target with a series of concentric circles on it. The main idea is the target's bull's-eye. Just like the archer, the preacher aims the arrow straight for the bull's-eye. If the arrow hits one of the outer circles, is the archer content or disappointed? The goal remains the same every time—to hit the center of the target. A sermon with a vague, imprecise main idea might land on an outer circle of the target, but it will not hit the bull's-eye until that unclear main idea becomes crystal clear to both the preacher and the listeners.

Now imagine a piece of wood in the hands of a professional woodworker. The woodworker creates a beautiful shape by devoting significant time and attention to whittling the wood. To whittle means to carve with the express purpose of creating a desired shape. When the shape does not look right or the sharp edges need to be smoothed out, the woodworker whittles the wood further until the correct shape emerges. If you want to develop a main idea that is both faithful to Scripture and memorable for listeners, keep whittling the wood until a beautiful shape emerges. An amorphous sermon is less impactful than one with a clearly defined shape.

So what will help us hit the target? How do we carve a beautiful shape? Here are a few recommendations. Remember that a main idea is not the same as a theme or topic. In the desire to be general, watch out that you do not neglect the opportunity to be specific. You have not hit the center of the target if you say, "Today, I am going to preach about God's grace." In this instance, grace is a theme or a topic of your sermon. In other words, you are still aiming at the outer circles rather than the bull's-eye. A lot of people have said a lot of things about God's grace. What will you say about God's grace that is clear and memorable for this particular group of listeners on this particular occasion with this particular text? What specific insight does *this* Scripture passage give you about God's grace that will provide people with hope and assurance between now and next Sunday? What do you want to say about God's grace based on what the passage of Scripture says about it? These deeper questions help preachers to understand the biblical text better and to craft a better main idea.

When it comes to developing main ideas that are both simple and sophisticated, preachers can learn a lot from communicators in other fields. In November 2012, I attended a conference on preaching and had the privilege of hearing Pete Docter, one of the keynote speakers at the event. Docter is a director at Pixar Animation Studios and has directed several blockbuster movies, including *Monsters, Inc.*; *Toy Story 2*; *Up!*; and *Inside Out*. Pixar has assembled quite a formula for its success. The expert animation and imaginative range of the characters (e.g., monsters, toys) reaches some of the youngest children, while at the same time the depth of storytelling and the attention to basic human needs appeal to adults.

As I listened to Docter tell the stories behind the films, it amazed me that each movie had a clear main idea. In *Monsters, Inc.*, we meet a monster named Sully who is addicted to his work but who experiences a life-changing transformation when he learns how to be a father figure to a little girl who is scared of him at first. Docter's autobiography intersected with the movie's plot in illuminating ways. His wife gave birth to their first child when he was working on the film. The central theme of the movie revealed itself in his personal life, and he felt led to weave it into the film. What is the main idea of *Monsters, Inc.*? "Life is about more than work."

Toy Story 2 defied the modest projections that movie critics forecasted for it. The film reached millions of viewers and was a huge success, a rarity for sequels. The story begins the way most stories begin: by introducing a conflict and complicating it. A boy named Andy is getting too old to play with toys, and the toys have to figure out what to do as a result of this sudden shift. The two main characters, toys named Woody and Buzz, must come to grips with the fact that Andy no longer attends to them as he once did. For good reasons, this development troubles them. In the midst of their crisis, they happen to meet a cowgirl named Jessie, a toy discarded by her owner, who tells them, "That's just how people are. They play with you and love you for a little while and then they cast you aside like all the other toys."[43] Why does *Toy Story 2* resonate so much with adults in addition to children? Because the question it raises touches on one of the most basic human fears: When I grow old, will anyone care enough about me to miss me, or will they completely forget about me? As the story progresses, the answer to this question is the main idea of the film: The people who love us most still care for us no matter what happens to us in life.

In the movie *Up!*, an introverted old man named Carl tries to escape to paradise in order to heal from the death of Ellie, his beloved wife of many decades, and to realize the original dream they shared of building a home

---

43. Lasseter, *Toy Story 2*.

in a far-off paradise. Carl finds healing in an unexpected place: a friendship with an extroverted and sometimes annoying little boy named Russell. Again, Docter's personal story intersected with the plot of the film. If I could paraphrase his comments at the conference, he said, "After a long day working with people and solving problems, all I wanted to do as an introvert was go into a room and be by myself. It was like I wanted to fly away to someplace where no one could find me." Docter's job as director of a major motion picture meant he was responsible for a team of close to one hundred people. His dream of being alone and uninterrupted had a direct impact on the plot of the film. That is to say, it is no accident that Carl is an introverted person who dreams of a paradise where he will be alone and uninterrupted. Then, a twist in the plot forces him to change his outlook. When he meets Russell, Carl is confronted with the needs and possibilities of friendship through those he is trying to escape. Docter did not say these exact words, but it seems as though the main idea of *Up!* is that life-giving friendship comes to us in unexpected ways through unexpected people.

What does Pixar have to do with preaching? The main connection is the emphasis on memorable main ideas. A few years ago, an elderly lady at my church greeted me at the door after the worship service and said, "Pastor, I was discouraged this morning when I came in here, but I am so glad that God used you to remind me that *God is not finished with me yet.*" Not only did her comments bless me; they also encouraged me as a preacher. I was thrilled! She heard and remembered the main idea of the sermon: *God is not finished with you yet.* She knew that was my central point, she heard me repeat it, and she was able to say the idea back to me. That does not happen to me every week, but I get really excited when it does.

> *Clear ideas have the power to minister to us in times of need: to make a home in our memories, capture our imaginations, and mark us on our faith journey.*

Clear ideas have the power to minister to us in times of need: to make a home in our memories, capture our imaginations, and mark us on our faith journey. A true idea shapes and even transforms our understanding of God and people. Do not underestimate the power of a sermon with a clear main idea, one that is both simple and sophisticated.

Commit to Brevity

The final mode of clarity is *commitment to brevity*. By brevity I do not mean that every preacher should preach short sermons. On a typical Sunday,

I preach in a context where the sermon runs thirty to thirty-five minutes long. Some preachers find themselves in contexts where the community expectation for a sermon is fifteen to twenty minutes, and others find themselves in contexts where forty to sixty minutes is the expectation. Our preaching contexts are so diverse and multifaceted that hard-and-fast rules on sermon length will only distract us. Commitment to brevity means: *make every minute count no matter the sermon length*. Remember Abraham Lincoln and Edward Everett? While most of us cannot preach a good sermon in two minutes, what we can do is develop a Lincoln-like approach to managing the twenty-minute, thirty-minute, or sixty-minute sermon.

Brevity adds precision to a sermon. Like an editor cutting away all of the footage from a movie that does not add to the plot, clear preachers pursue brevity with dedication and discipline. The saying in Hollywood is that many Oscar-winning performances have been left on the cutting-room floor. Why? Because the performances did not fit the plot, so they had to be removed. Part of our job as preachers is to ask ourselves what we need to cut from the sermon. Remove all extraneous words and competing ideas that keep your main idea from being as clear as possible.

You might be familiar with the story of a well-known speaker who was invited to speak at an important conference. The organizers asked him what his normal conference fee was. He answered, "If you want me to speak for thirty minutes, the fee is $10,000; if you want me to speak for twenty minutes, the fee is $15,000; and if you want me to speak for fifteen minutes, the fee is $20,000." The point of the story is simple. Those who speak as a profession know that time is a luxury. The greater the amount of time that is afforded, the more chances there will be to get your point across. The less time you have, the higher the difficulty for making your point in a way that is clear, engaging, and memorable. Brevity increases the burden on the preacher to communicate in a manner that is cogent and compelling. Make tough editorial decisions about what you will include and exclude from your sermon.

Imagine for a moment that I take you on a tour of my hometown: Princeton, New Jersey. When you come to visit, which tour should I give you—the ten-hour tour of Princeton or the one-hour tour? Which one would benefit you most? I have plenty that I could show you in Princeton: a Revolutionary War battlefield, Princeton University, Albert Einstein's house, Princeton Theological Seminary, a colonial museum, some beautiful churches, and several other historic sites. However, out of respect for you, I would have to make decisions about what to leave in and what to leave out in order to make the tour worth your time. I would have to resist the urge to show you everything in my town. I would owe that to you at the very least, since the tour would be for your benefit rather than mine. A similar case can be made for sermons. Remember that what is interesting to you is not necessarily interesting to your listeners. A lot of ideas do not need to make it into the final draft of your sermon, because they compete with the main idea. They confuse rather than clarify. They distract hearers rather than invite their participation.

Many of us fall into the information trap. We lock up our inner editor, and our sermons suffer as a result. In *Resonate*, Nancy Duarte's excellent book on being clear and compelling communicators, she claims, "Presentations fail because of too *much* information, not too little. Don't parade in front of the audience spewing every factoid you know on your topic. Only share the right information for that exact moment with that specific audience."[44]

The prolific Swedish film director Ingmar Bergman offers the following insights on the importance of editing in a 1964 interview: "Do you know what moviemaking is? Eight hours of hard work each day to get three minutes of film. And during those eight hours there are maybe only ten or twelve minutes, if you're lucky, of real creation. And maybe they don't come. Then you have to gear yourself for another eight hours and pray you're going to get your good ten minutes this time."[45]

What do Duarte and Bergman have to do with clarity in preaching? The main connection is this: sermons with memorable content and compelling main ideas are not memorable and compelling just because of what the preacher has left *in* the sermon. They are memorable and compelling because of what the preacher has left *out* of it. Beware of content tyranny! You do not need to make listeners aware of everything you learned about the passage. You do not have to mention every insight from every commentator that you read. Most listeners want you to be selective, not exhaustive. An exhaustive preacher produces exhausted listeners.

Commitment to brevity (which leads to greater clarity) requires an anti-verbosity bias. Our gifts in preaching and teaching are not an excuse for lengthy diatribes. In *Predicación y Misión: Una Perspectiva Pastoral* (*Preaching and Mission: A Pastoral Perspective*), the great Argentinian homiletician Osvaldo Mottesi exhorts preachers to avoid verbosity when he writes: "eliminate every tendency toward *being verbose* or the indiscriminate use of words and more words." Otherwise, claims Motessi, our verbosity will "dilute the depth of the message in a sea of prepositions, conjunctions, and especially

44. Duarte, *Resonate*, 176.
45. Cited in Currey, *Daily Rituals*, 13.

adjectives and adverbs. This transforms the sermon into speaking without telling, words without the Word."[46]

Guibert of Nogent points to the connection between verbosity in preachers and inefficacy for hearers: "As food when taken in moderation for the body's nourishment remains in the body but, gulped down in great quantities, turns harmful and causes vomiting, and sexual acts which are licit and not excessive produce offspring, whereas immoderate indulgence accomplishes nothing useful but pollutes the flesh, so *verbosity* cancels what had already been implanted in the hearts of the listeners and what could have been profitable."[47]

How much do we as preachers think about using words *in moderation*? Again, I do not wish to equate moderation with sermon length. Moderation matters whether we preach a sermon that lasts fifteen minutes or forty-five minutes. Our main problem with brevity is that many of us do not see verbosity as a vice; thus we do not see the need for an internal editor. If we lack discretion, we develop a reputation for prattling on in needless, purposeless, directionless meandering.

When I lived in Chicago and turned on sports talk radio one time, the cohosts said the following when the subject of church came up: "Why would I want to listen to a boring preacher deliver a boring sermon that puts me to sleep?" Do preachers really need to replicate that stereotype, or should they do something to reverse it?

Duarte challenges us to make the main idea central and to move everything else to the periphery. She writes, "The big idea is the well from which all supporting ideas spring, and it is also the filter to sort ideas down to the ones most applicable. Most presentations suffer from too many ideas, not too few. Even though you explored hundreds of potential ideas and left no rock unturned, don't convey every idea, only the most potent ones. Keep a stranglehold on the one big idea you need to convey and be relentless about building content that supports that one idea."[48]

If you want to learn to preach in moderation, ask yourself hard questions. Does all of the content in the sermon support the main idea of the sermon, or

46. Here is the quote in its context in Spanish: "Relacionada directamente con la pureza está *la claridad* del estilo, que demande entre otras cosas, economía con el uso de palabras, esto es, eliminar toda tendencia, a la 'verboragia,' o sea, el uso indiscriminado de palabras y más palabras. Esta obsesión por la forma 'florida' de la predicación puede diluir en un mar de preposiciónes, conjunciónes, y especialmente adjetivos y adverbios, el fondo del mensaje. Esto transforma el sermón en un hablar sin decir, palabras sin la Palabra." Mottesi, *Predicación y Misión*, 259 (emphasis added).
47. Guibert of Nogent, "How to Make a Sermon," 9:290 (emphasis added).
48. Duarte, *Resonate*, 122.

are there some ideas that might compete with the main idea? Here are some other questions to ask: If I tell a story that lasts five minutes, how might I tell the same story in two to three minutes so that only the most essential details remain? If my sermon lasts thirty minutes and my introduction takes ten minutes to complete, then is it really an introduction if it takes up one-third of the sermon? Which parts of the sermon need to be removed, even though I do not want to let them go? As it pertains to the last question, Duarte refers to this painful process as "murdering your darlings."[49] A provocative phrase, isn't it? These are the ideas that you worked long and hard to develop; nevertheless, their death will enhance the clarity of your sermon.[50]

One of the phrases I like to repeat with students is, "Engage in an economy of words." The American novelist Ernest Hemingway had a reputation for holding fast to this commitment. In most of his writing, he emphasized minimalism. He wrote short, simple sentences in his novels, and he usually avoided words with too many syllables. Yet he still used every word well. That is to say, he knew how to use simple words and sentences to communicate profound truths.

William Strunk Jr., a renowned English professor at Cornell University, also stressed an economy of words. E. B. White remembers being a student in Strunk's class in 1919 and hearing his teacher deliver a lecture on brevity. White writes, "He leaned over his desk, grasped his coat lapels in his hands, and in a husky, conspiratorial voice, said: 'Rule Seventeen! Omit needless words! Omit needless words! Omit needless words.'"[51]

Commitment to brevity should also impact the wording of our main ideas. The best main ideas are short and pithy. Challenge yourself to write a main idea that is *twelve words or less*. Can you state the main idea of your sermon in a single and memorable sentence using few words but without oversimplifying

---

49. Duarte, *Resonate*, 118.

50. Duarte writes,
    Make edits on behalf of the audience; they don't want everything. It's your job to be severe in your cuts. Let go of ideas even if you love them, for the sake of making the presentation better. Audiences are screaming "make it clear," not "cram more in." You won't often hear an audience member say, "That presentation would have been so much better if it were longer." Striking a balance between withholding and communicating information is what separates the great presenters from the rest. The quality depends just as much on what you choose to remove as what you choose to include. (*Resonate*, 119)
She borrows the phrase "murder your darlings" from Sir Arthur Quiller-Couch, who writes, "Whenever you feel an impulse to perpetrate a piece of exceptionally fine writing, obey it—wholeheartedly—and delete it before sending your manuscript to press. Murder your darlings." See Duarte, *Resonate*, 118–19.

51. Strunk and White, *Elements of Style*, xiv. White took Strunk's self-published book and introduced it to a wider audience in what is now a classic book.

or overgeneralizing? The task is much more difficult than people realize. Do not be legalistic about it, but do not be laissez-faire about it either. Whittle the wood of your main idea so that you eliminate as many extraneous words as possible. Not only should you be able to state what you want to say in a single sentence but you should also be able to hone and craft the main idea in such a way that someone who listens can say it back to you without much trouble.

Before concluding, let me share this example of the power of brevity. In his letter written from prison to the church in Philippi, the apostle Paul made a statement that persecuted Christians have repeated now for thousands of years. In Philippians 1:21, he wrote, "*To Zoen Christon, To Apothanein Kerdon.*" We know it in English as, "To live is Christ and to die is gain." In this one sentence, Paul takes a profound truth about his relationship with Christ and captures the power and impact of that relationship in just *six* words. We actually need nine words in order to translate what Paul was able to write in six words. Notice the parallelism and the poetics: three words followed by three words as well as alliteration and assonance. The sentence has a musical quality to it that makes it memorable and repeatable to the listeners. Philippians 1:21 serves as a perennial reminder that a simple sentence can still be a loaded sentence. As Leonardo da Vinci would say, "Simplicity is the ultimate sophistication." Think of the many loaded statements in Scripture. Here is just a small sample of them:

- Nehemiah 8:10: "Do not grieve, for the joy of the LORD is your strength."
- Psalm 23:1: "The LORD is my shepherd, I lack nothing."
- Proverbs 9:10: "The fear of the LORD is the beginning of wisdom."
- John 8:58: "'Very truly I tell you,' Jesus answered, 'before Abraham was born, I am!'"
- Romans 12:9: "Love must be sincere. Hate what is evil; cling to what is good."
- James 4:6 (quoting Prov. 3:34): "God opposes the proud but shows favor to the humble."

As was mentioned earlier, sophisticated simplicity occurs often in Scripture. Verbosity and lengthiness are not prerequisites for substance and gravitas. One can make profound statements through an economy of words.

Conclusion

The story is told of a spirited exchange between an English bishop and one of the local vicars (ministers) who pastored one of the churches under his supervision. The bishop traveled to the English Midlands to hear the vicar preach at a Sunday morning service, and when the service concluded, the bishop said, "Sir, I thought that was a very brief word which you gave to the people today." The vicar replied, "Your grace, better to be brief than to be boring." Without skipping a beat, the bishop answered, "Ah, but sir, you were both."[52]

It takes energy and effort to practice clarity in preaching, hard work to find the simplicity that exists on the other side of complexity. Whether you preach for fifteen minutes or forty-five minutes is immaterial to the larger point—being clear matters regardless of sermon length. In the nineteenth century, J. C. Ryle offered this warning: "You will never attain simplicity in preaching without plenty of trouble. Pains and trouble, I say emphatically, pains and trouble."[53] The pains and trouble you undergo in order to be clear are worthy of the time you invest. It is far better for you to go through pain and trouble for your listeners before they hear you than for your listeners to go through pain and trouble when they hear you. If you want to carve a beautiful shape, then spend more time whittling the wood.

Learning activities and sermon samples for this chapter are located at www.PracticesofChristianPreaching.com.

---

52. G. Taylor, "Freedom's Song," 164. This story shows up here and in various other audio recordings of Taylor sermons.

53. Ryle, *Simplicity in Preaching*, 41.

5

Preach Concretely

If I look at the mass, I will never act. If I look at the one, I will.

—Mother Teresa

The language of Scripture moves. It is concerned with concrete actions.

—Anna Carter Florence

Art Silverman needed to solve a problem. His research revealed dangerous trends in the American diet, but he did not know how to communicate its urgency in a way that would make people pay attention. It was 1994, and Silverman was directing a team of scientists trying to raise awareness about the dangers of saturated fat in the American diet. The team decided that the subject was too broad, so they narrowed their research to one particular area: the amount of saturated fat in movie popcorn. Although Silverman's team had already tried to sound the alarm in medical journals about health and wellness, none of their studies had gained traction in the media. Nobody seemed to care. The team's challenge: come up with an idea that would make inroads in the lives of everyday Americans. The data were not insignificant or unpersuasive. The team just needed to figure out how to communicate the significance of the data in a way that would make people listen. Their aim was simple: to explain an abstract concept in a concrete way. So they held a "food exposé."

Saturated fat is an abstract category to most of us. Butter, cheeseburgers, and bacon—these are familiar categories. To explain the unfamiliar with the familiar, Silverman's team set up a table. On one side of the table, they

Medium Popcorn
80g Saturated Fat

Figure 5.1. Visual Depiction of 80 Grams of Saturated Fat

placed a medium box of unbuttered movie popcorn along with a small sign that revealed the total grams of saturated fat, in this case 80 grams. On the other side, they demonstrated the equivalent of 80 grams of saturated fat by placing *six* Big Macs from McDonald's (see fig. 5.1).

The team thought that if people could see for themselves that a medium bag of unbuttered popcorn was equivalent to six Big Macs, perhaps it would shock them enough to compel them to act.

Then they took it a step further. They explained that when a movie theater adds butter to popcorn the saturated fat content rises from 80 grams to 143 grams. So they performed the same exercise, but this time with more food. They placed a medium box of buttered popcorn on one side of the table and on the other side placed one bacon-and-egg breakfast, six Big Macs, medium fries, and a steak dinner (see fig. 5.2).

People paid attention. All the regional and national news outlets picked up the story. It appeared in national newspapers and magazines as well as on major television stations. With all the negative press, most movie theaters changed their policies on saturated fat within a few months of the food exposé. Theaters changed how they popped the popcorn by moving mostly to air-popped options, and they switched from using saturated fats to unsaturated fats in their butter.[1]

Why was the study such a success? Put simply, the team discovered how to communicate the data in a way that people could understand. One hundred and forty-three grams of saturated fat does not mean anything to most of us; it is an unfamiliar category. We intuit that it is a lot, but it is difficult to know how much exactly. Movie popcorn sitting next to six Big Macs, a bacon-and-egg breakfast, medium fries, and a steak dinner—that is something most of us can taste, that we can see, that we have experienced. It provokes a visceral response and may even disturb us. One hundred and forty-three grams is abstract. Piles of food on a table is concrete.

1. Kurtz, "Great Exploding Popcorn Exposé."

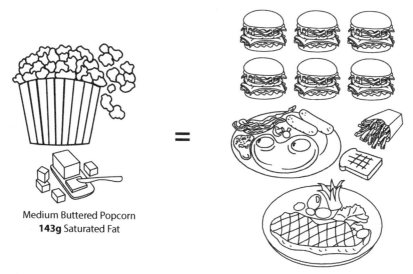

Medium Buttered Popcorn
143g Saturated Fat

Figure 5.2. Visual Depiction of 143 Grams of Saturated Fat

In this chapter, we will discuss why *concreteness* matters in preaching. "Concreteness" is the fourth *C* of the Five Cs of preaching. In my judgment, too many preachers suffer from a chronic case of abstraction. Although becoming more concrete does not require eliminating abstraction, it does mean that we guard ourselves against an overreliance on abstraction. The problem is not with abstraction per se but with chronic abstraction. The challenge here is not to be abstract *or* concrete. The challenge is to be *more* concrete.

Concreteness and Preaching

Concrete preaching helps our sermons matter more on Monday mornings. When we talk about God's grace, we should describe what God's grace looks like in bumper-to-bumper traffic during the morning commute. When we talk about justice, we should consider what it looks like for a financially disadvantaged family that has recently been the victim of credit-card fraud. When we talk about love, we should imagine what love looks like in a marriage characterized more by strife than by sacrifice and service. We have not done enough if all we ask is what grace, justice, or love looks like at thirty thousand feet. We also have to ask what they look like down at sea level.

I attended a wedding a few years ago, and my spouse was unable to join me because of a scheduling conflict. When I got home, she said, "So, tell me what you remember about the wedding." Let's just say that I did not have much to

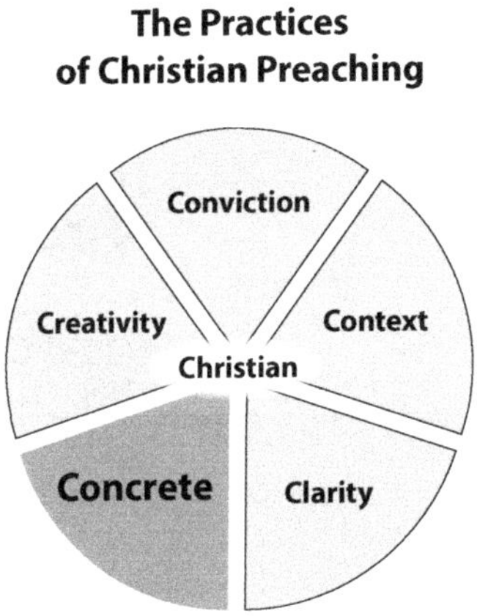

**The Practices
of Christian Preaching**

Figure 5.3. The Five Cs: Concreteness

offer by way of details. I remembered that the couple got married, but that was about it. Trying to jog my memory, she said, "So tell me about the dress." I said, "I don't know. It was white." Then she asked, "So, what did the dress look like?" I responded, "I don't know. I think it was a V-neck." Apparently, some male stereotypes exist for a reason. What was the issue? I was oblivious to important details. I could speak in generalities but not with precision. I had the broad brushstrokes down but was missing the finer points.

On another occasion, I received an email notifying me that one of our good friends had just had a baby. Later that night, I said to my wife, "Guess what? I have good news! Maria had a baby earlier today." She asked, "What is the baby's name?" I said, "I don't know. I know it was a boy, though." She said, "What about the weight or the height? How about the length?" I said, "I'm not sure they mentioned it. The baby's healthy and so is Maria, so I know that part." I probably could have guessed, but when I looked back at the email later that night, all of the information was there. I had just not paid sufficient attention to the details. If you think that details are not important, just ask a journalist, a surgeon, or my spouse.

Before continuing the discussion on concreteness, let me propose that there are theological reasons why concreteness matters to preaching. God commits to "specificity," to borrow a term that Martin Luther King Jr. was fond of using.[2] God takes the risk of specificity in the incarnation by becoming one of us through

2. Although others have used the term and have meant different things by it, King used this word to talk about the incarnation. King is cited as using this term by Gardner C. Taylor in a lecture titled "Recognizing and Removing the Presumptuousness of Preaching," in G. Taylor, *Words of Gardner Taylor*, 5:157.

Jesus Christ. God tabernacles with us. It is one thing to claim that God is a far-off, distant deity who rules over the universe. It is another thing altogether to say that God is with us, that the One who "sits enthroned above the circle of the earth" (Isa. 40:22) voluntarily enters into human frailty, willingly subjects the divine Godhead to time and space, and becomes like those whom God is trying to reach. As preachers, we already know that God is both transcendent and immanent. What we sometimes fail to appreciate, however, is the risk God takes in choosing immanence. The choice does not come without cost.

Reflecting on what it cost God to become incarnate, Gardner C. Taylor states, "For the divine Presence to be 'geography bound' and 'time capsulated' is something else, for this specificity risks that contempt which is born of familiarity and that suspicion which is associated with merely flesh and blood."[3] In the incarnation, God in Jesus Christ embraces the concrete, taking on flesh and blood, speaking a particular language, embracing a particular culture during a particular point in time. Jesus becomes "time-trapped, death eligible, pain capable for you and for me."[4]

In addition to the incarnation, think for a moment about some of the concrete ways that Scripture communicates the character of God and the nature of humanity. While some of the language is abstract, quite often biblical writers communicate categories like love, compassion, and grace in concrete ways. In Psalm 51, instead of "On account of humankind's fall and rebellion at creation, I am 'not able not to sin' (*non posse non peccare*)," the writer says, "Surely I was sinful at birth, sinful from the time my mother conceived me" (Ps. 51:5). In Psalm 139, instead of saying, "God is ineffable and omniscient with respect to my creatureliness," the writer says, "All the days ordained for me were written in your book before one of them came to be" (Ps. 139:16).

Jesus's teaching is concrete. Right after saying something abstract, "Do not worry about your life," Jesus adds, "Look at the birds of the air; they do not sow or reap or store away in barns, and yet your heavenly Father feeds them. Are you not much more valuable than they?" (Matt. 6:25–26). Later in Matthew's Gospel, when speaking of God's care, Jesus says, "Are not two sparrows sold for a penny? Yet not one of them will fall to the ground outside your Father's care. And even the very hairs on your head are all numbered. So don't be afraid; you are worth more than many sparrows" (Matt. 10:29–31). These examples are specific. God counts the hairs on our head, numbers our days aright, clothes us like the lilies of the field, and has compassion on us like a father has compassion on his children.

3. G. Taylor, *Words of Gardner Taylor*, 5:157.
4. G. Taylor, *Words of Gardner Taylor*, 2:100.

Just as specificity makes a difference in our understanding of God and how God relates to us, so also it makes a difference in preaching. An ability to preach at sea level may well determine the difference between an inaccessible sermon and an accessible one, a flat sermon and a textured one, a sermon that resides out there in the ether and one that breaks through and touches down in the neighborhoods where people live. It is much more difficult to make a difference in the lives of everyday people when your sermons do not come down to the level where they live.

Images of Concreteness: Ladders and Foundations

Climb down the Ladder of Abstraction

Japanese rhetorician S. I. Hayakawa uses the imagery of the ladder to talk about concreteness. Hayakawa argues that the best way to enhance communication is to "climb down the ladder of abstraction."[5] In other words, one increases the likelihood of connecting with one's listeners through being as concrete as possible. Hayakawa does not demand that we choose concreteness *over* abstraction. Rather, he invites us to balance abstraction *with* concreteness. The mistake that most communicators make, he claims, is imbalance—offering too much abstraction and not enough concreteness.

In *Language in Thought and Action*, Hayakawa gives an example of what climbing down the ladder of abstraction might look like. He starts with a category like wealth, which is an abstract concept at the top of the ladder. To climb down the ladder, one asks, "What kind of wealth?" In this case, Hayakawa lists "assets" as the source of wealth. A rung lower beneath assets is farm assets. Still, one asks, "Which farm assets produce the assets that lead to wealth?" So Hayakawa moves it down another step to livestock, and in particular to cows. The final rung, Hayakawa claims, is "Bessie" the cow. Figure 5.4 shows an adaptation of Hayakawa's ladder.

> *The best way to enhance communication is to "climb down the ladder of abstraction."*
> —S. I. Hayakawa

Art Silverman's team did exactly what Hayakawa recommends. Saturated fat is an abstract category at the top of the ladder. A food exposé with specific foods on a table is concrete and at the bottom of the ladder. In Hayakawa's example, wealth is abstract. Bessie is concrete. We can grasp what wealth is as a concept, but we can see and smell Bessie. Think of it this way: if you are going to talk about wealth in a sermon, you should also talk about Bessie.

5. Hayakawa, *Language*, 84–85.

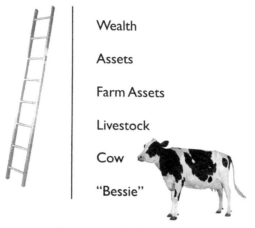

Figure 5.4. Ladder of Abstraction

Build the Foundations Before You Build the Roof

In 2007, Chip Heath and Dan Heath published a book titled *Made to Stick: Why Some Ideas Survive and Others Die,* in which they devoted an entire chapter to discussing why concreteness is important. If you want people to understand abstract concepts, Heath and Heath claim, you have to lay concrete foundations: "What makes something concrete? If you can examine something with your senses, it's concrete. A V8 engine is concrete. 'High performance' is abstract. Most of the time, concreteness boils down to specific people doing specific things. . . . [Nordstrom's] 'World-class customer service' is abstract. A Nordie ironing a customer's shirt is concrete."[6]

Concrete bricks undergirding abstract concepts are the building blocks to greater, higher-level thinking. Heath and Heath write, "Abstraction demands some concrete foundation. Trying to teach an abstract principle without concrete foundations is like trying to start a house by building a roof in the air."[7]

The temptation to build a roof in the air is especially dangerous for preachers. Even if we have spent hours studying the biblical text and consulting commentaries, we can still fail to lay concrete foundations for our listeners. As Heath and Heath remind us, "Abstraction is the luxury of the expert. If you've got to teach an idea to a room full of people, and you aren't certain what they know, concreteness is the only safe language."[8] Often, preachers

6. Heath and Heath, *Made to Stick,* 104. One of the stories that precedes this quotation is a story about a Nordstrom's employee, nicknamed a "Nordie," going the extra mile to iron a shirt for a customer who needed one for a meeting.

7. Heath and Heath, *Made to Stick,* 106.

8. Heath and Heath, *Made to Stick,* 104.

do not realize how much is at stake. Though they may be harsh, hear these words from an ancient Roman proverb: "If you do not wish to be understood, you deserve to be neglected."[9]

Get as specific as possible with your language when you preach. To improve at concreteness, Clarice Brantley and Michelle Miller recommend using "precise expressions" instead of "vague modifiers." Their communication research reveals two important findings about precise expressions: first, those who hear or read them "remember precise words more than they remember general words," and, second, "specific terms translate more easily than do broad general words."[10] In other words, people remember them more easily and the message gets through to them faster. Here are two among several examples that they mention to illustrate the contrast:

> Vague modifier: "Our storage facility offers *large* climate-controlled units. (Will [people] agree on what *large* means?)"
> Precise expression: "Our storage facility offers 15-by-20-foot climate-controlled units."
>
> Vague modifier: "The local travel agency offers *economical* packages for seven-day Alaskan cruises. (Will everyone have the same concept of *economical*? State an exact amount.)"
> Precise expression: "The local travel agency offers packages from $799 to $1,600 for seven-day Alaskan cruises."[11]

In your preaching, do you err on the side of precise expressions or vague modifiers? If you offer listeners lots of unfamiliar terms, abstract categories, or vague modifiers, then you will create hurdles to understanding.

How Do We Focus on Being Concrete?

How does one practice concreteness in a sermon? Ironically, so far in the chapter we have offered only abstract answers. Let me suggest three particular strategies: (1) focus on concrete details in the biblical text, (2) focus on using illustrations to climb down the ladder of abstraction, and (3) focus on using specific applications.

9. In Latin: "*Si non vis intelligi, debes negligi.*" Some attribute the quotation to Quintilian, the first-century Roman rhetorician.
10. Brantley and Miller, *Effective Communication for Colleges*, 45.
11. Brantley and Miller, *Effective Communication for Colleges*, 45 (emphasis in original).

Focus on Concrete Details in the Biblical Text

When reading the biblical text, the "small stuff" really does matter. As a case study, take a moment to examine Mark 4:35–41. This is the story in which Jesus and the disciples get on a boat on the Sea of Galilee, a "furious squall" hits the boat in the middle of the night, and the disciples fear that they will drown. This story is told in other Gospels, but in this instance we will keep Mark 4 as the primary text. Take a look at the story. Slow down long enough to notice the details:

[35]That day when evening came, he said to his disciples, "Let us go over to the other side." [36]Leaving the crowd behind, they took him along, just as he was, in the boat. There were also other boats with him. [37]A furious squall came up, and the waves broke over the boat, so that it was nearly swamped. [38]Jesus was in the stern, sleeping on a cushion. The disciples woke him and said to him, "Teacher, don't you care if we drown?"

[39]He got up, rebuked the wind and said to the waves, "Quiet! Be still!" Then the wind died down and it was completely calm.

[40]He said to his disciples, "Why are you so afraid? Do you still have no faith?"

[41]They were terrified and asked each other, "Who is this? Even the wind and the waves obey him!"

What details do you notice? If you take your time, perhaps you will notice some concrete details in the text that you might have missed if you read it in a hurry:

- 36a: "Leaving the crowd behind." A phrase like this one makes us ask where Jesus was before this scene unfolded. Is it possible that Jesus fell asleep because he was ministering to the crowds all day? We read about his ministry to the crowds just a few verses earlier.
- 36b: "There were also other boats with him." So many artists depict Jesus and the disciples alone on the Sea of Galilee but, according to Mark's account, there were other boats with him. This is the only account in the Gospels that includes this concrete detail.
- 37: "furious squall." This small detail helps readers understand that this is no ordinary storm. Wind, waves, and water filling the boat sounds a lot more like a hurricane than a rainstorm. The fact that most of those on the boat were experienced fishermen and that they were still afraid they were going to die helps us see that this was not a minor storm.

- 38a: "sleeping on a cushion." I remember hearing a preacher say one time, "Jesus didn't accidentally fall asleep. When someone falls asleep on a cushion, it means they are planning to get some rest."
- 39: "Quiet! Be still!" In the original language, the imperative "Be still!" can be translated as "Be muzzled." The same imagery that is used for muzzling a horse or a dog is also used for Jesus muzzling the wind and the waves.
- 41: "They were terrified." The disciples were not so much impressed or amazed; they were terrified. Some versions read that they were "filled with fear." The phrase here literally reads "they feared a great fear." In other words, they experienced reverential awe mixed with genuine fright over what happened. Perhaps they were more "frightened" than they were during the storm.
- 35: "Let us go over to the other side." Our thoughts on the story start to shift when we move out from the disciples' vantage point of fear and worry to the vantage point of Jesus. Long before the storm comes, Jesus tells them that they *will* get from one side of the Sea of Galilee to the other side.

We could miss great insights in the passage if we do not focus on the concrete details available to us. This is to say almost nothing about how in this passage Jesus displays his authority over nature or how this story participates in a larger theme in Mark 1–5 of Jesus's authority over disease, sin, nature, and death.

Here is another example, this time from the Old Testament: 2 Kings 4:1–7.

¹The wife of a man from the company of the prophets cried out to Elisha, "Your servant my husband is dead, and you know that he revered the Lord. But now his creditor is coming to take my two boys as his slaves."

²Elisha replied to her, "How can I help you? Tell me, what do you have in your house?"

"Your servant has nothing there at all," she said, "except a small jar of olive oil."

³Elisha said, "Go around and ask all your neighbors for empty jars. Don't ask for just a few. ⁴Then go inside and shut the door behind you and your sons. Pour oil into all the jars, and as each is filled, put it to one side."

⁵She left him and shut the door behind her and her sons. They brought the jars to her and she kept pouring. ⁶When all the jars were full, she said to her son, "Bring me another one."

But he replied, "There is not a jar left." Then the oil stopped flowing.

[7]She went and told the man of God, and he said, "Go, sell the oil and pay your debts. You and your sons can live on what is left."

What details do you notice? Which concrete details jump off the page? Here are just a few examples that make the story more vivid and concrete:

- 1a: "The wife of a man from the company of the prophets." We learn that the widow may not be a stranger to Elisha. Her husband belonged to the prophetical school in Israel. It is possible that Elisha knew him. Notice the relational language she uses later in verse 1: "*Your* servant my husband is dead, and *you know* that he revered the LORD."
- 1c: "Now his creditor is coming to take my two boys as his slaves." We know from this detail that the widow is in a desperate situation. We do not know why her husband owed money to a creditor, and we do not know how much he owed him. We do know that this widow lives in a patriarchal society in which widows were vulnerable and people took advantage of them. We also know that children were often sold into slavery to pay off debts according to Hebrew law (Exod. 21:7; Isa. 50:1; Neh. 5:5). She "cried out" to Elisha (v. 1) because she is in danger of losing the only family she has left.
- 2b: "small jar of olive oil." If we do some background work on this phrase, we learn that the only item she owned was worth about one day's wages, and it was small enough that she could hold it in one hand.
- 3a: "ask all your neighbors for empty jars. Don't ask for just a few." Notice that Elisha involves the woman's community in the miracle. It is difficult to imagine what it would have been like for her to ask them all for empty jars without an adequate explanation, but it is also interesting that more than her family is involved. Notice also that Elisha anticipates a bigger miracle when he tells her to make sure she does not get "just a few" jars from her neighbors. Background study on this text reveals that Elisha uses a different word for "jars" than the word that occurs for "small jar of olive oil" in verse 2. The word Elisha uses for "jars" can be translated as "storage containers." He expects something big to happen.
- 4a: "shut the door behind you and your sons." Elisha does not have to be present for her to experience the miracle. It requires faith for her to go out and get extra jars and then to go inside and proceed without Elisha by her side. It also takes humility on Elisha's part to get out of the way and to let God enact the miracle without him getting the credit.

- 7: "you and your sons can live on what is left." When the miracle takes place and afterward, the woman has agency and she has means. She is able to pay off her debt and rescue her sons from slavery. But notice that she does not receive an overabundance designed to make her super-rich after the miracle. Some preachers like to use stories like this to authorize prosperity gospel teachings such as, "If you have enough faith, God will multiply your small amount to a large amount." However, notice that she has *enough* rather than an overabundance—that is, she has enough money to pay off her debt and enough money to live on what is left rather than excessive wealth.

Remember Cecilio Arrastía's metaphor for exegesis from the chapter on clarity? When studying Scripture, the preacher is like a master jeweler who goes down into the mine of God in order to find the jewel, uncover its beauty, and study its many facets.[12] We cannot do what Arrastía describes without slowing down, taking our time, and studying the concrete details in the text.

Focus on Using Illustrations to Climb down the Ladder of Abstraction

The word "illustrate" means to shed light on something. An illustration sheds light on an abstract point or insight in the sermon. When we hear the word "illustration" with reference to preaching, many times we think of stories. While illustrations include stories, they are not limited to stories. Haddon W. Robinson argues that a preacher has the capacity to illustrate in at least six different ways.

DEFINITIONS

First, one can illustrate through *definitions*. Here is an example from an Earl F. Palmer sermon in which he defines *eros*: "*Eros* is love that is earned, love that is won from us. It is not the instinctive love that we have for our parents or our children, our family or our social or racial structure. It is not the kind of love we have for something like wisdom or mankind. It is love earned from us because of the compelling excellence of the person or thing or reality."[13] Notice that Palmer talks about what *eros* is and what *eros* is not in order to delimit his definition. He also uses contrast: *Eros* is this kind of love, not that kind of love. His definition sheds light on the abstract idea of love.

These days when I preach, I try to define terms a lot more than I used to, especially in an era of increasing biblical illiteracy. When I was a teaching pastor,

---

12. Arrastía, *Teoría y Práctica de la Predicación*, 27–28.
13. Palmer, *Love Has Its Reasons*, 38–39, as cited in H. Robinson, *Biblical Preaching*, 99–100.

I spent an entire summer preaching through the Sermon on the Mount. In the Beatitudes, Jesus uses the word "blessed" quite often, which creates a challenge: in the United States, too many people have a distorted understanding of blessing. So when I preached, I tried my best to define blessing concretely, but I tried to do it using my own words. I said that blessing as it is understood in the Bible can be defined as "God's presence and power are yours in increasing supply." Was it the perfect definition? No. The larger goal was to use the definition to help reframe the way that people understood the word. Rather than blessing meaning X, it means Y instead. I repeated the definition throughout individual sermons and throughout the sermon series. Whenever the word "blessed" came up, I would remind my listeners of the definition: "Blessing means that God's presence and power are yours in increasing supply."

I tried something similar when I preached a sermon about wisdom. The ancient Greeks connected wisdom to philosophy and knowledge. In many churches today, people associate wisdom with how much you know your Bible or how articulate you are in expressing your commitment to God. But the Bible defines wisdom differently. In Scripture, being wise not *only* means knowing about God, knowing and loving God, and trusting God's promises; it *also* means *doing* the will of God. To be wise is to listen to God's commands and to act on them. Jesus said in Matthew 7:24–29, "Anyone who hears these words of mine and *acts on them* is like a wise man who built his house upon the rock" (my paraphrase). He continues, "Anyone who hears these words of mine and *does not act on them* is like a foolish man who built his house on the sand." Wisdom is gained in doing, not just in knowing. A wise person knows and does the will of God. According to the biblical definition, wisdom means knowing and doing God's will in everyday life.

FACTS

Second, we illustrate through *appealing to facts*. This is especially useful if we want to prove something to be true—as long as we do not resort to "alternative facts" in order to make the case. For instance, if you want to talk about demographic shifts in the church in the United States and the need for multiethnic congregations that reflect daily realities on the ground, you can appeal to facts like these:

- Both the Latina/o population and the Asian American populations are expected to double between now and 2050.[14]

14. Statistics on Latinas/os and Asian Americans found in Passel and Cohn, "U.S. Population Projections."

- In 2012, about one in eight Americans was foreign born, but by 2050, at least one in five Americans will be foreign born.[15]
- In 2012, the median age for whites was about forty-two, for African Americans and Asians about thirty-two, and for Latina/os about twenty-eight. This year also marked the first time that more minority babies were born in the United States than majority culture babies.[16]
- School year 2014–15 was the first year that nonwhite minorities were the majority in US public schools.[17]
- The year 2042 is now projected as the latest year that minorities will become the majority in the United States.[18]

If you want to talk about injustice and mass incarceration in the United States, then you might use a fact like this one: The United States, the wealthiest nation in the world, does not lead the world in reading and math scores on standardized tests, but it *does* lead the world in the percentage of our population that we put in prison. The United States accounts for less than 5 percent of the world's population but about 25 percent of the world's incarcerated population.[19] If you want to get more specific, you can talk about racial and ethnic disparities in the prison population. You could use statistics to make a point about profiling or perhaps mass incarceration as a form of segregation.[20]

QUOTATIONS

Quotations are a third way that we illustrate. Imagine that you are preaching about the problem of greed. How might you climb down the ladder of abstraction? Perhaps you could say, "The ancient Romans had a proverb. They said that money was like seawater. The more a person drank it, the thirstier he became." Some preachers like to use cultural proverbs. For instance, imagine that you are preaching about the dangers of caricaturing a non-Christian's

15. Passel and Cohn, "U.S. Population Projections."
16. Morello and Mellnik, "Census."
17. As *Washington Post* journalist Valerie Strauss writes, "The U.S. Education Department projected that this fall [2014], the percentage of students who are white will drop from 51 percent in 2012 to 49.7. In 1997, white enrollment was 63.4 percent; by 2022, it is projected that minorities will constitute 54.7 percent of the public school student population and whites, 45.3 percent." See Strauss, "First Time."
18. Morello and Mellnik, "Census." For these and other statistics on rapid demographic changes in the United States in general and in the US church specifically, see Alcántara, *Crossover Preaching*, 24–25.
19. See Coates, "Black Family in the Age of Mass Incarceration."
20. Michelle Alexander takes note of these alarming trends—in particular, that of mass incarceration as a form of segregation—in *New Jim Crow*.

perspective without seeking to understand the person behind the perspective. One of the cultural proverbs in India goes like this: "There's no use punching someone in the nose and then giving him a rose to smell." It is a proverb about seeking to understand and respect people before engaging in debate with them. Some quotations provoke us to think. Martin Luther King Jr. talked a lot about the importance of changing laws at the national level. In an address delivered at Western Michigan University in December 1963, King said, "It may be true that a law cannot make a man love me, but it can keep him from lynching me, and I think that's pretty important."[21] Other quotations inspire us to live differently. I think of the missionary Jim Elliot writing in his journal just before leaving to serve the Huaroni people in Ecuador in the 1950s. Elliot wrote these oft-quoted words: "He is no fool who gives what he cannot keep to gain what he cannot lose."[22]

STORIES

A fourth way that we illustrate is by *telling stories*. Many of the stories that work well in a sermon are already available to us in the Bible. Do not miss out on the opportunity to use biblical texts as a way to illustrate abstract concepts. For instance, when I preached on the part of the Lord's Prayer where Jesus invites us to pray "forgive us our debts, as we also have forgiven our debtors" (Matt. 6:12), I illustrated it with a story from another passage. As an application point, I asked, "What happens when we fail to make a connection between vertical forgiveness from God and horizontal forgiveness toward those who have hurt us?" To get at the answer, I turned to a parable in the same Gospel, Matthew 18:21–35, the parable of the unmerciful servant. This parable reminds us of the definite and lasting consequences for those who fail to forgive a small debt when they have been forgiven a great debt. As a caveat: whenever you illustrate by using biblical stories, watch out that you do not assume that listeners have as a high a level of biblical literacy as you do.

We can also use modern stories. If we do a little searching, we will find stories of hope and transformation as well as stories of lostness and brokenness in our world. In my sermon on forgiveness and the Lord's Prayer, I told a story about Oshea Israel and Mary Johnson that I will also share here.[23]

21. For a complete transcript of King's address, see "MLK at Western." The quotation is from page 5.
22. Elliot, *Shadow of the Almighty*, 11.
23. I originally heard about their story in a sermon and later read about it in Ortberg, *Who Is This Man?*, 99–100.

In 1993, two young men living in Minneapolis got into a gang-related dispute, and one of them shot and killed the other. One was a teenager, and the other was twenty years old. The police informed the youth's mother, a woman named Mary Johnson, that her son, Marlon Byrd, had been shot and killed, and the police identified the killer: a teenage boy named Oshea Israel. The young man stood trial, was convicted of homicide, and was sent to the local penitentiary for the murder.

Mary said all the right things after her son died. She explained to people at the trial that she was a Christian; she was a "daughter of the church." Thus she would find space in her heart to forgive her son's killer. After all, that is what Christians do, or at least that is what they are supposed to do. But as time passed, Mary found bitterness and resentment eating away at her soul. It felt almost impossible to let go of the anger she felt. Her church did not help her much. Her pastor told her that her son was murdered because she did not pray enough. After she left that church, the people at the next church told her that she should just get over it and move on from the tragedy. She was hanging on to the past, they said.

Mary needed what so many of us need. She needed to be able to pray, "forgive us our debts, as we also have forgiven our debtors." Easier said than done. One day, Mary read a poem about two women who meet for the first time in heaven. When the women meet, they can tell from each other's crowns that they are both mothers of sons who have died. The poem reads:

> "I would have taken my son's place on the cross," said one.
> "Oh, you are the mother of Christ," said the other mother, falling to
>   her knee.
> Kissing the tear away, the first mother said, "Tell me who your son is,
>   that I may grieve with you also."
> "My son is Judas Iscariot."

That is how the poem ends. Something clicked inside Mary Johnson after she read it. She knew that something had to change. So she made a decision that most mothers of murdered children would not make. She decided to visit Oshea Israel in prison. She almost did not go through with it, but somehow she found the courage and strength to move forward. To her surprise, he expressed openness to the idea. She started their meetings with simple discussions designed to get to know each other. After a while, they became friends. On his release from prison, Oshea had no place to go, so Mary convinced her landlord to let him move in to the apartment next door. Today, the two check in with each other on a regular basis. Oshea can never undo what he

Figure 5.5. Mary Johnson and Oshea Israel

did to her son in the past, and he can never replace her son in the present. But by the grace of God, it is as if Oshea has become an *adopted* son through Mary's resilient and persistent decision to forgive. The photo of Mary and Oshea provides a visual depiction of what forgiveness looks like when we attach names and faces to an abstract concept.

What else besides Jesus's vertical forgiveness can compel such dangerous horizontal forgiveness toward a sister or brother who has hurt us so deeply?

ANALOGIES

The fifth way we illustrate is through *analogies*. An analogy is a comparison between two things for the purpose of explanation or clarification. Robinson writes, "If you wanted to argue that truth is equally valid but not equally valuable, you might [say,] A penny and a dollar bill are both genuine . . . but they are not of equal worth. Therefore we must distinguish between penny- and dollar-truth."[24] We also see the writers of Scripture using analogies. Consider these words from Amos 5:18–20:

> Woe to you who long
> for the day of the LORD!
> Why do you long for the day of the LORD?
> That day will be darkness, not light.

24. H. Robinson, *Biblical Preaching*, 108.

> It will be as though a man fled from a lion
>   only to meet a bear,
> as though he entered his house
>   and rested his hand on the wall
>   only to have a snake bite him.
> Will not the day of the LORD be darkness, not light—
>   pitch-dark, without a ray of brightness?

Did you notice that the writer does not describe the day of the Lord in an abstract way but in a poetic way? The day of the Lord can be compared to a man fleeing from a lion only to meet a bear, or to one resting his hand on the wall only to be bitten by a snake.

People use analogies all the time. I remember having a conversation with the president of a well-known college. I will never forget the analogy he gave for what it is like to be president of a university. He said, "When you start out, it's like you're running on a treadmill as fast as you can. Then they ask you to run faster." He shared that analogy with me twenty years ago, and I still remember it.

Metaphor

The final way we illustrate is through *metaphor*. As the French philosopher Paul Ricoeur reminds us, "The symbol gives rise to thought."[25] A metaphor used in the right way can open a new world of possibilities in people's minds. Think for a moment about the beautiful metaphors in the Bible. Exodus is not just an event—it is a metaphor. Exile is not just an event—it is a metaphor. Resurrection is not just an event—it is a metaphor. You get the idea. Take a look at several metaphors in one passage, 1 Corinthians 5:6–8: "Your boasting is not good. Don't you know that a little yeast leavens the whole batch of dough? Get rid of the old yeast, so that you may be a new unleavened batch—as you really are. For Christ, our Passover lamb, has been sacrificed. Therefore let us keep the Festival, not with the old bread leavened with malice and wickedness, but with the unleavened bread of sincerity and truth."

Those of us who grew up in church heard plenty of metaphors designed to help us understand Christian faith: "Jesus is the good shepherd"; "God is our stronghold"; "We have been adopted"; "We are no longer slaves but free"; "We are the children of God." Consider using more metaphors when you preach as a way to help people understand abstract concepts.

25. Ricoeur, *Symbolism of Evil*, 347.

Focus on Using Specific Applications

If we want to practice concreteness in preaching, then we also need to focus on concrete application. A lot of sermons fall short in this key area, including many that I have preached. Let me recommend two questions in particular that will help us to make better applications.

The first question is, *How might this be heard by . . . ?* Take as an example a well-known verse, James 1:2–3: "Consider it pure joy, my brothers and sisters, whenever you face trials of many kinds, because you know that the testing of your faith produces perseverance." The question, "How might this text be heard by high school juniors and seniors in the United States?" has a different answer than, "How might this text be heard by Syrian Christian refugees fleeing persecution?" Both groups need to hear the promise that the testing of one's faith produces perseverance. However, each group will look on their testing differently. Some applications might touch down similarly to how this text touched down in the first century if it is being heard in the context of heavy persecution. The reason we ask the question is that it forces us to think more strategically about how to apply this passage to our listeners.

Another example is the parable of the prodigal son in Luke 15:11–32. One reason why this parable is a good example is that the original listeners heard it in different ways. We read in Luke 15:1–2, "Now the tax collectors and sinners were all gathering around to hear Jesus. But the Pharisees and the teachers of the law muttered, 'This man welcomes sinners and eats with them.'" Immediately after Luke introduces this detail, he has Jesus tell the parable of the lost sheep (Luke 15:3–7), the parable of the lost coin (Luke 15:8–10), and the parable of the prodigal son (Luke 15:11–23) in succession. In these three stories, the accent is mainly on the audacious and even reckless love of the one searching for what is lost: the shepherd leaving the ninety-nine for the one sheep, the woman searching desperately for her lost coin, and, of course, the father lowering himself to the point of indignity to restore his younger *and* his older son. All three parables tell us about the deep and abiding love of the Father, a love that is willing to risk everything in order to seek and find us.

Even though the accent is on the father in the story of the prodigal son, think for a moment about how the original audience might have heard it. The father has two sons, one who disregards the rules of his house, squanders himself in licentiousness, wrecks his life, and repents, and another who is so insulted by his father's mercy that he would rather be indignant and bitter than joyful and accepting of a prodigal brother. Which brother do the tax collectors and sinners most resemble, and which brother do the Pharisees and teachers of the law most resemble? You do not need to be a rocket scientist to know the answer.

When it comes to applying this text to a modern congregation, we might also ask ourselves which brother we most resemble. We like to think the answer is the former rather than the latter. Doing so would let us off the hook. But what if we are most like the older brother? If that is the case, then we have some soul-searching to do. Regardless of which person we resemble most, the father offers his love to both and invites both to the banquet.

Also remember that different communities will hear the text in different ways, and they might apply it in different ways. Consider an example from Luke 19:1–10, the story of Zacchaeus the tax collector:

> Jesus entered Jericho and was passing through. A man was there by the name of Zacchaeus; he was a chief tax collector and was wealthy. He wanted to see who Jesus was, but because he was short he could not see over the crowd. So he ran ahead and climbed a sycamore-fig tree to see him, since Jesus was coming that way.
>
> When Jesus reached the spot, he looked up and said to him, "Zacchaeus, come down immediately. I must stay at your house today." So he came down at once and welcomed him gladly.
>
> All the people saw this and began to mutter, "He has gone to be the guest of a sinner."
>
> But Zacchaeus stood up and said to the Lord, "Look, Lord! Here and now I give half of my possessions to the poor, and if I have cheated anybody out of anything, I will pay back four times the amount."
>
> Jesus said to him, "Today salvation has come to this house, because this man, too, is a son of Abraham. For the Son of Man came to seek and to save the lost."

Now that you have read the text, ask yourself: How might this text be heard by different communities? How might it be heard by a community that struggles with excluding people? How might it be heard by a group of misfits or outcasts? How might the "one percent" hear the text? What about young children in kids' church? How would retirees hear it, or people in banking or big business? The text resonates in different ways among different communities. In his commentary on the Gospel of Luke, Robert C. Tannehill writes, "For exclusionary communities, this story is a reminder of Jesus' mission. For outcasts, this is a story of hope. For people with wealth, it's a story of generosity."[26]

When it comes to preaching, it helps to ask *how the text might be heard* by our listeners. How might senior citizens in my church hear the text? How

26. Tannehill, *Luke*, 278.

might kids who just graduated from kids' church and are now worshiping with their parents hear it? How might the passage be heard by the poor? the rich? the single mom? the widower? the unmarried person? the abused? When we think of our communities as diverse and multifaceted, this adds texture and nuance to the way that we apply the sermon. Just as different communities hear the text differently, so also different communities apply the text differently.

The second question is, *What does that look like?* If preachers talk to their listeners about becoming people who commit themselves to doing justice, "What does that look like?" Or if we talk to our congregations about hospitality and welcoming the stranger, then, "What does that look like?" Paul says to the Romans, "Love must be sincere. Hate what is evil; cling to what is good" (Rom. 12:9). So, what does it look like to hate evil? For that matter, what does it look like to cling to what is good? Sometimes we find clues in the passage that help us answer the question, but other times there are no good clues. Even with good clues, we still need to think through what it might look like in a twenty-first-century context. Later in Romans, Paul says, "Mourn with those who mourn" (Rom. 12:15). What does it look like in the twenty-first century to mourn with those who mourn? The point in asking this question is *not* to make people believe in only one possible answer, the "right" answer. We can help listeners to imagine *more than one* appropriate way to apply this passage in their lives.

> *When we think of our communities as diverse and multifaceted, this adds texture and nuance to the way that we apply the sermon.*

In some of my preaching classes, I try an exercise with students. I read Micah 6:8: "He has shown you, O mortal, what is good. And what does the LORD require of you? To act justly and to love mercy and to walk humbly with your God." After reminding the students of the importance of solid exegesis in the book of Micah, I ask them a few simple questions:

- What does it look like today to act justly, and what does it look like today to act *un*justly?
- What does it look like today to love mercy, and what does it look like today to *hate* mercy?
- What does it look like today to walk humbly with God, and what does it look like today to walk *proudly*?

Then I invite them to come up with answers. Of course, their answers vary since they come from different social locations and life experiences, but usually the diversity of their answers provokes more thought and discussion. Preaching students generate lots of great possibilities, answers that I would never think of on my own. What does it look like to act justly? Here are some of their answers:

- Sell something at its proper selling price, and don't inflate or gouge the price to make a bigger profit.
- Rally to stop gun violence.
- Seek funding for low-income schools.
- Find shelter for those who are homeless.
- Seek reparations for victims of police brutality.
- Organize and educate people on systemic injustice.
- Advocate for legislation that stands against oppression of minorities.
- Respect your leaders both at work and at church, whether they are rich or poor.
- Do your work without abusing the clock for overtime.
- Start a farmer's market in your church's neighborhood, because in the middle of a large city poor people have a hard time getting access to fresh produce.
- Adopt a girl from a place where girls are considered worthless.

These are just a few possibilities for what acting justly might look like on a daily basis. Some answers will be better than others. The simple process of generating answers helps us get from thirty thousand feet down to sea level.

Pastor Jill Briscoe knows how to preach at sea level. She and her husband, Stuart, served as co-pastors for many years at Elmbrook Church in Brookfield, Wisconsin. In a sermon on the parable of the good Samaritan (Luke 10:25–37), Briscoe offers some modern answers to the lawyer's question to Jesus in Luke 10:29, "And who is my neighbor?"[27] In answering it, she borrows the imagery of the ditch from the parable in order to make her application more vivid. Who is my neighbor? The person in the ditch.

Go to www.Practices ofChristianPreaching .com to hear Jill Briscoe as she describes who the person in the ditch might be in a twenty-first-century context.

Briscoe's larger point is that our love for God is shown when we care for the person in the ditch. But notice how concrete she is when she talks about who that person in the ditch might be today. It might be someone we know. She gets context specific in order to answer the question in much the same way that Jesus does in the parable.

27. Jill Briscoe's sermon, "Loving God with Your Whole Heart," delivered at the Chicago Sunday Evening Club, is available at www.preachingtoday.com.

The two questions I mentioned—*How might this be heard by . . . ?* and *What does that look like?*—are two possible questions designed to help preachers focus on using specific applications. These questions help us climb down the ladder of abstraction, to return to Hayakawa's phrase.

Conclusion

Effective sermons include abstraction and concreteness. The choice is not either-or; it is both-and. Here is what Hayakawa says about joining the two together: "The informative speakers . . . operate on all levels of the abstraction ladder, moving quickly and gracefully in orderly fashion from higher to lower, from lower to higher—with minds as lithe and deft and beautiful as monkeys in a tree."[28] In other words, good communicators know how to balance abstraction and concreteness without sacrificing one for the other.

Too many sermons major on abstraction and minor on concreteness. We usually come up short in the latter rather than the former. More often than we realize, our sermons take off from the runway, stay at thirty thousand feet, and never land in the neighborhoods where people live. To illustrate and apply effectively in a sermon means that we eventually find a way back down to sea level. If your genuine desire is to make your sermons more accessible to listeners, then strive to make them more concrete. If you remember to talk about Bessie and food exposés from time to time, your listeners will thank you for it.

Learning activities and sermon samples for this chapter are located at www .PracticesofChristian Preaching.com.

28. Hayakawa, *Language*, 190.

6

Preach Creatively

The Christian vocation is above all a vocation to imagine—to see what God sees when God looks at the world, and to believe that God's dreams can come true.

—Barbara Brown Taylor, *The Preaching Life*

No one in society has as much responsibility as the preacher for altering our perception of the world around us from that of a chemical-physical accident to the handiwork of a loving, caring God.

—Samuel D. Proctor, *The Certain Sound of the Trumpet*

Imagination bodies forth the form of things unknown, the poet's pen turns them into shapes, and gives to airy nothing a local habitation and a name."[1] These words penned by William Shakespeare in *A Midsummer Night's Dream* describe the beauty and wonder of creativity. Human beings have a remarkable capacity to create, to fashion, to shape "the form of things unknown." But many of us overlook and even suppress our creativity. Sometimes we miss it even when it is right in front of our faces. I will mention just one example.

On January 12, 2007, two men conducted a social experiment outside an arcade in a Metro subway station in Washington, DC, a little before 8:00 a.m. on a Friday during rush hour. Joshua Bell, one of the world's great classical

1. Shakespeare, *William Shakespeare*, 327.

Figure 6.1. Joshua Bell in Leipzig (2016)

violinists, served as the main actor, and Gene Weingarten, a journalist for the *Washington Post*, documented and wrote about it afterward. Bell walked into the subway station wearing jeans, a long-sleeved T-shirt, and a Washington Nationals baseball cap, a uniform quite different from the formal attire that he normally wears in concert-hall performances. He also brought his Stradivarius violin, an instrument valued at $3.5 million in 2007. Three days earlier, Weingarten notes, "Bell had filled the house at Boston's stately Symphony Hall, where merely pretty good seats went for $100."[2] Normally, he performs in some of the most prestigious concert halls in the world.

2. Weingarten, "Pearls Before Breakfast."

After laying out his case for donations and putting in a "few dollars and pocket change as seed money," Bell started playing. For forty-three minutes, he played breathtaking pieces of classical music. The sound in the Metro that morning must have been glorious. A total of 1,097 people passed through the subway entrance on their way to work. Want to guess how many stopped? *Seven.* Just over one half of one percent broke free from their harried morning commute to listen to the music. Adding insult to injury, only twenty-seven people put money in his case. Joshua Bell makes about $1,000 per minute in concert-hall performances. In his Metro performance, he made $32 and change.

What induces such a poor response to such a compelling performance? Did the radical shift in location prevent people from hearing the music? Did the time constraints keep them from stopping even if they wanted to? Perhaps the part of the brain connected to habit held too strong a sway. Presumably, all of these factors played *some* part in what transpired. Whatever the reasons, the story itself reminds us of how easy it is to turn a blind eye to the creativity that resides in us or in others, even when it is three feet in front of us.

The subject of this chapter is *creativity*, and its aim is to help preachers engage in the creative process with greater interest and impact. Creativity is the fifth and final C of the Five Cs of preaching.

The word "create" comes from the past participle *creatum*, a conjugation of the verb *creare*, "to produce, to make." But the word "creative" implies more than doing or making. If we choose to be more formal in our description of the word, we can point to scholarly consensus on the definition. Most creativity researchers agree that creative work displays at least three main traits: novelty, quality, and relevance.[3] One displays creativity through engaging in expert performance or production that is new and innovative (novelty), excellent as agreed on by the community and usually by fellow experts (quality), and appropriate to the domain in which it takes place (relevance). Applied to preaching, this definition means that creative preachers prepare and deliver sermons that are fresh, high in quality, and valuable to the community. If we choose to be less formal in our description, I like Ken Robinson's succinct definition of creativity: "putting your imagination to work."[4] Creative preachers put their imagination to work.

3. In the preface to *The Cambridge Handbook of Creativity*, James C. Kaufman and Robert J. Sternberg write, "Most definitions of creative ideas comprise three components. First, creative ideas must represent something different, new, or innovative. Second, creative ideas are of high quality. Third, creative ideas must also be appropriate to the task at hand or some redefinition of that task. Thus, a creative response is novel, good, and relevant" (xiii). Many consider Kaufman and Sternberg to be two of the leading creativity researchers today.
4. K. Robinson, *Out of Our Minds*, 142.

**The Practices
of Christian Preaching**

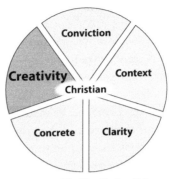

Figure 6.2. The Five Cs: Creativity

In this chapter, we will present a short history of creativity, discuss opportunities for practicing creativity in preaching, describe obstacles that stifle creativity, and recommend ideas for practicing creativity in preaching.

A Short History of Creativity and Its Relevance for Preaching

Creativity has a long and complex history in both religious and secular spheres, so what follows is a brief and largely Western story of creativity. I have divided this unscientific history into five phases—Greek, Judeo-Christian, medieval, early modern (pre-1950), and late modern (post-1950).

Greek Creativity

The best-known classical Greek philosophers treated creativity and imagination with caution and sometimes suspicion. Both Plato and Aristotle believed that art always took second place to reason.[5] Plato reserved some of his harshest judgments for artists. He chose outright negativity and even hostility.[6]

---

5. Appeals to reason led to the true and the real, whereas appeals to imagination led to imitations of the true and illusions of the real. See Kearney, *Wake of Imagination*, 91–92. In Plato's world, Kearney writes, "Reason alone has access to divine Ideas. And imagination, for its part, is condemned to a pseudo-world of imitations." *Wake of Imagination*, 88.

6. In Book 10 of *The Republic*, Plato writes, "The artist's representation is a long way removed from truth, and he is able to reproduce everything because he never penetrates beneath the superficial appearance of anything." In the same paragraph, Plato suggests that artists usually operate from ignorance and sometimes contribute to deceiving "children or simple people" because their imitations trick people into confusing the false with the real. See Plato, *Republic*, 396–405.

Aristotle opted for nuanced ambivalence. He believed that imagination functioned as a mediator between sensation and reason, two higher faculties.[7] Although Aristotle was more nuanced, both he and Plato ranked reason high above imagination.[8]

Judeo-Christian Creativity

To understand and appreciate creativity in the Judeo-Christian worldview, one must begin at the beginning.[9] In Genesis 1, God created the world ex nihilo (out of nothing). God made human beings with the capacity to create, although this creative capacity was limited. We can make something out of something but not something out of nothing. The two primary Hebrew words for "create" illustrate the differences. The Hebrew verb *bara* means to create something ex nihilo. It occurs almost exclusively with reference to God's action (e.g., Gen. 1:1, 21, 27 [3x]; 5:1–2; Num. 16:30; Deut. 4:32; Ps. 148:5; Isa. 4:5; Mal. 2:10). Only God creates new things out of nothing. The second Hebrew verb, *yetser*, means to form or shape.[10] The Old Testament writers use it to refer to divine *and* human creating.[11] When used for human creating, *yetser* has positive and negative uses depending on *what* is formed or shaped.[12] Human beings can shape objects common to daily life, such as reservoirs (Isa. 22:10), pots (Isa. 29:16), or weapons for battle (Isa. 54:17), but

7. Aristotle argued that art (e.g., poetry) *can* have a positive role as a societal good on one condition: it leads to truth and re-presents reality. *Poetics*, 37–39, 59–61.

8. For both philosophers, writes Kearney, "imagination remains largely a *reproductive* rather than a *productive* activity, a servant rather than a master of meaning, imitation rather than origin." *Wake of Imagination*, 113 (emphasis in original).

9. Creativity researchers Mark A. Runco and Robert S. Albert observe, "The earliest Western conception of creativity was the Biblical story of creation given in *Genesis*, from which followed the idea of the artisan doing God's work on earth." "Creativity Research," 5. In the words of French historian Jacques Le Goff, "To study the imagination of a society is to go to the heart of its consciousness and historical evolution. It is to go to the origin and profound nature of man, created 'in the image of God.'" *Medieval Imagination*, 6.

10. For a fuller word study of *yetser*, *bara*, other Hebrew words for create/imagination, as well as Greek cognates in the New Testament, see Searle, *The Eyes of Your Heart*, 32–34.

11. In Genesis 2, God forms human beings from the dust of the earth (Gen. 2:7; cf. also Ps. 103:14), trees (Gen. 2:9), and wild beasts (Gen. 2:16).

12. In a section within his classic text *Good and Evil*, Martin Buber writes, "Imagination is not entirely evil, it is good and evil, for in the midst of it and from out of it decision can arouse the heart's willing direction toward him, master the vortex of possibility and realize the human figure purposed in creation, as it could not yet do prior to the knowledge of good and evil . . . greatest danger and greatest opportunity at once. . . . To unite the two urges of the imagination implies to equip the absolute potency of passion with the one direction that renders it capable of great love and great service. Thus and not otherwise can man become whole." "The Good and Evil Imagination," 93, 97.

they can also create idols (Isa. 44:9) and negative dispositions in their hearts and minds (Gen. 6:5; 8:21; Deut. 31:21; Isa. 26:3).

Medieval to Renaissance Creativity

The church fathers fused together insights from Christian theology and Greek philosophy to form their understanding of creativity. Influential church leaders like Saint Augustine and Thomas Aquinas argued that "the creature cannot itself create [*creatura non potest creare*]."[13] God creates. Human beings represent, imitate, and mirror God's creative work. Craftsmen, artists, and teachers "create" in a purposeful and disciplined manner that is supposed to reflect a reverent separation between the Creator and the created. Imagination remains "under the strict supervision of reason and revelation, to instruct the faithful." An untamed imagination is vulnerable to "irrational passion (even demonic possession)."[14]

Eastern Orthodox Christianity placed fewer restrictions and suspicions on creativity. Iconography arose in the early church and continues to this day. For various reasons, which are too tangential to repeat here, most Orthodox Christians experienced less anxiety about the creation of artistic images for worship. Even so, iconographers never saw themselves as "artists" in the modern sense of the word. For the first few centuries, those who made icons refused to attach their names to the works they created, unlike in the West, where theological books bore the name of the author. They made icons as sacrifices to God, and they saw what they created as "the work of the Holy Spirit rather than of an individual man."[15] Eventually the Western church relaxed *some* of its fears regarding the arts. Many of the great sculptors and painters in both the East and the West saw themselves not as artists but as craftsmen.[16]

---

13. Pope, *Creativity*, 45. For more on Augustine's understanding of the imagination, and in particular his account of it in *De Genessi ad litteram*, see Meconi and Stump, *Cambridge Companion to Augustine*, 130–31.

14. As Kearney observes, "Many classical and medieval thinkers considered imagination an unreliable, unpredictable and irreverent faculty. . . . As Thomas Aquinas observed in a resonant phrase, imagination makes 'everything other than it is.'" *Poetics of Imagining*, 3.

15. Kearney, *Wake of Imagination*, 134.

16. "Until the end of the 15th century in Europe," write Sami Abuhamdeh and Mihaly Csikszentmihalyi, the great artists and sculptors were still "considered to be merely craftsmen" and the work they performed "required the collaboration of several individuals." "The Artistic Personality," 31. Arnold Hauser, the prominent sociologist of art, notes, "The artist's studio in the early Renaissance is still dominated by the communal spirit of the mason's lodge and guilded workshop; the work of art is not yet the expression of an independent personality." *Social History of Art*, 54–55, cited in Abuhamdeh and Csikszentmihalyi, "Artistic Personality," 31.

Early Modern (Pre-1950) Creativity

In the early 1800s, understandings of creativity shifted dramatically from collective collaboration to individual inspiration. The craftsman in community gave way to the artistic personality in isolation.[17] Academics started weighing in on the power of the imagination.[18] At the popular level, the conditions were nearly perfect for "the lone genius myth" to take root, with its emphases on individual reclusiveness, artistic temperament, and mental illness as inextricably linked to the highest forms of creative capacity.[19] The myth sounded something like this: the true artist commits to self-expression, nonconformity, reclusiveness, and originality by "rising above the limiting, stultifying forces of the conforming masses."[20] As early as the Romantic period, Dean Keith Simonton observes, "the notion of the mad genius had become virtual dogma."[21] By the end of the nineteenth century, notes Simonton, many experts in psychology, including the Italian criminologist Cesare Lombroso, argued that genius was a "mental disorder" that could be ascribed to a "congenital neuropathology."[22] In other words, *the modern Western idea of*

17. To use M. H. Abrams's imagery in *The Mirror and the Lamp*, the paradigm shifted from the mirror to the lamp, from creativity as representation and reflection (mirror) to creativity as individual expression and production (lamp). Kearney uses the same metaphors to describe the shift. He writes, "The *mimetic* paradigm of imagining is replaced by the *productive* paradigm. . . . Now imagination is deemed capable of inventing a world out of its human resources, a world answerable to no power higher than itself. Or to cite the canonical metaphor, the imagination ceases to function as a mirror reflecting some external reality and becomes a lamp which projects its own internally generated light onto things." *Wake of Imagination*, 155.

18. Kearney points to a significant number of nineteenth- and twentieth-century thinkers from several different countries who write about the imagination in the areas of philosophy or poetics: Immanuel Kant, Friedrich Wilhelm Joseph Schelling, Johann Gottlieb Fichte, Samuel Coleridge, Charles Baudelaire, Gaston Bachelard, and Paul Ricoeur. See Kearney, *Poetics of Imagining*, 1–6, 98–101, 165–77.

19. See also Montuori and Purser, "Deconstructing the Lone Genius Myth."

20. Montuori and Purser, "Deconstructing the Lone Genius Myth," 74.

21. Simonton, *Greatness*, 284. The fact that early Greco-Roman thinkers connected genius to "madness" only added to the problem of creativity mythology. Aristotle believed that all great politicians, poets, and artists shared "tendencies toward melancholia." *Problems*, Book 30, line 1, in Ross and Smith, *Works of Aristotle*, 953a. In "Of Peace of Mind," Seneca also claimed, "If we trust Aristotle, no great genius has ever been without a touch of insanity" (287). See also Simonton, *Greatness*, 284. The seventeenth-century English poet John Dryden also sowed seeds for the mythology when he wrote in 1681, "Great wits are sure to madness near allied, And thin partitions do their bounds divide." "Absalom and Ahithophel," in Hammdon, *Poems of John Dryden*, 469. See also the Dryden citation in Simonton, *Greatness*, 284.

22. According to Simonton, Lombroso's book "emphatically affirmed that genius could be linked with 'degenerative psychosis,' especially that of the 'epileptoid group.'" *Greatness*, 285. In 1891, Lombroso wrote, "The frequency of delusions in their multiform characters of degenerative characteristics, of the loss of affectivity, of heredity, more particularly in the children of inebriate, imbecile, idiotic, or epileptic parents, and above all, the peculiar character

creativity with its individualistic, personality-based, lone genius bias comes to us as a recent phenomenon. The noun "creativity" did not appear in the *Oxford English Dictionary* until 1875, and it did not become widely popularized until the 1940s and 1950s.[23]

Late Modern (Post-1950) Creativity

The year 1950 represents an important turning point in modern creativity work, especially in social psychology. J. P. Guilford's presidential address to the American Psychological Association that year sparked an academic movement.[24] Since Guilford's address, modern creativity research has grown at an exponential rate, with researchers proposing new theories,[25] scholars

---

of inspiration, show that genius is a degenerative psychosis of the epileptoid group." *Man of Genius*, 359. Unfortunately, the myth of the mad genius did not end with Lombroso and his colleagues in the nineteenth century; it continues to this day. As social psychologist and creativity researcher James C. Kaufman observes, "The idea of the mad genius (particularly the mad artist) has been prevalent in the research literature for more than one hundred years (e.g., Lombroso, 1891). . . . Regardless of empirical evidence, most people believe in the mad genius theory. The image of the mad genius or tormented artist persists in media, popular culture, and psychology." *Creativity 101*, 124–25.

23. Rob Pope observes, "It is an arresting fact that the abstract noun 'creativity' was not widely current until the 1940s and 1950s (it did not appear at all in the 1933 edition of *The Oxford English Dictionary*), and when it was used it was invoked in contexts and with applications that were highly specific to that time. In this respect, 'creativity' (narrowly conceived) is a product of the mid-twentieth century and the modern West." *Creativity*, 19.

24. In that address, Guilford lamented the lack of scholarly research on creativity in academic journals, discussed possibilities for opening up new areas of scholarship, and highlighted the important connections between creativity and education. Pope refers to Guilford as "the founder of modern creativity research." *Creativity*, 19. Kaufman observes, "Before Guilford, less than 0.2% of all entries of *Psychological Abstracts* concentrated on creativity. He helped move the field forward." *Creativity 101*, 11. A few years later, in 1956, Guilford proposed a Structure of the Intellect Model of creativity that still wields influence today whenever psychologists discuss differences between convergent and divergent thinking. See Guilford, *Intelligence, Creativity, and Their Educational Implications*. See also Baer, *Domain Specificity of Creativity*, 8, 105–12; Kaufman, *Creativity 101*, 13–15.

25. In 2010, Aaron Kozbelt, Ronald A. Beghetto, and Mark A. Runco pointed to at least ten *major* categories of creativity theories in their field in "Theories of Creativity." I will only mention some of the more popular and influential theories here. In *Creativity in Context*, Teresa Amabile presents a model that highlights how social factors (e.g., motivation) shape creativity. In *Flow*, Mihaly Csikszentmihalyi proposes a systems model of creativity that consists of domain, field, and individual. In their article "Toward a Broader Conception of Creativity," Ronald Beghetto and James C. Kaufman offer a multitiered 3-C model of creativity to distinguish various types: Big-C, little-c, and mini-c. John Baer and James C. Kaufman provide a model they call Amusement Park Theory in "Bridging Generality and Specificity." R. Keith Sawyer highlights the importance of improvisational group creativity through what he calls "collaborative emergence." *Explaining Creativity*, 4. See also Sawyer, "Individual and Group Creativity," 366–80.

collaborating to launch new journals,[26] and at least some theorists challenging Western understandings.[27]

The late twentieth and early twenty-first centuries have seen an exponential rise in creativity research.[28] According to R. Keith Sawyer, creativity research has undergone at least three major shifts since Guilford. In the 1950s and 1960s, they focused on the *personalities* of some of the most creative people in society. In the 1970s and 1980s, they adopted more of a *cognitive* approach focused on "internal mental processes that occur while people are engaged in creative behavior." In the 1980s and into the 1990s, they adopted a *sociological* approach, emphasizing the conditions in which creativity either flourished or languished.

Relevance for Preaching

So what does creativity research have to do with preaching? More than we think. In the last few decades, a number of homileticians have brought modern understandings of creativity and imagination into dialogue with preaching.[29] In fact, the list of those who have written about imagination and preaching is quite long.[30] Rather than replicate what other homileticians have said, I will offer my own perspectives. I will discuss opportunities for practicing creativity, the obstacles that prevent it, and I will offer some ideas for how to cultivate it in preaching.

---

26. Some of the newer journals are *Creativity Research Journal, The Journal of Creative Behavior, Empirical Studies of the Arts,* and *Imagination, Creativity, and Personality.*

27. For example, Todd Lubart has written a fascinating book chapter on the connection between the lone genius myth and the Western emphasis on individualism over against collectivism. In collectivistic cultures in other parts of the world, the society does not elevate "special people" to the level of creative savant. Lubart writes, "In contrast, according to some reports in other cultures, everyone is naturally creative in all activities of life, such that the question itself of nominating creative people is odd and often meets with no response." "Cross-Cultural Perspectives on Creativity," 269–70. See also James C. Kaufman's discussion of Eastern and Western understandings of creativity in *Creativity 101,* 155–59.

28. Sawyer, "Emergence of Creativity," 453. See also Sawyer, *Improvised Dialogues.*

29. For an overview of imagination and preaching, see Lose, "Imagination and Preaching."

30. Although *creativity* shows up often in homiletics textbooks, conversations around *imagination* recur with greater frequency in homiletical discussions. Of course, one can detect a lot of overlap between these two terms. Barbara Brown Taylor has written about developing "everyday imagination," Thomas H. Troeger the need for "imaginative theology," Mary Catherine Hilkert the value of "sacramental imagination," Paul Scott Wilson the "imagination of the heart," Richard Eslinger the connection between narrative and imagination, Geoff New the importance of imaginative preaching, and Walter Brueggemann the "practice of prophetic imagination." These are just some of those who have written on these topics. See B. Taylor, *Preaching Life,* 15; Wilson, *Imagination of the Heart;* Hilkert, *Naming Grace;* Eslinger, *New Hearing;* New, *Imaginative Preaching;* Brueggemann, *Practice of Prophetic Imagination.*

Opportunities to Practice Creativity in Preaching

In his book *Preaching with Passion*, Alex Montoya argues that preachers must learn to be "skillful artists." He writes, "Preaching is an art, not just an act. Congregations have long moved beyond the simple lecture on the Bible and the 'sharing of a few nuggets' from the Word."[31] A preacher without a good imagination is like a concert pianist without three octaves on the piano. One *technically* can play a sonata with twenty-four fewer notes, but how beautiful can the music really be without the full range of possibilities? No matter how accomplished the musician, a limited range stifles the creation of beautiful music. Preachers need the notes they are used to using—exegetical, biblical, rational, practical, and so on—but they also need access to the notes of their imagination. What happens when we fail to access our imagination? More harm than we realize. Amos N. Wilder writes, "When imagination fails doctrine becomes ossified, witness and proclamation wooden, doxologies and litanies empty, consolations hollow, and ethics legalistic."[32] In other words, we lose the vitality and vibrancy of our Christian witness. Does the world really need more colorless, boring preaching?

So how do we expand our imaginative capacity as preachers? To answer this question, as well as move us toward a more creative mind-set in preaching, let me suggest five possibilities for expanding our imaginative range: biblical, poetic, theological, prophetic, and pastoral.

Expand Our Biblical Imagination

How can a preacher expand his or her range of biblical imagination? *Involve listeners in the world of the biblical text.* That is one tangible strategy. Some preaching traditions already know how to do this quite well. Historically, African American preaching has excelled at involving the community of faith in the world of the Bible. Richard Lischer observes, "The cruelties of slavery made it imperative that African Americans not *step back* but *step into* the Book and its storied world of God's personal relations with those in trouble."[33] In such a context, the preacher's task was to enroll the community of faith in that world. The preacher's world, writes Lischer, does not "merely correspond to the world of the Bible, it is *enrolled* in the world of the Bible."[34]

31. Montoya, *Preaching with Passion*, 84.
32. Wilder, *Theopoetic*, 2.
33. Lischer, *Preacher King*, 200 (emphasis in original).
34. Lischer, *Preacher King*, 200–201.

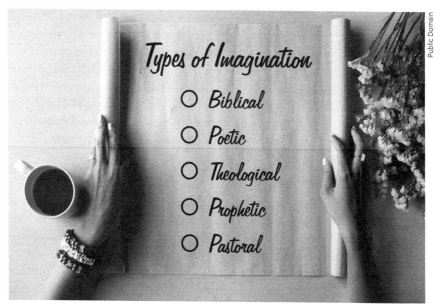

Figure 6.3. Ways to Practice Creativity

To enroll listeners in the world of the text means that a preacher helps listeners see themselves as participants instead of passive spectators. Does your preaching carry people to the desert where Hagar wandered alone, the shore of the Red Sea as it parted, the cleft of the rock as the Lord passed by Moses, the fields where Ruth gleaned the grain, the lonely palace where Esther risked her life, the cave where Jesus was born, the garden where Jesus sweat drops of blood the night before his death, the cross on which he hung, or the garden tomb that he emptied on Easter Sunday? Creative preaching leads listeners into the biblical story so that what mattered then will matter now. It enrolls them in the world of the text. Too many sermons sound like historical reports on data from the past. Preachers bring worlds together: the world of the biblical text and the world in which people live their lives. Preachers show how this world relates to that one, and they also involve people who live in this world in the stories of people who lived in that world.

Creative preaching leads listeners into the biblical story so that what mattered then will matter now.

Osvaldo L. Mottesi claims that a robust imagination grants a preacher the ability "to reproduce, even in the smallest details, the multiform quadrants that the Bible presents to us, or to walk in the sandals of biblical personalities, that is, to enter into 'existential harmony' with the biblical world."[35] When was the last time you helped your listeners to walk in the sandals of the authors of Scripture or the sandals of the characters in the stories themselves? My point here is not to suggest that preachers should use their imagination to say anything and everything they want. Mottesi warns that an unwieldy imagination is "good for science fiction but not for preaching."[36] Rather, my point is to push preachers to "walk up and down the street where a text lives" and not just report on an ancient event from thousands of years ago.[37]

Expand Our Poetic Imagination

From time to time, young preachers would ask Gardner C. Taylor, one of the great American preachers of the twentieth century, why he did not sing or whoop when he preached. Singing, chanting, and whooping are popular in a lot of black preaching circles, especially among folk preachers toward the close of sermons. Taylor answered, "Your words should sing!"[38] Let me suggest that the primary way to expand your poetic imagination is to *invest your time and energy in making your words "sing."* Devote yourself to crafting sermonic language known for its care, precision, and artfulness. Words are more powerful than we realize. As the writer of Proverbs reminds us, "The tongue has the power of life and death, and those who love it will eat its fruit" (Prov. 18:21). Words have the power of life or death.

If the gospel comes to us in poetic language quite often, should not the preaching of the gospel come to us in poetic forms as well? Perhaps you are

---

35. Here is the quote in its context in Spanish: "Con ella [la imaginación] somos capaces de reproducir, aun en sus detalles más mínimos, los cuadros multiformes que la Biblia nos presenta, o caminar en las sandalias de los personajes bíblicos, es decir, entrar en 'sintonía existencial' con el mundo bíblico." Mottesi, *Predicación y Misión*, 233.

36. Mottesi writes that a "fantastical imagination" (*imaginación fantástica*) is "buena para la ciencia ficción, per no para la predicación." *Predicación y Misión*, 233. Barbara Brown Taylor makes a similar argument when she writes, "The Bible reminds us that we are not free to imagine anything we like. We may not imagine that God speaks only through cats, for instance, or that turning three circles before walking out the front door will protect us from harm each day. By keeping us rooted in our historical tradition, the Bible helps us know the difference between imagination and delusion; by tethering our imaginations to that of the whole people of God, the Bible teaches us to imagine the God who was and is and who shall be." *Preaching Life*, 53–54.

37. Gardner C. Taylor puts it this way: "A wise preacher of another generation ago suggested that one ought to 'walk up and down the street where a text lives.' The surrounding terrain ought to be taken into account. What is the block like on which the text is located? . . . Does one hear light and merry music in the neighborhood of the text or are there solemn cadences of some sad and mournful time?" "Shaping Sermons by the Shape of Text and Preacher," in G. Taylor, *Words of Gardner Taylor*, 5:45–46.

38. Alcántara, *Learning from a Legend*, 65. See also Massey, "Composing Sermons That Sing!"

accustomed to more of a "plain style" approach. If that is your context, you may have to err more on the side of precision than artfulness. Even so, every preacher should love the sense and sound of words. As Angel Mergal observes, "The sermon is more than art, but never can it be less than art. If it is less than art, it is neither art nor a sermon."[39] Remember that God spoke the world into existence through words: "And God said . . ." If words matter to God to the extent that God uses them to bring new life into existence, then perhaps they should matter to us as well.

Some preachers come from a tradition in which they receive homiletical training early on in a rhetorical style. In *I Believe I'll Testify*, Cleophus J. LaRue observes, "Blacks are taught early on to love words—to love how they sound, how they feel, how they create reality, and how they give voice to the deepest expression of one's inner being."[40] A preacher with a robust poetic imagination takes care of words in order to become more effective at preaching. Perhaps more preachers should be known for their ability to take care of words in their sermons: *what* words they say and *how* they say them.[41] This may require writing out a verbatim manuscript, incorporating more rhetorical devices, or exegeting the images and metaphors in the text instead of the abstract ideas alone. To turn your speech into song, challenge yourself to take better care of the words you choose and how you say them.[42]

Expand Our Theological Imagination

Theology at its best clarifies our vision of God, humanity, the world, and eternity. An expanded theological imagination *invites congregants to abandon a false vision of reality and to embrace a God-shaped vision of reality*. It provides a corrective prescription. The people to whom we preach are constantly bombarded by false visions of success, pleasure, fulfillment, desire, image, and happiness. If we are honest, so are we. These false illusions vie for our attention, and they are so subtle and pervasive that we fail to realize how much they hold us captive.

---

39. Here is the quote in Spanish: "Cierto, el sermón es más que arte, pero nunca puede ser ménos que arte. Si es ménos que arte, ni será arte ni sermón." Mergal, *Arte Cristiano de la Predicación*, 47.

40. LaRue, *I Believe I'll Testify*, 93.

41. In the words of Gardner C. Taylor, "Words are cheap? That depends on whether or not we cheapen them." As quoted in Sallquist, *Classroom Classics*, 80.

42. Leonard Sweet observes that many postmodern listeners are drawn to images and metaphors much more than they are drawn to abstraction and proposition. He writes, "Propositions are lost on postmodern ears, but metaphor they will hear; images they will see and understand. Image dictionaries are replacing word dictionaries, and image banks are becoming as valuable as money banks (just ask Bill Gates)." *Post-Modern Pilgrims*, 86.

A robust theological imagination compels preachers and listeners alike to surrender false visions of the way life *seems to be* in order to embrace a kingdom vision of the way life really is. Barbara Brown Taylor claims that faith at its core is a "surrender of one set of images and the acceptance of another. It is a matter of learning to see the world, each other, and ourselves as God sees us, and to live as if God's reality were the only one that mattered."[43] By helying to open the eyes of faith, the preacher helps listeners shake loose from a vision that ruins and destroys both the soul and society. A robust theological imagination wakes us up to what really matters in life and for eternity. As Kevin Vanhoozer puts it, "[theology] is all about waking up to the real, to *what is*—specifically, to *what is* 'in Christ.'"[44]

> *Faith at its core is a "surrender of one set of images and the acceptance of another."*
>
> —Barbara Brown Taylor

What is a God-shaped vision of reality? The answer demands more time and space than is allotted here, but for the sake of clarification, let me suggest several possibilities. A God-shaped vision sees, honors, and dignifies those whom society ignores, such as the undocumented, the widow, the orphan, the mentally ill, and the disabled. It names and exposes sin, whether in us or in others, for what it is—the "culpable disturbance of shalom"—and seeks to advance God's vision for shalom in the world through Christ followers who act justly, love mercy, and walk humbly with God (Mic. 6:8).[45] It confronts the idols that we worship individually and corporately by demanding that we choose the God who has made us over the gods we have made for ourselves. It longs for human beings, especially the least, the lonely, and the lost, to experience restored and reconciled relationships with God and with others. It takes our most cherished markers of identity and does *not* ask us to erase them—thanks be to God—but *does* ask us to reorient and reframe them in such a way that Christ can occupy the central place. It prays what the Lord Jesus asked the disciples to pray: "your kingdom come, your will be done, on earth as it is in heaven" (Matt. 6:10).

---

43. B. Taylor, *Preaching Life*, 42 (emphasis in original). See also James D. Whitehead's definition: "Faith is the enduring ability to imagine life in a certain way." "Religious Imagination," cited in B. Taylor, *Preaching Life*, 42.

44. Vanhoozer, "In Bright Shadow," 97.

45. Cornelius Plantinga defines sin as the "culpable disturbance of shalom—that is, culpable in the eyes of God." *Not the Way It's Supposed to Be*, 18. According to Kenyatta Gilbert, the job of preachers is to "name reality in a tone-deaf culture." To elaborate on what he means, Gilbert writes, "To name reality is to identify root causes of injustice, concretely pointing out places where society's most vulnerable populations are caught in the crosswinds of greed, violence, and abuses of power." *Exodus Preaching*, 67.

Expand Our Prophetic Imagination

Prophetic imagination functions in much the same way as theological imagination in that it names the way things really are in Christ, but it also adds another important layer to the Christian account of reality: it envisions God's future invading our present. Preachers with prophetic imagination *invite listeners to embrace the future hope that the God of creation is also the God of new creation.* Biblical faith requires eschatological vision. Here is how Barbara Brown Taylor puts it in *The Preaching Life*: "In faith, we imagine ourselves whole, imagine ourselves in love with our neighbors, imagine ourselves bathed and fed by God, imagine the creation at peace, imagine the breath of God coinciding with our own, imagine the heart of God beating at the heart of the world."[46]

Think about Job. It took a strong theological imagination to say in the midst of suffering, "I know that my redeemer lives." But it also took a strong *prophetic* imagination to believe "in the end he will stand on the earth. And after my skin has been destroyed, yet in my flesh I will see God" (Job 19:25–26). Job believed in a future that would invade the now, but he also lived as if the light had already dawned. In a sense, he performed God's hopeful future in the pain-filled present. Prophetic imagination insists that the new creation has somehow invaded the present even and especially in the midst of desperate situations.

In its ideal form, prophetic preaching does not consist of moralistic bromides against the culture or social action preaching of the sort that weighs people down with heavy loads impossible for them to carry. A more expansive and hope-filled vision is required. According to Old Testament scholar Walter Brueggemann, those who preach with prophetic imagination dare to make the faith-filled assertion that God's light has dawned on painful and sometimes impossible circumstances. Brueggemann describes prophetic imagination in preaching as "the enactment of hope in contexts of loss. It is the declaration that God can enact a *novum* in our very midst, even when we judge that to be impossible."[47]

Consider Nelson Mandela, who survived twenty-seven years of imprisonment, eighteen of which were spent on Robben Island. I mentioned Mandela in chapter 2 when we discussed the practice of conviction. The government in South Africa sent him to prison in 1964 because of his antiapartheid activism. At Robben Island, especially in the early years, the guards subjected Mandela and his colleagues to cruel and inhuman treatment: small prison cells, slop

46. B. Taylor, *Preaching Life*, 50.
47. Brueggemann, *Practice of Prophetic Imagination*, 110.

buckets, work crushing rocks in the quarry, nothing to read, and several trips to solitary confinement. Yet Mandela refused to see the guards in the same way that they saw him. Even when it looked like no changes were imminent, he acted like the changes had come. He treated everyone around him as if they were already living in the new South Africa.[48] That is prophetic imagination.

Expand Our Pastoral Imagination

We preach not to a generic group of any people but to a particular group of people at a particular point in time. According to 1 John 3:1, preachers and listeners alike are children of God *right now* (not in the distant future) because of God's love for us in Christ. Yet the next verse reminds us of the reason for maintaining a healthy pastoral imagination: "Dear friends, now we are children of God, and what we will be has not yet been made known. But we know that when Christ appears, we shall be like him, for we shall see him as he is" (1 John 3:2). Notice especially the phrase "what we will be has not yet been made known." How do preachers engage their pastoral imagination? *Remember that your listeners are always more than they appear to be.* They are children of God right now, and what they will be has not yet been made known.

Peggy Fullman mentored me when I was a teenager. She served as the pastor of Christian education at my home church, and she used to sit on ordination councils for our denomination. After I answered a call to pastoral ministry at the age of eighteen, I would ask her questions about church ministry whenever I came home from college on break. One time, our conversation shifted to the work she did on ordination councils. Whenever the council met with a prospective candidate for ordination, the committee would meet on the second floor of the denominational office. When it was her turn, she would ask every candidate the same question. She would ask the person to look out the window to the people passing one another on the sidewalks below, and she would say, "What do you see?" Then she would tell me, "Their answer to that question always told me how fruitful they would be in pastoral ministry. If they said things like, 'These are people made in the image of God,' or 'people whom God loves,' or 'people for whom Christ died,' then they would be fine. If their answers were more abstract, distanced, or detached, that's when I would need to follow up with more probing questions."

No doubt it is difficult for preachers to see people that way all the time—the way God sees them—especially when it comes to people for whom extra grace

48. Katongole and Rice, *Reconciling All Things*, 97.

is required. However, pastors *have* to believe that God is doing much more than is within their capacity to see. Long-term pastoral ministry demands a rich pastoral imagination for the people to whom we minister. Otherwise, disillusionment or discouragement sets in and blurs our ability to see people through the eyes of faith.

Obstacles to Practicing Creativity in Preaching

Imagine for a moment that you are riding on a bike path. You want to find the right speed, get where you want to go, and enjoy yourself, all at the same time. If the ride goes well, you will not have to *think* about accomplishing any of these things. You will experience what creativity researcher Mihaly Csikszentmihalyi refers to as "flow," or the ability to concentrate on an activity and absorb oneself completely in it in such a way that it is effortless and unobstructed.[49] Now imagine that the bike path is difficult. It requires great effort and is filled with lots of obstacles. It seems like every other mile consists of jagged rocks, slippery surfaces, low-hanging branches, or downed trees that require getting off your bike at various points. As you ride, the last thing you feel is flow. The obstacles prevent you from having an ideal experience.

In a similar way, various obstacles exist in preaching that prevent us from experiencing flow.

Perceived Lack of Creativity

First, preachers psychologically impede themselves from being creative when they repeat the common refrain "But I'm not creative." Many preachers say it for the same reason that others do: they believe creativity is a specialized field reserved for artistic personalities, or they associate creativity with music, painting, dance, or storytelling. They will never be as creative as true artists, they say. Of course, it is good medicine to admit that we will probably never sing like Mahalia Jackson, paint like Joan Miró, dance like Mikhail Baryshnikov, or write like Isabel Allende. I could try to sound like Charlie Parker, but I will never be able to change jazz music the way that he did. The world should acknowledge and celebrate boundary-spanning, generationally transcending artists, and it should distinguish between history-shaping art and everyday art. However, cultural adulation and historical recognition are not prerequisites for creativity, especially if you believe that you are made in the image of God. Can a preacher reconcile the phrase "But I'm not creative"

49. See Csikszentmihalyi, *Flow*.

with the God-given capacity granted at creation to form and shape (*yetser*) the world? Human beings form and shape all the time, even if they do not realize they are doing it. Everyday creativity is still creativity, even if acclaim does not result from it. Perhaps the phrase "But I'm not creative" comes from being socialized into the lone genius myth and its overemphasis on the exceptional, individualistic, unstable, and culture-challenging work of social misfits. Preachers more than most people should know how much forming and shaping they do. They constantly create.

We cannot reach our threshold of creativity in preaching and achieve the flow we desire if we do not first believe that we possess *some* measure of creative potential and even capacity. Granted, it might not look the same as the artistic creativity celebrated in the larger society, but it is still creativity. Creative potential does not come from the privileged dispensation of experts. Everyone has creative potential. As British educator and researcher Ken Robinson reminds us, "Everyone has huge creative capacities as a natural result of being a human being. The challenge is to develop them." Robinson compares it to a scenario in which someone says they cannot read or write. You do not assume that they lack the capability; you assume that they never learned and that no one taught them. "It is the same with creativity," he writes. "When people say to me they are not creative, I assume they just haven't yet learnt what is involved."[50]

Perceived Lack of Faithfulness to the Text

The second obstacle on the bike path is another common and oft-repeated refrain: "But creative preachers are not faithful preachers." Many preachers worry that they will somehow wander from the responsibility they have to be faithful to the biblical text(s) that they preach and the gospel that they steward. For this reason (and others), too many preachers fear the imagination. When backed into a corner, they stick with logical deduction and proposition over imagination and creativity. These anxieties are difficult to overcome, and they are not new worries. Remember Plato's suspicion of the imagination and his disdain for artists? He believed that imagination was deceptive and that reason always triumphed. Appeals to reason led to the true and the real. Appeals to the imagination led to imitations of the true and illusions of the real. Some translations of the Bible, perhaps influenced by Platonic views, made a negative view of the imagination more plausible.

---

50. K. Robinson, *Out of Our Minds*, 4. See also Runco, who demystifies the lone genius myth when he writes, "Who is creative? Everyone. Everyone is creative." "Everyone Has Creative Potential," 22.

For instance, the King James Version described the imagination of the human heart as evil (Gen. 6:5; 8:21) and those who rejected their Creator as "vain in their imaginations"[51] (Rom. 1:21).

One reason many preachers place reason and imagination in opposition to each other arises from a false dichotomy as old as the ancient Greek philosophers. This dichotomy says that reason always brings us to the home of truth whereas imagination brings us near the neighborhood of truth when it is at its best and to the wrong neighborhood of "vain imaginings" at its worst. But remember that the misuse of creativity does not justify its abandonment. Systematic theologian Kevin Vanhoozer points out that, while there will always be "vain imaginings" of one kind or another, "this no more disqualifies the imagination from serving theology than the existence of logical fallacies disqualifies reason."[52] One does not have to choose between biblical faithfulness and creativity in preaching, between reason and imagination. Why not opt for a healthy diet of both? Listeners need both, and so do preachers. Imagination allows us to "feel as true what reason treats only as abstractions."[53] When we maintain a holistic understanding of the imagination, writes Vanhoozer, we "do more justice to the image of God in humanity and to the nature of Scripture itself."[54]

Chronic Distraction

The third obstacle to creativity in preaching is *chronic distraction*—in particular, distraction through media designed to entertain us and keep us from boredom. Without a doubt, hyper-connection (i.e., constant connectivity to social media, mobile phones, email, and internet) brings many benefits with it such as virtual friendships, the ability to collapse time and space barriers, and the democratization of information, just to name a few. I reap these benefits and give thanks for them. But hyper-connection also has a shadow side. At its worst, it compels constant attention, inhibits deep thought, feeds anxiety, and nurtures a constant thirst for entertainment.[55] A hyper-connected

51. I owe this insight on the King James Version's use of the word "imagination" to Vanhoozer, "Imagination in Theology," 441. The Authorized Standard Version and Revised Standard Version use the word "imagination(s)" in Genesis 6:5 and 8:21. The Amplified Version uses the word "imagination" in Genesis 6:5.
52. Vanhoozer, "Imagination in Theology," 442.
53. Vanhoozer, "In Bright Shadow," 95.
54. Vanhoozer, "Imagination in Theology," 443.
55. Drawing from recent research by communication scholars, homiletician Jeffrey D. Arthurs claims that we are living in an "a-literate" society that has lost the capacity to read and write. More people than ever process information in small chunks and through sound bites, as

society excels at processing information, attaining efficiency, and achieving new technological milestones, but quite often lags behind at seeking wisdom, practicing community, and pursuing creativity. The point here is not to sound like a Luddite but to add the costs to the benefits. In *The Four Quartets*, originally published in 1943, T. S. Eliot describes human beings as "distracted from distraction by distraction"—and that was more than seventy-five years ago.[56] Distraction is not a new problem. But is the problem worse or better than it was in 1943? Human beings have an inbuilt desire to distract themselves from themselves. Hyper-connection takes that inbuilt desire and exponentially increases opportunities for it to proliferate.

So what does constantly being "on" have to do with creativity? While hyper-connection *does* foster creativity through tools, access, and collaboration, it can also impede and even kill creativity through the chronic distraction it facilitates. For instance, when was the last time you were truly bored? How can you think, pray, ponder, daydream, brainstorm, meditate, or people watch if you never look up from a screen? It is so much faster, easier, and more entertaining *not* to do those things. The absence of boredom from a preacher's life through constant connection slowly empties his or her reservoir of creative potential.[57]

A growing body of research observes the significant connections between the experience of boredom and the process/performance of creativity.[58] Several researchers point out that the "daydreaming" that often arises from boredom produces a "propitious mental state for creativity, insight and problem solving" and that "truly novel solutions and ideas emerge" from a human brain with enough space and time to think, create, and wonder.[59] Think about the connection between the two for a moment, especially for children. On a winter day, with nothing to do, young children turn a pile of snow into a snow fort. On a rainy day, a set of dining room chairs transforms into a train, or a couple of laundry baskets become a school bus. On a summer day, a pile of sticks and rocks change into the materials for a project, or a mound of sand

---

opposed to following complex arguments as one might find in a lengthy speech, a book, or an essay. See Arthurs, *Preaching with Variety*, 29–37.

56. See Book 1, "Burnt Norton," III.1.101, in Eliot, *Four Quartets*, 17.

57. In 1985, Neil Postman predicted that our society was becoming too addicted to self-entertainment: "Our politics, religion, news, athletics, education, and commerce have been transformed into congenial adjuncts of show business, largely without protest or even much popular notice. The result is that we are a people on the verge of amusing ourselves to death." *Amusing Ourselves to Death*, 3–4.

58. See Mann and Cadman, "Does Being Bored Makes Us More Creative?"; Smallwood and Schooler, "Restless Mind"; Toohey, *Boredom*.

59. Begley et al., "Will the Blackberry Sink the Presidency?," 36.

becomes an opportunity to spend a few hours building a sandcastle. Boredom *increases* the possibilities for creativity when a person is not chronically distracted because it sparks invention, encourages experimentation, and feeds the imagination. If you want to cultivate creativity in preaching, find a way to liberate yourself from distraction.

Environmental Obstacles

The fourth obstacle to creativity is *environment*. Like so many other things in life, creativity flourishes best in the right ecosystem under the right conditions. According to Teresa M. Amabile, a social psychologist at Harvard University, "largely because they affect motivation, social factors can have a powerful impact on creativity."[60] She tells the story of Albert Einstein, whose interest in physics was almost completely destroyed during his adolescent years when he attended a school in Munich, Germany, known for its strict, controlled, authoritarian approach. He shrank under the constant pressure of exams and the overbearing methods modeled by his teachers. He almost completely lost his love for learning. Einstein writes, "This coercion had such a deterring effect upon me that, after I passed the final examination, I found the consideration of any scientific problems distasteful to me for an entire year."[61] He tried transferring to a Polytechnic Institute in Zurich when he was fifteen but failed the entrance exam. When he was finally able to enroll in a "Swiss school for remedial coursework," it turned out to be one of the best things that ever happened to him. The school was "humanistic in orientation" and emphasized the "individual's unencumbered search for knowledge." The teachers also related to the students in a different way: "little emphasis on memorization, much emphasis on individual laboratory work, and a concentration on the development of relaxed, democratic exchanges between students and teachers."[62] Einstein was equally smart at both schools. The difference was environment. In one ecosystem, his gifts withered and almost died; in the other ecosystem, his gifts thrived and flourished. In fact, in the Swiss remedial school, Einstein conducted the first *Gedankenexperiment* that would eventually lead him to the theory of relativity later in his life.[63] To use

60. Amabile, *Creativity in Context*, 3.
61. As cited in Amabile, *Creativity in Context*, 7.
62. Amabile, *Creativity in Context*, 7.
63. In his book *Roots of Things*, Grometstein defines a *Gedankenexperiment* ("thought experiment") as one that "can be thought through without using equipment such as test tubes, voltmeters, flywheels, etc., and which may lead to insights into the nature of things" (82). For the use of this word in the story about Einstein's childhood schooling, see Amabile, *Creativity in Context*, 7.

Amabile's language, "social factors" had a powerful impact on Einstein's creativity because of the impact they had on his level of motivation.

What environmental obstacles prevent creativity in our preaching? We have already considered chronic distraction. Think through which environments are least conducive to focus, flow, and freedom. Amabile lays out nine environmental obstacles to creativity, most of which are relevant to business settings instead of churches—she teaches at the Harvard Business School. I will mention just three obstacles, because they seem to be the ones most relevant to preaching ministry:

1. *Constraint* is a "lack of freedom in deciding what to do or how to accomplish the task; a lack of a sense of control."[64] You might struggle to practice creativity if you feel like you have little to no creative control or autonomy over the sermon. Perhaps you feel that you cannot be yourself, that you have to sound like your former teachers or mentors, or that you have to conform to a style that is wholly different from your personality. Certain constraints can be good in preaching, but too many constraints, whether self-imposed or imposed by others, stifle rather than empower.

2. *Time pressure* is another inhibitor. By this, Amabile means "insufficient time to think creatively about a problem, too great a workload within a realistic time frame, high frequency of 'fire fighting.'"[65] Many preachers can relate to the idea of being time poor, having too great a workload, suffering under the tyranny of the immediate, and engaging in the constant firefighting that happens in ministry. That stated, the odds go way down that your sermons will be creative if you do not budget sufficient time to think creatively. There is a noticeable difference between food cooked in a slow cooker and food cooked in a microwave. Creative sermons come to you because you have cooked them in a slow cooker. Give yourself sufficient time to prepare your heart and soul and to feed your imagination when you write sermons. If you want to be more creative, resist the urge to write "Saturday night specials."

3. *Overemphasis on the status quo* is the "reluctance of managers or coworkers to change their way of doing things; an unwillingness to take risks."[66] Creative preachers push themselves to break free from the status quo through risk-taking. Does every outline look the same no matter what the text or genre of Scripture? Does every sermon sound like it is about the

64. Amabile, *Creativity in Context*, 232.
65. Amabile, *Creativity in Context*, 232.
66. Amabile, *Creativity in Context*, 232.

same subject: prayer, spiritual warfare, or social justice? Preachers cannot become more creative if they refuse to challenge their comfort levels, if they always insist on their normal way of doing things, if they never take risks in preaching or never experiment with new ways of preaching.

What environmental obstacles exist in your preaching? Is it one of these three inhibitors, chronic distraction, or something else? In general, preachers do a better job of interrogating the spiritual, psychological, and intellectual inhibitors but do not spend enough time interrogating the environmental inhibitors. Remember the bike path? In order to achieve creative flow, take a proactive approach to removing the obstacles that prevent it.

Some Ideas for Cultivating Creativity in Preaching

Now we will consider some ideas to catalyze creativity in preaching. What is the easiest and fastest recommendation? Just do the opposite of the obstacles mentioned above. In other words, believe you are creative, avoid the false dichotomy between faithfulness and imagination, steer clear of chronic distraction, and interrogate environmental inhibitors. Without a doubt, following these recommendations will help, but focusing on what to avoid instead of what to pursue can also be limiting. The opposite of bad is usually not-bad rather than excellent, so we need more guidance. Here are several ideas for how to cultivate creativity in preaching.

Seek Out Diverse Voices and Perspectives

According to Ken Robinson, "Creativity thrives on diversity."[67] The most creative individuals and teams bring together "people who think differently, who may be of different ages and genders, and with different cultural backgrounds and professional experiences."[68] When it comes to preaching, do you read, listen to, or bounce ideas off people who look just like you and believe the exact same things as you, or do you expose yourself to diverse voices and perspectives? This does not mean that a preacher has to know eighteen major (and divergent) interpretations of a given passage of Scripture or solicit half a dozen perspectives from the congregation for every sermon. Most pastors are too busy to do that monthly, let alone weekly. Instead, the aim should be to engage diverse perspectives as we are able through what we read, the people

---

67. K. Robinson, *Out of Our Minds*, 231.
68. K. Robinson, *Out of Our Minds*, 233.

we talk to, how we prepare our sermons, and who we mention and do not mention in our sermons. If the only people we talk to, listen to, or read look just like us, then we have stunted our capacity to be creative. Joel C. Gregory recommends reading widely and deeply in a variety of disciplines from a variety of perspectives. He writes, "Creativity begets creativity. There may be some credence to the 'Mozart Effect.' Preachers who regularly expose themselves to other creative circles may find themselves thinking creatively."[69] In addition to engaging diverse perspectives through your reading, build friendships with pastors and laypeople from diverse backgrounds.

Collaborate Instead of Isolate

Present your sermon ideas to others with the expectation that their feedback will help a bad idea become a good idea or a good idea become a great idea. Collaboration in community enhances the potential for creativity, whereas detachment in isolation suppresses creativity.

The animation company I mentioned in my chapter on clarity—Pixar—has produced hit movies for decades. Part of its success is due to the emphasis placed on collaborative work. Those who work there believe that every good movie has the potential to become a great movie when a team of people exercises creativity in a strategically collaborative environment. Even if the idea is good, it can always be better. In fact, collaboration almost always makes it better. As a result, Pixar has adopted this motto: *Elixius non dilitus,* or "Alone no longer." Creativity does not arise from geniuses working in isolation but in communities transforming good ideas into great ideas.

If you are a solo pastor, try meeting with another pastor to talk about your preaching. If you are on a pastoral staff, consider studying biblical texts in community and exposing yourself to what others see. Also try presenting the gist of your sermon to a smaller group before you preach it to the whole church. Invite feed-forward and feedback from members of the congregation, people who are not preachers, as a way to hear and see things through their eyes and ears. Test your ideas with friends or family members who are interested and invested in your growth. Creativity quotients rise when collaborative ideas emerge in community.

Recover Some Childlike Creativity

Sometimes when I teach students about creativity in preaching, I hand them blank sheets of paper and some pencils or crayons and then ask them to spend

---

69. Gregory, "Measuring a Preacher's Creativity," 40.

several minutes drawing a sketch of a butterfly. Almost every class has one student who is skillful at drawing, so there is almost always one excellent sketch. To be candid, most of the drawings are terrible, and the students know it. After they share their drawings with the rest of the class, I show them a picture of a butterfly that my daughter drew when she was six years old (see fig. 6.4).

My daughter is a good artist, but her drawing abilities as a six-year-old should probably not be better than those of undergraduates or seminarians. After the students participate in this learning activity, their two most common responses are, "What is wrong with me?" and, "What happened to me?" They find it difficult to wrap their minds around the fact that much of their childlike creativity has eroded now that they are adults. Keith Johnstone, an improvisational artist and director, makes a similar observation. "Most people lose their talent at puberty," Johnstone writes. "I lost mine in my early twenties. I began to think of children not as immature adults, but of adults as atrophied children."[70] Elsewhere in the same book, Johnstone claims that "most children can operate in a creative way until they're eleven or twelve, when suddenly they lose their spontaneity, and produce imitations of 'adult art.'"[71]

What would it look like to recover some childlike creativity? Some preachers choose to journal as a way to capture their thoughts, express their emotions, and engage their imaginations. Others create through music, painting, drawing, or craftsmanship simply for the sheer joy of creating. It is a source of input rather than output for them. Others read short stories or poetry. Still others engage in imaginative play with their children. Especially when my kids were younger, in addition to reading well-known children's books, I would make up stories right before they went to bed.

Engage the Senses through Images and Visuals

When was the last time you used an image or a visual in a sermon? Besides helping those who are visual learners, visuals and images engage more than one of the senses. If you want to share a quote from a poet like Maya Angelou or an activist like Bartholomé de las Casas, why not offer your listeners an image of the person? Think of all the images in Scripture: sheep, shepherds, mustard seeds, fig trees, the Sea of Galilee, the Dead Sea, the Jordan River, the trees of Lebanon, pomegranates. Examples abound. Who ever said that preachers could not show these images to those who listen to their sermons? Also consider using visuals as object lessons. An image does not *have to* appear

70. Johnstone, *Impro*, 25.
71. Johnstone, *Impro*, 77.

Figure 6.4. Butterfly Sketched by My Daughter at Age Six

on a screen, especially if your church does not use projectors and screens. You can use a visual that you hold in your hand or that stands next to you.

Observe Daily Lived Experience (La Vida Cotidiana)[72]

Too many preachers know how to study books, but they do not know how to study people.[73] When was the last time you people watched? Before mobile

72. *Lo cotidiano* and *la vida cotidiana* are terms that many Latinx theologians use to describe "daily lived experience" for Latinx Christians. For instance, the Catholic *mujerista* theologian Ada María Isasi-Díaz writes, "It is in the lived experience of the everyday life of *lo cotidiano* [daily lived experience] that we relate to God, that we come to know who God is and what God is like." *La Lucha Continues*, 51. Elsewhere, Isasi-Díaz writes, "In *mujerista* theology *lo cotidiano* has made it possible to appeal to the daily-lived experience of Latinas as an authentic source without ignoring social location. On the contrary, *lo cotidiano* makes social location explicit, for it is the context of the person in relation to physical space, ethnic space, social space." "Mujerista Theology," 244. See also Nanko-Fernández, *Theologizing en Espanglish*, 2–3.

73. Osvaldo Mottesi argues that preachers develop better sermons through "our observation of daily lived experience" ("nuestra observación de la vida cotidiana,"). He writes, "If we have developed the capacity to reflect biblically and theologically on human realities, which is a basic requirement for preaching, that which occurs in our immediate or distant surroundings will be excellent for explaining, illustrating, or showing the truths or aspects of our theme." Here is the quote in Spanish: "Si hemos desarrollado la capacidad de reflexionar bíblica y teológicamente

phones and tablets, people used to have nothing better to do at shopping malls, in public parks, or at airports. Some people still do it, but it is a lost art. Find a place indoors or outdoors where you can people watch. What do you notice about them? What makes them different from other people around them? What do they share in common with those around them? Find ways to relate what you see back to the sermon.

Walk Your Way to Creativity

I know several preachers who walk, jog, or ride a bike as a way to generate new ideas or transform good ideas into better ideas. Although it may be difficult to find the time if you are a busy, full-time pastor, bi-vocational, have young kids, or minister in a place where outdoor activity is difficult some parts of the year because of bad weather, it is still critical that you create time and space to think. Rebecca Solnit observes, "Walking allows us to be in our bodies and in the world without being made busy by them. It leaves us free to think without being wholly lost in our thoughts."[74] The temptation is to believe that you will be less productive if you schedule time like this into your daily routine. Why walk (or exercise another way) when you can work? But what if the real thief of productivity is *not* the time wasted through activities like walking? What if the real thief is the absence of time to think?

In the 1950s, Princeton University professor and physicist Albert Einstein walked around town so much that he became a local celebrity. The nineteenth-century Russian composer Pyotr Ilyich Tchaikovsky went on a two-hour walk every day after lunch regardless of the weather. The nineteenth-century British author Charles Dickens wrote an average of two thousand words per day and wound up writing fifteen novels, yet he still went on a daily three-hour walk at 2:00 p.m. around the countryside and through the streets of London. The nineteenth-century Danish philosopher and preacher Søren Kierkegaard lived each day "dominated by two pursuits: writing and walking. Typically, he wrote in the morning, set off on a long walk through Copenhagen at noon, and then returned to his writing for the rest of the day and into the evening. The walks were where he had his best ideas."[75] One does not have to choose productivity over time to think. The two can go together.

---

sobre las realidades humanas, lo cual es requisito básico para la predicación, lo que ocurre a nuestro derredor inmediato o lejano será material excelente para explicar, ilustrar, o demostrar las verdades o aspectos de nuestro tema." *Predicación y Misión*, 230.

74. Solnit, *Wanderlust*, 5.

75. Currey, *Daily Rituals*, is my source for the Einstein (pp. 196–97), Tchaikovsky (pp. 171–73), Dickens (pp. 160–62), and Kierkegaard (p. 19) references.

Produce from Your Thinking Instead of Thinking without Producing

Creative thinking without creative action leads to creative impotence. Much like the myth mentioned earlier that carving out time to think somehow leads to less productivity, another creativity myth that needs to be refuted is that quality of work and quantity of work do not overlap. Most of the time, creative thinking and creative processing correspond to creative production.

In what is now considered a classic study, psychologist Dean K. Simonton studied the lives and music of ten famous classical composers (Bach, Beethoven, Mozart, Haydn, Brahms, Handel, Debussy, Schubert, Wagner, and Chopin) and was able to demonstrate a connection between quality of work and quantity of work. He looked at five-year segments of each composer's musical compositions and made the following discovery: "The composers who wrote the most music also wrote the best music (with *best* being defined as most-cited and discussed across 15 different reference works). The most fertile time periods in terms of production were also marked by the best work. . . . Two-time Nobel Prize winner Linus Pauling may have sensed this phenomenon, once saying, 'The best way to get a good idea is to get a lot of ideas.'"[76]

When we apply this insight to preaching, we see the connection between quality and quantity. A preacher should practice creativity in higher *quantity* in order to practice creativity of higher *quality*. Growth in imagination most often arises from growth in creative production.

As you implement some of these ideas as well as ideas that you generate on your own, remember that the goal is to cultivate creativity over time rather than achieve excellence right away. Remember the four commitments that Ericsson sets forth as constitutive of deliberate practice and apply them to growth in creativity: well-defined and specific goals, focused attention, a consistent feedback loop, and a willingness to get out of one's comfort zone.

Creativity in preaching is more like a marathon than a four-hundred-meter dash. On an Olympic-size track, a competitive runner runs one lap in order to run four hundred meters. If the same runner wants to run a marathon, he or she runs 105½ laps to complete the race. To get better at this practice, you must train for and race 105½ laps instead of one lap. Creativity takes a long time to develop.

Some psychologists of creativity like to refer to the "ten-year rule" whenever they talk about creative leaders who end up being influential in their field. According to James C. Kaufman, excellence "requires a tremendous amount of knowledge and practice. On average, this process requires approximately

---

76. Cited in Kaufman, *Creativity 101*, 44. For Simonton's study, see Simonton, "Creativity, Productivity, Age, and Stress."

10 years from beginning to enter a field to making any kind of substantial contribution."[77] Kaufman argues that it takes an *additional* ten years to move from good to great in one's field: "Just as there is evidence that creators take 10 years from the time they put the pen to the paper, there may also be evidence that another 10 years pass before a truly elite work is produced."[78] Do not be surprised if it takes a long time to become more creative than you are now. Focus on small wins over time as opposed to exponential change right now.

Conclusion

As we conclude this chapter, we return to a Washington, DC, subway and to Gene Weingarten and Joshua Bell's social experiment. It produced a surprising result that neither participant anticipated. The purpose of the experiment, Weingarten wrote, was to conduct an "experiment in context, perception and priorities—as well as an unblinking assessment of public taste: In a banal setting at an inconvenient time, would beauty transcend?" Weingarten and Bell expected much higher response rates than they received, which interested them but was not the unanticipated surprise they discovered as a result of conducting the experiment. While there were no ethnic, racial, or gender differences to distinguish the people who stopped from those who continued walking, Weingarten noticed one group in particular that stopped more than any other: "Every single time a child walked past, he or she tried to stop and watch. And every single time, a parent scooted the kid away."[79]

Why were children more tuned in to beautiful music than adults? Perhaps it was because young children focus more on being rather than doing. The clock and the schedule do not hold them captive in the same way they do adults. Perhaps, unlike their parents, they did not have to worry much about how to stay safe, how to get through a crowd of people, how to stay together, or how to get on the right train at the right time. Presumably, these factors all played a part in their response. But what if the children could hear the music for a different reason? Unlike their parents, they had not yet lost their sense of wonder or drained their reservoir of imaginative potential. As Ken

---

77. Kaufman, *Creativity 101*, 56.
78. Kaufman, *Creativity 101*, 58. Angela Duckworth writes, "The dancer Martha Graham declared, 'It takes about ten years to make a mature dancer.' More than a century ago, psychologists studying telegraph operators observed that reaching complete fluency in Morse code was rare because of the 'many years of hard apprenticeship' required. How many years? Our evidence, the researchers concluded, 'is that it requires ten years to make a thoroughly seasoned press dispatcher.'" *Grit*, 119.
79. Weingarten, "Pearls Before Breakfast."

Robinson puts it, "We don't grow *into* creativity. We grow *out* of it. Often, we are educated out of it."[80] Pablo Picasso once commented that all children are born artists. The problem is that they grow up and lose what once came naturally to them.[81]

What if preachers do not need to acquire creativity but rather need to regain the creativity they once possessed? What if in all of our busyness, over-scheduling, and chronic distraction, we have suppressed an instinct that should come naturally to us, especially as divine image-bearers? In our haste, what if we have forgotten to stop and listen to the music?

Learning activities and sermon samples for this chapter are located at www .PracticesofChristian Preaching.com.

---

80. K. Robinson, *Out of Our Minds*, 49 (emphasis in original).

81. Attributions abound, but the original quotation is undocumented. For one attribution, see K. Robinson, *Out of Our Minds*, 50.

Conclusion

Warren MacKenzie loved to make pots. MacKenzie began working in ceramics in his early twenties, when he enrolled for the first time in a ceramics program at the Art Institute in Chicago. He wanted a spot in the painting program, but it was wait-listed, so he tried ceramics. Until his death in late 2018 at the age of ninety-four, he lived in Stillwater, Minnesota, where he made pots in his home studio.[1]

In the early years, MacKenzie and his first wife, Alix, tried their hand at lots of different trades: "When you're young, you think you can do anything, and we thought, oh, we'll be potters, we'll be painters, we'll be textile designers, we'll be jewelers, we'll be a little of this, a little of that. We were going to be renaissance people."[2] After a while, they concluded that "doing one thing better and better might be more satisfying than staying an amateur at many different things." According to Mackenzie, "that [pottery] was where we felt our true interest lay."[3] It turns out they made a good decision. A medium-sized Warren MacKenzie–stamped water pitcher costs about $3,000. You can also buy less expensive pieces, but most of the preachers I know do not have an extra $450 lying around in their couch cushions for a ceramic teapot.

From the very beginning, MacKenzie believed that most of his pottery was not good enough for a gallery or a museum, but he never let this belief deter him from the regular habit of continuous creative production. Art enthusiasts enjoy quoting his now-popular statement: "The first 10,000

---

1. He moved there in 1953 with his first wife, Alix, to join the faculty at the University of Minnesota.
2. Quotation taken from MacKenzie's one-on-one interview with Duckworth in *Grit*, 43.
3. Duckworth, *Grit*, 43.

Figure C.1. Warren MacKenzie at the Leach Pottery (2013)

pots are difficult and then it gets a bit easier."[4] On a good day, MacKenzie sat at his Leach wheel and made about forty or fifty pots—"some of them are good and some of them are mediocre and some of them are bad." He thought that only a couple of pots were worth selling and, among those sold, just a few "engage the senses after daily use." In an interview, he explained that he did not want to be remembered as one of those master potters who produced just one or two pieces over a lifetime; he believed that quality, quantity, and usefulness are all connected. "I'm striving to make things which are the most exciting things I can make that will fit in people's homes," he said.[5] MacKenzie bears a striking resemblance to at least two other people:

4. Lauer, "Living with Pottery."
5. Duckworth, *Grit*, 43.

Figure C.2. Ray Allen

Ray Allen, an NBA basketball player, and Martha Graham, an American dancer and teacher.

Many in the basketball world agree that Allen (now retired) is one of the greatest three-point shooters of all time. When he was getting close to breaking the record for three-point shots, ESPN columnist Jackie MacMullin ran a story about his illustrious career and his quest to break the record.

In an interview with Allen, MacMullin told him that another basketball commentator complimented him for his "natural shot"—the commentator believed that he was "born with a shooting touch . . . an innate gift for three-pointers." Allen balked at the suggestion, telling MacMullin, "I've argued this with a lot of people in my life. When people say God blessed me with a beautiful jump shot, it really pisses me off. I tell those people, 'Don't undermine the work I put in every day.' Not some days. Every day. Ask anyone who has been on a team with me who shoots the most. Go back to Seattle and Milwaukee, and ask them. The answer is me."[6] MacMullin also contacted Allen's high school basketball coach for the story, and she discovered that Allen's shot was not any better than his teammates' when he first started playing—in fact, it was worse. Allen had turned a bad shot into a good shot and then into a great shot.

Martha Graham first excelled as a dancer. Then she transformed the American dance scene through pioneering work in choreography, creating the "Graham technique" for learning dance, mentoring scores of dancers and choreographers, and revitalizing dance around the world through her unparalleled expertise and contagious enthusiasm. She died in 1991, but many artists and academics still point to her unique contributions in her field and speak her name in hushed, reverential tones.

Graham never believed that dance comes easily to people, at least not the sort of dance that is truly great. In her essay "I Am a Dancer" she writes, "Dancing appears glamorous, easy, delightful. But the path to the paradise of achievement is not easier than any other. There is fatigue so great that the body cries, even in its sleep. There are times of complete frustration; there are daily small deaths. . . . It takes about ten years to make a mature dancer."[7]

Maturity in dance comes in two phases, she says. At the beginning, one must study the craft with such precision and relentlessness that "movement becomes clean, precise, eloquent, truthful."[8] Then a dancer must pursue the "cultivation of the being from which whatever you have to say comes."[9] True maturity, she argues, demands technical study and artistry, commitment and expression, setbacks and progress.

What do MacKenzie, Allen, and Graham have to do with preaching? The answer might surprise you. MacKenzie spent more than one hundred thousand hours sitting at his Leach wheel throwing tens of thousands of ceramic pots. Allen arrived early to the gym and stayed late over a long and distinguished NBA career. Graham danced, choreographed, and taught with such a high degree of excellence and commitment that the name "Martha Graham"

---

6. Cited in Ericsson and Pool, *Peak*, xviii–xix.
7. Graham, "I Am a Dancer," 95.
8. Graham, "I Am a Dancer," 95.
9. Graham, "I Am a Dancer," 96.

Figure C.3. Portrait of Martha Graham by Nickolas Muray in *Shadowland* (1922)

became synonymous with modern dance throughout the world. What binds them together is not that they were successful, though each of them became leaders in their respective fields; nor is it that they were born with such talent that their likes will never be seen again, though each person did have the right skills to do the right things at the right time in the right ways; it is not even that their art captivates experts and novices alike, though watching them do what they do best is indeed a privilege.

So then what does bind them all together? The answer leads us back to the primary claim of this book. If we want to use academic language, we could say that the common bond that unites them is their commitment to *deliberate*

Figure C.4. Charlie Parker Redux

practice, to return to K. Anders Ericsson's phrase.[10] All three of them ascribed to the four commitments that Ericsson lifts up as critical to expertise in performance: well-defined and specific goals, focused attention, a consistent feedback loop, and a willingness to get out of one's comfort zone. But if we prefer to use the language of the Reno Jazz Club in Kansas City, we could also say that all three of them spent a long time in the "woodshed"—just as Charlie Parker did. They honed and mastered their craft through practicing differently and not just practicing harder.

Those who spend time in the woodshed will learn, grow, and get better at preaching—maybe not perfectly overnight, but progressively over a lifetime. As I stated in the introduction, *preachers who cultivate life-giving preaching habits through deliberate practice will enhance their proficiency, grow in their commitment, and flourish in their homiletical ministry.* Along with Warren MacKenzie, many of us will need to make at least ten thousand pots before we show marked improvement. Those who have already made ten thousand pots would do well to remember that repetition without deliberateness usually leads to a level of automaticity and diminished returns rather than measurable improvement and continued growth—our task is never complete. It is

10. Ericsson and Pool, *Peak*, xxi–xxiii.

not at all sacrilegious to conceive of preaching this way especially if we bring to mind again some phrases that are easy to miss in the book of Romans: "If it is possible, as far as it depends on you . . ." (Rom. 12:18). Preachers who trust God with the *event* of preaching are also called to believe that God has entrusted them with agency in the *process* of preparing.

In this book, I have recommended five deliberate practices—conviction, contextualization, clarity, concreteness, and creativity—which are all undergirded by the resolute belief that our preaching should remain unambiguously Christian at its core. I have presented these as practices that preachers can cultivate over time in order to make their preaching more proficient, effective, and rewarding. We do not master a method; neither do we ever "arrive." Instead, we cultivate life-giving habits that will serve us now and in the future.

No doubt this book proposes a different way to get to where you are going than the typical roadmap you will find elsewhere. Most introduction to preaching books are method-focused, single author, monocultural, text-based, and monolingual whereas the book you have just read is consciously practice-centered, intentionally collaborative, strategically diverse, technologically interactive, and purposefully multilingual. It also encourages a commitment to a "growth mindset" rather than a "fixed mindset" in our preaching in terms of how we think about our own agency, development, and capacity to thrive in the humbling task to which God has called us.[11] I have structured it this way on account of my conviction that deliberate practice over time creates more space for growth than a particular method does, that creative ideas emerge through an encounter with a multiplicity of perspectives, that preachers get better not just through reading but also through hearing and seeing, that difference is an opportunity rather than a threat.

For those who are new to the preparation and delivery of sermons, an introductory homiletics book may feel a lot like a driver's education course. It helps you learn the rules, makes you aware of the dangers, and gives you some much-needed guidance. Then, after a short time together, it sends you on your way, even though much more could be said in addition to what has been presented to you. "Best wishes driving!" you are told as someone hands you the keys. Some preachers figure out how to drive right away; it comes easy to them. Others struggle for a while until they get the hang of it. No matter who is driving, no matter what their skill level, the fastest and best way to get better at driving is to drive deliberately. In much the same way, I have argued

11. For the language of "growth mindset" versus "fixed mindset," see Dweck, *Mindset*, 6–7. See also my more expansive explanation of these two terms in note 12 of the introduction to this book.

here that the fastest and best way for a preacher to get better at preaching is to preach deliberately.

Most jazz historians agree that Charlie Parker expressed little to no interest in organized religion; he probably would have balked at any association with preachers. But if someone told Parker that you were woodshedding your sermons, that you had committed yourself to the relentless pursuit of practice because you believed that preaching was worth all the hours and energy you could give to it, I wonder if you would have earned his respect. Perhaps he would have smiled and said, "Keep up the good work, a few extra hours in the woodshed never hurt anybody."

Bibliography

Abrams, M. H. *The Mirror and the Lamp: Romantic Theory and the Critical Tradition*. New York: Oxford University Press, 1953.

Abuhamdeh, Sami, and Mihaly Csikszentmihalyi. "The Artistic Personality: A Systems Perspective." In *Creativity: From Potential to Realization*, edited by Robert J. Sternberg, Elena Grigorenko, and Jerome L. Singer, 31–42. Washington, DC: American Psychological Association, 2004.

Adamopoulos, John, and Yoshihisa Kashima, eds. *Social Psychology and Cultural Context*. Thousand Oaks, CA: Sage Publications, 1999.

Adeleye, Femi B. *Preachers of a Different Gospel: A Pilgrim's Reflections on Contemporary Trends in Christianity*. Grand Rapids: Hippo Books, 2011.

Alcántara, Jared E. *Crossover Preaching: Improvisational-Intercultural Homiletics in Conversation with Gardner C. Taylor*. Downers Grove, IL: IVP Academic, 2015.

————. *Learning from a Legend: What Gardner C. Taylor Can Teach Us about Preaching*. Eugene, OR: Wipf & Stock, 2016.

Alexander, Michelle. *The New Jim Crow: Mass Incarceration in the Age of Colorblindness*. New York: New Press, 2012.

Allen, Ronald J. *Interpreting the Gospel: An Introduction to Preaching*. St. Louis: Chalice, 1998.

Amabile, Teresa M. *Creativity in Context*. Boulder, CO: Westview, 1996.

American Heritage Dictionary. New York: Houghton Mifflin Company, 2006.

"American Preaching: A Dying Art?" *Time*, December 31, 1979, 67.

Andrews, William, ed. *Sisters of the Spirit*. Bloomington: Indiana University Press, 1986.

Aristotle. *Poetics*. In *Aristotle: Poetics; Longinus: On the Sublime; Demetrius: On Style*, edited by Jeffery Henderson. Loeb Classical Library. Cambridge, MA: Harvard University Press, 1995.

———. *Problems.* In *The Works of Aristotle*, edited by W. D. Ross and J. A. Smith. Oxford: Clarendon Press, 1910.

Arnold, Thomas Kerchever. *Cornelius Nepos: With Answered Questions and Imitative Exercises.* New York: Appleton, 1867.

Arrastía, Cecilio. *Teoría y Práctica de la Predicación.* Miami: Editorial Caribe, 1992.

Arthurs, Jeffrey D. *Preaching as Reminding: Stirring Memory in an Age of Forgetfulness.* Downers Grove, IL: InterVarsity, 2017.

———. *Preaching with Variety: How to Re-Create the Dynamics of Biblical Genres.* Grand Rapids: Kregel, 2007.

Augustine. *On Christian Teaching.* New York: Oxford University Press, 2008.

Baer, John. *Domain Specificity of Creativity.* New York: Academic Press, 2016.

Baer, John, and James C. Kaufman. "Bridging Generality and Specificity: The Amusement Park Theoretical (APT) Model of Creativity." *Roeper Review* 27, no. 3 (Spring 2005): 158–63.

Bailey, Kenneth E. *Jesus through Middle Eastern Eyes: Cultural Studies in the Gospels.* Downers Grove, IL: InterVarsity, 2008.

———. *Paul through Mediterranean Eyes: Cultural Studies in 1 Corinthians.* Downers Grove, IL: IVP Academic, 2011.

Barth, Karl. *Church Dogmatics.* Vol. III, 4, *The Doctrine of Creation*, edited by G. W. Bromiley and Thomas F. Torrance. Peabody, MA: Hendrickson, 2010.

———. *Church Dogmatics.* Vol. IV, 3, *The Doctrine of Reconciliation*, edited by G. W. Bromiley and Thomas F. Torrance. Peabody, MA: Hendrickson, 2010.

Basil. *Saint Basil, The Letters.* Translated by Roy J. Deferrari. Vol. 1. Loeb Classical Library. New York: G. P. Putnam and Sons, 1926.

Bass, Diana Butler. *Christianity After Religion: The End of the Church and the Birth of a New Spiritual Awakening.* New York: HarperOne, 2012.

Baxter, Richard. *The Reformed Pastor.* Carlisle, PA: Banner of Truth, 1974.

Beghetto, Ronald A., and James C. Kaufman. "Toward a Broader Conception of Creativity: A Case for 'mini-c' Creativity." *Psychology of Aesthetics, Creativity, and the Arts* 1, no. 2 (2007): 73–79.

Begley, Sharon, Holly Bailey, Daniel Stone, and Jeneen Interlandi. "Will the Blackberry Sink the Presidency?" *Newsweek*, February 16, 2009, 36.

Benner, David G. *The Gift of Being Yourself.* Downers Grove, IL: InterVarsity, 2004.

Berliner, Paul. *Thinking in Jazz: The Infinite Art of Improvisation.* Chicago: University of Chicago Press, 1994.

Bevans, Stephen B. *Models of Contextual Theology.* Maryknoll, NY: Orbis, 2002.

Bonhoeffer, Dietrich. *Christ the Center.* New York: Harper & Row, 1966.

———. *The Cost of Discipleship.* New York: MacMillan, 1949.

———. *Letters and Papers from Prison.* Edited by Eberhard Bethge. New York: MacMillan, 1971.

———. *Life Together*. New York: Harper & Row, 1954.

Bonilla, Plutarco A. "Cecilio Arrastía: El Hombre, El Escritor, y El Predicador." *Revista Pastoralia* 9, no. 4 (1982): 6–35.

Boreham, F. W. *Pathway to Roses*. West Yorkshire, UK: Emerald Publishing House, 1997.

Bosch, David J. *Transforming Mission: Paradigm Shifts in Theology of Mission*. Maryknoll, NY: Orbis, 1991.

Bowler, Kate. *Blessed: A History of the American Prosperity Gospel*. New York: Oxford University Press, 2013.

Boyd, Gregory A. *The Myth of a Christian Nation: How the Quest for Political Power Is Destroying the Church*. Grand Rapids: Zondervan, 2005.

Brantley, Clarice, and Michele Miller. *Effective Communication for Colleges*. Mason, OH: Thomson-Southwestern, 2008.

Brekus, Catherine A. *Strangers and Pilgrims: Female Preaching in America, 1740–1845*. Chapel Hill: University of North Carolina Press, 1998.

Broadus, John. *A Treatise on the Preparation and Delivery of Sermons*. Philadelphia: Smith, English & Company, 1871.

Brown, Robert McAfee. *Gustavo Gutiérrez: An Introduction to Liberation Theology*. Maryknoll, NY: Orbis, 1990.

Brown, Sally A., and Luke A. Powery. *Ways of the Word: Learning to Preach for Your Time and Place*. Minneapolis: Fortress, 2016.

Brown, Teresa L. Fry. *Delivering the Sermon: Voice, Body, and Animation in Proclamation*. Minneapolis: Fortress, 2008.

Brueggemann, Walter. *The Practice of Prophetic Imagination: Preaching an Emancipatory Word*. Minneapolis: Fortress, 2012.

Brunner, Emil. *The Divine Imperative*. London: Lutterworth, 1937.

Buber, Martin. "The Good and Evil Imagination." In *Good and Evil*, translated by R. G. Smith, 93–97. New York: Scribner and Sons, 1952.

Buechner, Frederick. *Wishful Thinking: A Theological ABC*. New York: Harper & Row, 1973.

Burns, Bob, Tasha D. Chapman, and Donald C. Guthrie. *Resilient Ministry: What Pastors Told Us about Surviving and Thriving*. Downers Grove, IL: InterVarsity, 2013.

Cacioppo, John T., and William Patrick. *Loneliness: Human Nature and the Need for Social Connection*. New York: W. W. Norton, 2008.

Calvin, John. *The Institutes of Christian Religion*. Edited by John T. McNeill. Translated by Ford Lewis Battles. Vol. 1. Philadelphia: Westminster, 1960.

Carrington, Damien. "Da Vinci's Parachute Flies." BBC News, June 27, 2000. http://news.bbc.co.uk/2/hi/science/nature/808246.stm.

Chalmers, Thomas. *Sermons and Discourses*. Vol. 2. New York: Robert Carter, 1844.

Chapell, Bryan. *Christ-Centered Preaching: Redeeming the Expository Sermon*. Grand Rapids: Baker Academic, 2005.

Charles, H. B., Jr. *On Pastoring: A Short Guide to Living, Leading, and Ministering as a Pastor*. Chicago: Moody, 2016.

Clance, Pauline Rose. *Impostor Phenomenon*. Atlanta: Peachtree, 1985.

Coates, Ta-Nehisi. "The Black Family in the Age of Mass Incarceration." *The Atlantic*, October 2015. https://www.theatlantic.com/magazine/archive/2015/10/the-black-family-in-the-age-of-mass-incarceration/403246.

Collier-Thomas, Bettye. *Daughters of Thunder: Black Women Preachers and Their Sermons, 1850–1979*. San Francisco: Jossey-Bass, 1998.

Corrigan, Kevin. *Evagrius and Gregory: Mind, Soul, and Body in the 4th Century*. Burlington, VT: Ashgate, 2009.

Costas, Orlando E. *Christ outside the Gate: Mission beyond Christendom*. Eugene, OR: Wipf & Stock, 2005.

———. *Comunicación por Medio de la Predicación*. Miami: Editorial Caribe, 1973.

Covey, Stephen R. *The 8th Habit: From Effectiveness to Greatness*. New York: Free Press, 2004.

Craddock, Fred B. *Preaching*. Nashville: Abingdon, 1985.

Csikszentmihalyi, Mihaly. *Flow: The Psychology of Optimal Experience*. New York: Harper Perennial, 1991.

Currey, Mason. *Daily Rituals: How Artists Work*. New York: Alfred A. Knopf, 2013.

Davis, H. Grady. *Design for Preaching*. Philadelphia: Muhlenberg, 1958.

Dean, Kenda Creasy. *Almost Christian: What the Faith of Our Teenagers Is Telling the American Church*. New York: Oxford University Press, 2010.

DeBose, Charles E. "Codeswitching: Black English and Standard English in the African-American Linguistic Repertoire." *Journal of Multilingual and Multicultural Development* 13 (1992): 157–67.

Deissmann, Adolf. *The New Testament in Light of Modern Research*. Garden City, NY: Doubleday, Doran, & Co., 1929.

de Vet, Thérèse. "Context and the Emerging Story: Improvised Performance in Oral and Literate Societies." *Oral Tradition* 23, no. 1 (2008): 159–79.

Donne, John, and John Carey. *Selected Poetry*. New York: Oxford University Press, 1996.

Douglass, James W. *The Nonviolent Coming of God*. Eugene, OR: Wipf & Stock, 2006.

Douthat, Ross. *Bad Religion: How We Became a Nation of Heretics*. New York: Free Press, 2013.

Duarte, Nancy. *Resonate: Present Visual Stories That Transform Audiences*. Hoboken, NJ: John Wiley & Sons, 2010.

Duckworth, Angela. *Grit: The Power of Passion and Perseverance*. New York: Scribner, 2016.

Durso, Keith E. *Thy Will Be Done: A Biography of George W. Truett*. Macon, GA: Mercer University Press, 2009.

Dweck, Carol S. *Mindset: The New Psychology of Success*. New York: Ballantine Books, 2016.

Edwards, J. Kent. *Deep Preaching: Creating Sermons That Go beyond the Superficial*. Nashville: B&H Academic, 2010.

Edwards, Jonathan. *Jonathan Edwards' Resolutions and Advice to Young Converts*. Edited by Stephen J. Nichols. Phillipsburg, NJ: P&R, 2001.

———. *The Works of Jonathan Edwards: Religious Affections*. Edited by John E. Smith. Vol. 2. New Haven: Yale University Press, 1959.

Eliot, T. S. *Four Quartets*. New York: Harcourt, 1971.

Elliot, Elisabeth. *Shadow of the Almighty: The Life and Testament of Jim Elliot*. Peabody, MA: Hendrickson, 2008.

Emerson, Michael O., and Christian Smith. *Divided by Faith: Evangelical Religion and the Problem of Race in America*. New York: Oxford University Press, 2001.

Ericsson, K. Anders. "The Influence of Experience and Deliberate Practice on the Development of Superior Expert Performance." In *The Cambridge Handbook of Expertise and Expert Performance*, edited by K. Anders Ericsson, Neil Charness, Robert R. Hoffman, and Paul J. Feltovich, 685–705. New York: Cambridge University Press, 2006.

———, ed. *The Road to Excellence: The Acquisition of Expert Performance in the Arts and Sciences, Sports, and Games*. New York: Psychology Press, 2014.

Ericsson, Anders, and Robert Pool. *Peak: Secrets from the New Science of Expertise*. New York: Houghton Mifflin Harcourt, 2016.

Eslinger, Richard L. *A New Hearing: Living Options in Homiletic Method*. Nashville: Abingdon, 1987.

Fee, Gordon D. *Listening to the Spirit in the Text*. Grand Rapids: Eerdmans, 2000.

Flemming, Dean E. *Contextualization in the New Testament: Patterns for Theology and Mission*. Downers Grove, IL: InterVarsity, 2005.

Florence, Anna Carter. "The Preaching Imagination." In *Teaching Preaching as a Christian Practice: A New Approach to Homiletical Pedagogy*, edited by Thomas G. Long and Leonora Tubbs Tisdale, 116–33. Louisville: Westminster John Knox, 2008.

Forbes, James. *The Holy Spirit and Preaching*. Nashville: Abingdon, 1989.

Fordham, John. "A Teenage Charlie Parker Has a Cymbal Thrown at Him." *The Guardian*, June 16, 2011. https://www.theguardian.com/music/2011/jun/17/charlie-parker-cymbal-thrown.

Frye, Nancy Kettering. *An Uncommon Woman: The Life and Times of Sarah Righter Major*. Elgin, IL: Brethren Press, 1997.

Gibson, Scott M. "The Landscape of the Character of Preaching." Unpublished Papers of the Annual Meeting of the Evangelical Homiletics Society, 46–62. Chicago, IL, October 9–11, 2014.

Gilbert, Kenyatta R. *Exodus Preaching: Crafting Sermons about Justice and Hope.* Nashville: Abingdon, 2018.

———. *The Journey and Promise of African American Preaching.* Minneapolis: Fortress, 2011.

Gomes, Peter J. *The Scandalous Gospel of Jesus: What's So Good about the Good News?* New York: HarperOne, 2007.

Goodstein, Laurie. "Billy Graham, 99, Dies; Pastor Filled Stadiums and Counseled Presidents." *New York Times*, February 21, 2018. https://www.nytimes.com/2018/02/21/obituaries/billy-graham-dead.html.

Graham, Martha. "I Am a Dancer." In *The Routledge Dance Studies Reader*, edited by Alexandra Carter and Janet O'Shea, 95–100. New York: Routledge, 2010.

Graves, Mike. *The Fully Alive Preacher: Recovering from Homiletical Burnout.* Louisville: Westminster John Knox, 2006.

Greer, Peter, and Chris Horst. *Mission Drift: The Unspoken Crisis Facing Leaders, Charities, and Churches.* Bloomington, MN: Bethany House, 2014.

Gregory, Joel C. "Measuring a Preacher's Creativity with a Borrowed Ruler." In *Our Sufficiency Is of God: Essays on Preaching in Honor of Gardner C. Taylor*, edited by Timothy George, James Earl Massey, and Robert Smith Jr., 23–44. Macon, GA: Mercer University Press, 2010.

Griffiths, Thomas Sharp. *A History of Baptists in New Jersey.* Hightstown, NJ: Barr, 1904.

Grometstein, Alan A. *The Roots of Things: Topics in Quantum Mechanics.* New York: Springer Science & Business Media, 1999.

Guibert of Nogent. "How to Make a Sermon." In *Early Medieval Theology*, edited by George E. McCracken, 9:285–99. Philadelphia: Westminster, 1957.

Guilford, J. P. *Intelligence, Creativity, and Their Educational Implications.* San Diego: Robert R. Knapp, 1968.

Hamman, Jaco J. *Becoming a Pastor: Forming Self and Soul for Ministry.* Cleveland: Pilgrim, 2007.

Hammdon, Paul. *The Poems of John Dryden: Volume One: 1649–1681.* New York: Routledge, 2014.

Hartmann, Douglas, and Christopher Uggen, eds. *The Contexts Reader.* New York: W. W. Norton, 2012.

Hauser, Arnold. *The Social History of Art.* New York: Knopf, 1951.

Hayakawa, S. I. *Language in Thought and Action.* London: George Allen & Unwin, 1964.

Haywood, Chanta M. *Prophesying Daughters: Black Women Preachers and the Word, 1823–1913.* Columbia: University of Missouri Press, 2003.

Heath, Chip, and Dan Heath. *Made to Stick: Why Some Ideas Survive and Others Die.* New York: Random House, 2007.

Hiebert, Paul G. *Anthropological Reflections on Missiological Issues.* Grand Rapids: Baker, 1994.

———. "Critical Contextualization." *International Bulletin of Missionary Research* 11, no. 3 (July 1987): 104–12.

Higginbotham, Evelyn Brooks. *Righteous Discontent: The Women's Movement in the Black Baptist Church, 1880–1920.* Cambridge, MA: Harvard University Press, 1993.

Hildebrand, Stephen M. *Basil of Caesarea.* Grand Rapids: Baker Academic, 2014.

Hilkert, Mary Catherine. *Naming Grace: Preaching and the Sacramental Imagination.* New York: Continuum, 1997.

Hofstede, Geert H. *Culture's Consequences: Comparing Values, Behaviors, Institutions, and Organizations across Nations.* Thousand Oaks, CA: Sage Publications, 2001.

Hubbard, David Allan. Foreword to *The Word among Us: Contextualizing Theology for Mission Today*, edited by Dean Gilliland and David Allan Hubbard, vii–viii. Eugene, OR: Wipf & Stock, 1989.

Hughes, Richard T. *Christian America and the Kingdom of God.* Chicago: University of Illinois Press, 2009.

Hulst, Mary S. *A Little Handbook for Preachers.* Downers Grove, IL: InterVarsity, 2016.

Irigaray, Luce. *The Forgetting of Air in Martin Heidegger.* Austin: University of Texas Press, 1999.

Isasi-Díaz, Ada María. *La Lucha Continues: Mujerista Theology.* Maryknoll, NY: Orbis, 2004.

———. "Mujerista Theology: A Challenge to Traditional Theology." In *Introduction to Christian Theology: Contemporary North American Perspectives*, edited by Roger A. Badham, 244–52. Louisville: Westminster John Knox, 1998.

Jacks, G. Robert. *Just Say the Word! Writing for the Ear.* Grand Rapids: Eerdmans, 1996.

"James Farmer Jr., Freedom Ride Organizer on Non-Violent Resistance." NPR. Accessed March 4, 2018. https://www.npr.org/templates/transcript/transcript.php ?storyId=135836458.

Jeter, Joseph R., Jr., and Ronald J. Allen. *One Gospel, Many Ears: Preaching for Different Listeners in the Congregation.* St. Louis: Chalice, 2002.

Jobes, Karen H. *Esther.* The NIV Application Commentary. Grand Rapids: Zondervan, 1999.

Johnston, Scott Black, Ted A. Smith, and Leonora Tubbs Tisdale, eds. *Questions Preachers Ask: Essays in Honor of Thomas G. Long.* Louisville: Westminster John Knox, 2016.

Johnstone, Keith. *Impro: Improvisation and the Theatre.* New York: Routledge, 1992.

Kagawa, Toyohiko. *Meditations on the Cross.* New York: Willett, Clark, & Company, 1935.

Karr, Mary. *Lit: A Memoir*. New York: Harper Memorial, 2009.

Katongole, Emmanuel, and Chris Rice. *Reconciling All Things: A Christian Vision for Justice, Peace and Healing*. Downers Grove, IL: InterVarsity, 2008.

Kaufman, James C. *Creativity 101*. New York: Springer, 2009.

Kaufman, James C., and Robert J. Sternberg. Preface to *The Cambridge Handbook of Creativity*, edited by James C. Kaufman and Robert J. Sternberg, xiii–xv. New York: Cambridge University Press, 2010.

Kaveny, Cathleen. *Prophecy without Contempt: Religious Discourse in the Public Square*. Cambridge, MA: Harvard University Press, 2016.

Kearney, Richard. *Poetics of Imagining: Modern to Post-Modern*. New York: Fordham Press, 1998.

———. *The Wake of Imagination: Toward a Postmodern Culture*. Minneapolis: University of Minnesota Press, 1988.

Kim, Matthew D. *Preaching with Cultural Intelligence*. Grand Rapids: Baker Academic, 2017.

King, Martin Luther, Jr. *A Knock at Midnight: Inspiration from the Great Sermons of Reverend Martin Luther King, Jr.* Edited by Clayborne Carson and Peter Holloran. New York: Warner, 2000.

———. "Letter from a Birmingham Jail." In *On Being Responsible: Issues in Personal Ethics*, edited by James M. Gustafson and James T. Laney, 256–74. New York: Harper & Row, 1968.

———. *Strength to Love*. Philadelphia: Fortress, 1981.

Koyama, Kosuke. *Mount Fuji and Mount Sinai*. Maryknoll, NY: Orbis, 1984.

Kozbelt, Aaron, Ronald A. Beghetto, and Mark A. Runco. "Theories of Creativity." In *The Cambridge Handbook of Creativity*, edited by James C. Kaufman and Robert J. Sternberg, 20–47. New York: Cambridge University Press, 2010.

Kurtz, Howard. "The Great Exploding Popcorn Exposé." *Washington Post*, May 12, 1994, C1.

Lane, Patty. *A Beginner's Guide to Crossing Cultures: Making Friends in a Multicultural World*. Downers Grove, IL: InterVarsity, 2002.

Larson, Rebecca. *Daughters of Light: Quaker Women Preaching and Prophesying in the Colonies and Abroad, 1700–1775*. Chapel Hill: University of North Carolina Press, 2000.

Larson, Thomas E. *History and Tradition of Jazz*. Dubuque, IA: Kendall Hunt, 2002.

LaRue, Cleophus J. *I Believe I'll Testify: The Art of African American Preaching*. Louisville: Westminster John Knox, 2011.

Lasseter, John, dir. *Toy Story 2*. Emeryville, CA: Pixar Animation Studios, 1999. VHS/DVD release 2000.

Lauer, Alex. "Living with Pottery: Warren MacKenzie at 90." *Sightlines*, February 6, 2014. https://walkerart.org/magazine/living-with-pottery-warren-mackenzie-at-90.

Lee, Jarena. *The Life and Religious Experience of Jarena Lee, a Colored Lady*. Cincinnati: self-published, 1839.

Le Goff, Jacques. *The Medieval Imagination*. Chicago: University of Chicago Press, 1988.

Lewis, C. S. *The Collected Letters of C. S. Lewis*. Edited by Walter Hopper. Vol. 3, *Narnia, Cambridge, and Joy*. San Francisco: HarperCollins, 2007.

———. *God in the Dock: Essays on Theology and Ethics*. Grand Rapids: Eerdmans, 2014.

———. *Mere Christianity*. New York: HarperOne, 2001.

———. *The Problem of Pain*. New York: HarperCollins, 1996.

———. *Surprised by Joy: The Shape of My Early Life*. New York: Harcourt, Brace, 1955.

Lidz, Franz. "Will the Real Abraham Lincoln Please Stand Up?" *Smithsonian Magazine*, October 2013. http://www.smithsonianmag.com/history/will-the-real-abraham -lincoln-please-stand-up-3431.

Lischer, Richard. *The Preacher King: Martin Luther King Jr. and the Word That Moved America*. New York: Oxford University Press, 1995.

Livermore, David A. *Expand Your Borders: Discover Ten Cultural Clusters*. East Lansing, MI: Cultural Intelligence Center, 2013.

Lloyd-Jones, D. Martyn. *Preaching and Preachers*. London: Hodder and Stoughton, 1971.

Lombroso, Cesare. *The Man of Genius*. London: Walter Scott, 1891.

Long, Thomas G. "No News Is Bad News." In *What's the Matter with Preaching Today?*, edited by Mike Graves, 145–58. Louisville: Westminster John Knox, 2004.

———. "The Preaching of Jesus." Paper presented at the National Symposium on Preaching, Truett Theological Seminary, Waco, September 11–12, 2017.

Lose, David J. "Imagination and Preaching." In *A Handbook for Catholic Preaching*, 190–99. Collegeville, MN: Liturgical Press, 2016.

Lovelace, Richard F. *The Dynamics of the Spiritual Life*. Downers Grove, IL: InterVarsity, 1979.

Lowry, Eugene L. *The Homiletical Plot: The Sermon as Narrative Art Form*. Louisville: Westminster John Knox, 2001.

Lubart, Todd. "Cross-Cultural Perspectives on Creativity." In *The Cambridge Handbook of Creativity*, edited by James C. Kaufman and Robert J. Sternberg, 265–78. New York: Cambridge University Press, 2010.

Luchetti, Lenny. *Preaching Essentials*. Indianapolis: Wesleyan Publishing House, 2012.

Luther, Martin. *The Bondage of the Will*. Grand Rapids: Baker Academic, 2012.

———. *Luther's Works*. Edited by Theodore G. Tappert. Vol. 54, *Table Talk*. Philadelphia: Fortress, 1967.

Mandela, Nelson. *In His Own Words*. Edited by Kader Asmal, David Chidester, and Wilmot James. New York: Little, Brown, 2003.

Mann, Sandi, and Rebekah Cadman. "Does Being Bored Make Us More Creative?" *Creativity Research Journal* 26, no. 2 (2014): 165–73.

Martínez, Juan Francisco. *Walk with the People: Latino Ministry in the United States.* Nashville: Abingdon, 2008.

Martyn, J. Louis. "The Apocalyptic Gospel in Galatians." *Interpretation* 54, no. 3 (July 2000): 246–66.

Massey, James Earl. *The Burdensome Joy of Preaching.* Nashville: Abingdon, 1998.

———. "Composing Sermons That Sing!" In *Our Sufficiency Is of God: Essays on Preaching in Honor of Gardner C. Taylor*, edited by Timothy George, James Earl Massey, and Robert Smith Jr., 11–22. Macon, GA: Mercer University Press, 2010.

Maxwell, Jaclyn L. *Christianization and Communication in Late Antiquity: John Chrysostom and His Congregation in Antioch.* Cambridge: Cambridge University Press, 2006.

Mbiti, John S. "Theological Impotence and the Universality of the Church." In *Mission Trends, No. 3: Third World Theologies*, edited by Gerald H. Anderson and Thomas F. Stransky, 6–18. Grand Rapids: Eerdmans, 1976.

McCheyne, Robert Murray. *The Works of Rev. Robert Murray McCheyne.* Edited by Andrew A. Bonar. New York: Robert Carter & Brothers, 1874.

McClure, John S. *The Roundtable Pulpit: Where Leadership and Preaching Meet.* Nashville: Abingdon, 1995.

McMickle, Marvin. "What Shall They Preach?" In *Our Sufficiency Is of God: Essays on Preaching in Honor of Gardner C. Taylor*, edited by Timothy George, James Earl Massey, and Robert Smith Jr., 103–22. Macon, GA: Mercer University Press, 2010.

Meconi, David Vincent, and Eleanor Stump, eds. *The Cambridge Companion to Augustine.* New York: Cambridge University Press, 2014.

Mergal, Angel M. *Arte Cristiano de la Predicación.* México: Comité de Literatura de la Asociación de Iglesias Evangélicas de Puerto Rico, 1951.

Meyer, Jason C. *Preaching: A Biblical Theology.* Wheaton: Crossway, 2013.

Miller, Calvin. *Table of Inwardness.* Downers Grove, IL: InterVarsity, 1984.

Mitchell, Henry H. "African American Preaching." *Interpretation* 51, no. 4 (October 1997): 371–83.

"MLK at Western." Western Michigan University Archives and Regional History Collections and University Libraries, http://www.wmich.edu/sites/default/files/attachments/MLK.pdf.

Montoya, Alex. *Preaching with Passion.* Grand Rapids: Kregel, 2000.

Montuori, Alfonso, and Ronald E. Purser. "Deconstructing the Lone Genius Myth: Toward a Contextual View of Creativity." *Journal of Humanistic Psychology* 35, no. 3 (July 1, 1995): 69–112.

Morello, Carol, and Ted Mellnik. "Census: Minority Babies Are Now Majority in United States." *The Washington Post*, May 17, 2012, http://www.washingtonpost

.com/local/census-minority-babies-are-now-majority-in-united-states/2012/05/16
/gIQA1WY8UU_story.html.

Morgan, G. Campbell. "The Possibility of Prayer." In *Northfield Echoes, Vol. 8: Conference Addresses for 1901*, edited by Delavan L. Pierson and Paul D. Moody, 380–87. East Northfield, MA: East Northfield Bookstore, 1901.

Mottesi, Osvaldo Luis. *Predicación y Misión: Una Perspectiva Pastoral: Un Texto Didactico Sobre la Predicación Pastoral.* Miami: LOGOI, 1989.

Mounce, Robert H. *So They Say.* Eugene, OR: Resource Publications, 2014.

Mulholland, M. Robert, Jr. *The Deeper Journey: The Spirituality of Becoming Your True Self.* Downers Grove, IL: InterVarsity, 2006.

Nanko-Fernández, Carmen. *Theologizing en Espanglish: Context, Community, and Ministry.* Maryknoll, NY: Orbis, 2010.

New, Geoff. *Imaginative Preaching.* Carlisle, UK: Langham Partnership, 2015.

Newbigin, Lesslie. *Foolishness to the Greeks: The Gospel and Western Culture.* Grand Rapids: Eerdmans, 1986.

———. *A Word in Season.* Grand Rapids: Eerdmans, 1994.

Nicolay, John G., and John Hay. *Complete Works of Abraham Lincoln.* Vol. 9. Harrogate, TN: Lincoln Memorial University, 1894.

Niebuhr, H. Richard. *The Kingdom of God in America.* New York: Harper & Row, 1959.

Nieman, James R. *Knowing the Context: Frames, Tools, and Signs for Preaching.* Minneapolis: Fortress, 2008.

Northcutt, Kay L. *Kindling Desire for God: Preaching as Spiritual Direction.* Minneapolis: Fortress, 2009.

Old, Hughes Oliphant. *The Reading and Preaching of the Scriptures in the Worship of the Christian Church.* Vol. 2, *The Patristic Age.* Grand Rapids: Eerdmans, 1998.

———. *The Reading and Preaching of the Scriptures in the Worship of the Christian Church.* Vol. 7, *Our Own Time.* Grand Rapids: Eerdmans, 2010.

Orleck, Annelise. *Rethinking American Women's Activism.* New York: Taylor & Francis, 2015.

Ortberg, John. *Who Is This Man? The Unpredictable Impact of the Inescapable Jesus.* Grand Rapids: Zondervan, 2012.

Osborne, Grant R. *The Hermeneutical Spiral: A Comprehensive Introduction to Biblical Interpretation.* Downers Grove, IL: InterVarsity, 2006.

Padilla, C. René. "Hacia una Definición de la Misión Integral [Toward a Definition of Integral Mission]." In *El Proyecto de Dios y las Necesidades Humanas: Más Modelos de Ministerio Integral en América Latina*, edited by C. René Padilla and Tetsunao Yamamori, 19–34. Buenos Aires: Kairos, 2000.

Palmer, Earl F. *Love Has Its Reasons.* Waco: Word, 1977.

Parker, T. H. L. *Calvin's Preaching.* Louisville: Westminster John Knox, 1992.

Passel, Jeffrey S., and D'Vera Cohn. "U.S. Population Projections: 2005–2050." *Pew Research Center*, February 11, 2008, http://www.pewsocialtrends.org/2008/02/11/us-population-projections-2005-2050/.

Perkins, William. *"The Art of Prophesying," and "The Calling of the Ministry."* Edinburgh: Banner of Truth, 1996.

Pitt-Watson, Ian. *Preaching: A Kind of Folly*. Philadelphia: Westminster, 1978.

Plantinga, Cornelius. *Not the Way It's Supposed to Be: A Breviary of Sin*. Grand Rapids: Eerdmans, 1995.

Plato. *Republic: Books 6–10*. Edited by Chris Emlyn-Jones and William Preddy. Loeb Classical Library. Cambridge, MA: Harvard University Press, 2013.

Pope, Rob. *Creativity: Theory, History, Practice*. New York: Routledge, 2005.

Pope-Levison, Priscilla. "Sojourner Truth." In *Handbook of Women Biblical Interpreters: A Historical and Biographical Guide*, edited by Marion Ann Taylor and Agnes Choi, 509–11. Grand Rapids: Baker Academic, 2012.

Porter, Stanley E. Katallasso *in Ancient Greek Literature, with Reference to the Pauline Writings*. Cordoba: Ediciones el Almendro, 1994.

Postman, Neil. *Amusing Ourselves to Death: Public Discourse in the Age of Show Business*. New York: Penguin, 1985.

Proctor, Samuel D. *The Certain Sound of the Trumpet: Crafting a Sermon of Authority*. Valley Forge, PA: Judson Press, 1994.

Rah, Soong-Chan. *Prophetic Lament: A Call for Justice in Troubled Times*. Downers Grove, IL: IVP Press, 2015.

Randolph, David James. *The Renewal of Preaching in the Twenty-First Century: The Next Homiletics*. Eugene, OR: Wipf & Stock, 2009.

Reed, Angela H. *Quest for Spiritual Community*. New York: T&T Clark, 2011.

Reeves, Michael. *Rejoicing in Christ*. Downers Grove, IL: InterVarsity, 2015.

Reid, Robert Stephen, and Lucy Lind Hogan. *The Six Deadly Sins of Preaching*. Nashville: Abingdon, 2012.

Richards, E. Randolph, and Brandon J. O'Brien. *Misreading Scripture with Western Eyes: Removing Cultural Blinders to Better Understanding the Bible*. Downers Grove, IL: InterVarsity, 2012.

Ricoeur, Paul. *The Symbolism of Evil*. Boston: Beacon, 1967.

Robinson, Haddon W. *Biblical Preaching: The Development and Delivery of Expository Messages*. Grand Rapids: Baker Academic, 2014.

Robinson, Ken. *Out of Our Minds: Learning to Be Creative*. Chichester, UK: Capstone, 2011.

Romero, Oscar. *The Violence of Love*. Maryknoll, NY: Orbis, 2004.

Rose, Lucy Atkinson. *Sharing the Word: Preaching in the Roundtable Church*. Louisville: Westminster John Knox, 1997.

Runco, Mark A. "Everyone Has Creative Potential." In *Creativity: From Potential to Realization*, edited by Robert J. Sternberg, Elena Grigorenko, and Jerome L. Singer, 21–30. Washington, DC: American Psychological Association, 2004.

Runco, Mark A., and Robert S. Albert. "Creativity Research: A Historical View." In *The Cambridge Handbook of Creativity*, edited by James C. Kaufman and Robert J. Sternberg, 3–19. New York: Cambridge University Press, 2010.

Ryle, J. C. *Simplicity in Preaching: A Few Short Hints on the Subject*. London: William Hunt, 1882.

Sallquist, Gary. *Classroom Classics*. Bloomington, IN: 1st Books Library, 2003.

Sanneh, Lamin O. *Translating the Message: The Missionary Impact on Culture*. Maryknoll, NY: Orbis, 2008.

Sawyer, R. Keith. "The Emergence of Creativity." *Philosophical Psychology* 12, no. 4 (1999): 447–69.

———. *Explaining Creativity: The Science of Human Innovation*. New York: Oxford University Press, 2012.

———. *Improvised Dialogues: Emergence and Creativity in Conversation*. Westport, CT: Ablex, 2003.

———. "Individual and Group Creativity." In *The Cambridge Handbook of Creativity*, edited by James C. Kaufman and Robert J. Sternberg, 366–80. New York: Cambridge University Press, 2010.

Scharf, Greg R. "'Double Listening' Revisited: Hearing Listeners without Compromising Faithfulness to the Biblical Text." *Trinity Journal* 33, no. 2 (September 2012): 181–97.

———. *Let the Earth Hear His Voice: Strategies for Overcoming Bottlenecks in Preaching God's Word*. Phillipsburg, NJ: P&R, 2015.

Scherer, Paul. *We Have This Treasure*. New York: Harper and Brothers, 1944.

———. *The Word God Sent*. New York: Harper & Row, 1965.

Schlipp, Paul Arthur. *Albert Einstein: Philosopher-Scientist*. Evanston, IL: Library of Living Philosophers, 1949.

Schreiter, Robert J. *Constructing Local Theologies*. Maryknoll, NY: Orbis, 2015.

Schulenburg, Jane Tibbetts. *Forgetful of Their Sex: Female Sanctity and Society ca. 500–1100*. Chicago: University of Chicago Press, 1998.

Searle, Alison. *The Eyes of Your Heart: Literary and Theological Trajectories of Imagining Biblically*. Eugene, OR: Wipf & Stock, 2008.

Seneca. "Of Peace of Mind." In *Minor Dialogues: Together with the Dialogue on Clemency*, translated by Aubrey Stewart, 250–87. London: George Bell and Sons, 1889.

Shaddix, Jim, and Jerry Vines. *Progress in the Pulpit: How to Grow in Your Preaching*. Chicago: Moody, 2017.

Shakespeare, William. *William Shakespeare: Four Comedies: "The Taming of the Shrew," "A Midsummer Night's Dream," "As You Like It," and "Twelfth Night."*

Edited by G. R. Hibbard, Stanley Wells, H. J. Oliver, and M. M. Mahood. New York: Penguin Classics, 1996.

Simonton, Dean Keath. "Creativity, Productivity, Age, and Stress: A Biographical Time-Series Analysis of 10 Classical Composers." *Journal of Personality and Social Psychology* 35 (1977): 791–804.

———. *Greatness: Who Makes History and Why*. New York: Guilford, 1994.

Simpson, D. P. *Cassell's Latin Dictionary*. New York: MacMillan, 1982.

Smallwood, Jonathan, and Jonathan W. Schooler. "The Restless Mind." *Psychological Bulletin* 132 (2006): 946–58.

Smith, Christian, with Melinda Lundquist Denton. *Soul Searching: The Religious and Spiritual Lives of American Teenagers*. New York: Oxford University Press, 2009.

Smith, James K. A. *You Are What You Love: The Spiritual Power of Habit*. Grand Rapids: Brazos, 2016.

Solnit, Rebecca. *Wanderlust: A History of Walking*. New York: Viking Penguin, 2000.

Soskice, Janet Martin. "The Truth Looks Different from Here, or, On Seeking the Unity of Truth from a Diversity of Perspectives." In *Christ and Context: The Confrontation between Gospel and Culture*, edited by Hilary D. Regan and Alan J. Torrance, 43–59. Edinburgh: T&T Clark, 1993.

Stewart, James. *Heralds of God*. New York: Scribner's, 1946.

Stott, John R. W. *Between Two Worlds: The Art of Preaching in the Twentieth Century*. Grand Rapids: Eerdmans, 1982.

———. *The Contemporary Christian: Applying God's Word to Today's World*. Downers Grove, IL: InterVarsity, 1992.

Strauss, Valerie. "For First Time, Minority Students Expected to Be Majority in U.S. Public Schools This Fall." *The Washington Post*. August 21, 2014, https://www.washingtonpost.com/news/answer-sheet/wp/2014/08/21/for-first-time-minority-students-expected-to-be-majority-in-u-s-public-schools-this-fall/?noredirect=on&utm_term=.e496fa7aa8c0.

Strunk, William, Jr., and E. B. White. *The Elements of Style*, rev. ed. New York: Penguin, 2007.

Sunukjian, Donald. *Invitation to Biblical Preaching*. Grand Rapids: Kregel, 2007.

Sweet, Leonard. *Post-Modern Pilgrims*. Nashville: Broadman & Holman, 2000.

Tannehill, Robert C. *Luke*. Abingdon New Testament Commentaries. Nashville: Abingdon, 1996.

Tanner, Kathryn. *Theories of Culture: A New Agenda for Theology*. Minneapolis: Fortress, 1997.

Taylor, Barbara Brown. *The Preaching Life*. Cambridge, MA: Cowley, 1993.

Taylor, Gardner C. "Freedom's Song." In *How Long This Road: Race, Religion, and the Legacy of C. Eric Lincoln*, edited by Alton B. Pollard III and Love Henry Whelchel, 163–70. New York: Palgrave Macmillan, 2003.

———. "The Sweet Torture of Sunday Morning (Interview)." *Leadership* 2, no. 3 (Summer 1981): 16–29.

———. *The Words of Gardner Taylor*. Edited by Edward L. Taylor. Vol. 2, *Sermons from the Middle Years, 1970–1980*. Valley Forge, PA: Judson Press, 2004.

———. *The Words of Gardner Taylor*. Edited by Edward L. Taylor. Vol. 5, *Lectures, Essays, and Interviews*. Valley Forge, PA: Judson Press, 2004.

Tertullian. "On Prayer (Chapter 29)." In *The Ante-Nicene Fathers*. Vol. 3, *Latin Fathers*, edited by Alexander Roberts, James Donaldson, and Arthur Cleveland Coxe, 681–92. New York: Cosimo Classics, 2007.

Thomas, Gerald Lamont. *African American Preaching: The Contribution of Dr. Gardner C. Taylor*. New York: Peter Lang, 2004.

Throntveit, Mark A. *Ezra-Nehemiah*. Louisville: John Knox, 1992.

Tisdale, Leonora Tubbs. *Preaching as Local Theology and Folk Art*. Minneapolis: Fortress, 1997.

———. *Prophetic Preaching: A Pastoral Approach*. Louisville: Westminster John Knox, 2010.

Toohey, Peter. *Boredom: A Lively History*. New Haven: Yale University Press, 2011.

Torrey, R. A. *How to Succeed in the Christian Life*. Springdale, PA: Whitaker House, 1984.

Troeger, Thomas H., and Leonora Tubbs Tisdale. *A Sermon Workbook: Exercises in the Art and Craft of Preaching*. Nashville: Abingdon, 2013.

Truett, George W. *Follow Me*. New York: Long and Smith, 1932.

Tutu, Desmond. *Hope and Suffering: Sermons and Speeches*. Grand Rapids: Eerdmans, 1984.

Vanhoozer, Kevin J. "Imagination in Theology." In *New Dictionary of Theology: Historical and Systematic*, edited by Martin Davie, Tim Grass, Stephen R. Holmes, John McDowell, and T. A. Noble, 441–43. Downers Grove, IL: IVP Academic, 2016.

———. "In Bright Shadow: C. S. Lewis on the Imagination for Theology and Discipleship." In *The Romantic Rationalist: God, Life, and Imagination in the Work of C. S. Lewis*, edited by John Piper, David Mathis, and Kevin J. Vanhoozer, 81–104. Wheaton: Crossway, 2014.

Villafañe, Eldin. *Seek the Peace of the City: Reflections on Urban Ministry*. Grand Rapids: Eerdmans, 1995.

Vitale, Tom. "The Birth of Bird: Young Charlie Parker Found Focus, Faith in Music." NPR. October 19, 2013. https://www.npr.org/2013/10/19/237040499/the-birth-of-bird-young-charlie-parker-found-focus-faith-in-music.

Voltaire. *Oeuvres Complètes de Voltaire: Vol. 1*. Edited by Armand Aubrée. Paris: J. Lefebvre et Cie, 1830.

Wallis, Jim. *America's Original Sin: Racism, White Privilege, and the Bridge to a New America*. Grand Rapids: Brazos, 2016.

Walton, Jonathan L. *Watch This!: The Ethics and Aesthetics of Black Televangelism.* New York: NYU Press, 2009.

Weingarten, Gene. "Pearls Before Breakfast: Can One of the Nation's Great Musicians Cut through the Fog of a DC Rush Hour? Let's Find Out." *Washington Post*, April 8, 2007. https://www.washingtonpost.com/lifestyle/magazine/pearls-before-break fast-can-one-of-the-nations-great-musicians-cut-through-the-fog-of-a-dc-rush -hour-lets-find-out/2014/09/23/8a6d46da-4331-11e4-b47c-f5889e061e5f_story .html.

Wesley, John. *Wesley's Standard Sermons.* Edited by Edward H. Sugden. Vol. 1. London: Epworth, 1951.

Whitehead, James D. "The Religious Imagination." *Liturgy*, 1985, 54–59.

Widmer, Ted. "The Other Gettysburg Address." *New York Times*, November 19, 2013. http://opinionator.blogs.nytimes.com/2013/11/19/the-other-gettysburg-ad dress/?_r=0.

Wilder, Amos N. *Theopoetic.* Philadelphia: Fortress, 1976.

Willard, Dallas. *The Spirit of the Disciplines: Understanding How God Changes Lives.* San Francisco: Harper & Row, 1988.

Willimon, William H. *How Odd of God: Chosen for the Curious Vocation of Preaching.* Louisville: Westminster John Knox, 2015.

Wilson, Paul Scott. *Imagination of the Heart: New Understandings in Preaching.* Nashville: Abingdon, 1988.

Winnicott, D. W. "The Capacity to Be Alone." *International Journal of Psychoanalytic Development* no. 39 (1958): 416–20.

Wisdom, John. *Paradox and Discovery.* Oxford: Basil Blackwell, 1965.

Witten, Marsha G. *All Is Forgiven: The Secular Message in American Protestantism.* Princeton: Princeton University Press, 1993.

Wright, N. T. *After You Believe.* New York: HarperCollins, 2010.

Yancey, Philip. *Disappointment with God.* Grand Rapids: Zondervan, 2015.

Yeginsu, Ceylan. "U.K. Appoints a Minister for Loneliness." *New York Times*, January 17, 2018. https://www.nytimes.com/2018/01/17/world/europe/uk-britain-lone liness.html.

Young, Vershawn Ashanti, Rusty Barrett, Y'Shanda Young-Rivera, and Kim Brian Lovejoy. *Other People's English: Code-Meshing, Code-Switching, and African American Literacy.* New York: Teachers College Press, 2013.

Zink-Sawyer, Beverly. *From Preachers to Suffragists: Woman's Rights and Religious Conviction in the Lives of Three Nineteenth-Century American Clergywomen.* Louisville: Westminster John Knox, 2003.

Index

Abrams, M. H., 161
abstraction, 15n8, 26n35, 30n43, 105, 116, 131–33, 137–38, 153
 ladder of, 136–37, 142–48, 153
Abuhamdeh, Sami, 160n16
academic language, 97, 112, 115–16, 117–18, 119, 120
accessible language, 110–13, 115–20
accountability, 61, 64
Adeleye, Femi B., 33
Africa, 48, 88
 South Africa, 70–71, 109, 169–70
African Americans, 80n22, 144
 preaching, preachers, 59, 111–12, 164, 166
 See also specific individuals
African Methodist Episcopal (AME) church, 48–49
air metaphor, 79–81, 91, 96
Albert, Robert S., 159n9
Alexandru, Joan, 48
Allen, Ray, 187–88
Allen, Ronald J., 78n14, 83n32
Amabile, Teresa, 162n25, 175–77
American Dream mythology, 27–29
Amos (prophet), 44
analogies, 147–48
Andrews, William, 49n14
antinomianism, 12–13, 33
apartheid, South African, 70–71, 169–70

application, 149–53
Aristotle, 158–59, 161
Arrastía, Cecilio, 38, 48, 114, 142
arrogance, 51, 56–57, 61–62
Arroyo, Gonzalo, 91
Arthurs, Jeffrey D., 173n55
artists, 158–59, 160–63, 164, 171–72, 183–84
 lone genius myth, 161–62, 163n27, 172, 178
Asian Americans, 143, 144
Augustine, 6, 30n43, 68, 104, 160

Baer, John, 162n25
Bailey, Kenneth E., 92
balance, 87–88, 136, 153
Baptists, 30, 48
 Hopewell Old School Baptist Meeting House, Hopewell, New Jersey, 11–13
Barnabas, 45, 59
Barth, Karl, 15, 19n17, 26n35
Bartow, Charles L., 39–40
Basil of Caesarea, 68, 110
Baxter, Richard, 58
Beghetto, Ronald A., 162n25
Bell, Joshua, 155–57, 183–84
Benner, David G., 62
Bereans, 69
Bergman, Ingmar, 125
Bernard of Clairvaux, 50
Bethune, Mary McLeod, 49

Bible, 22, 36–37, 38–39, 148
 analogies, 147–48
 characters as examples, 44–47, 109–10
 clarity, 109–10, 113–14, 128
 concreteness, 135, 139–42, 145
 context, 75–77, 139–40
 original languages, 69, 115, 118–19
 study, 67–70, 71, 139–42
biblical illiteracy, 142–43, 145
biblical imagination, 164–66
Bonhoeffer, Dietrich, 20, 35, 53–54, 64, 65
Bonilla, Plutarco, 48n13
Boreham, F. W., 48
boring, boredom, 101, 173–75
Bosch, David, 82, 88n47, 91n54
Bowler, Kate, 28
Boyd, Gregory A., 27–28
Brantley, Clarice, 138
Brekus, Catherine, 49–50
brevity, 123–28
Briscoe, Jill, 152
Broadus, John, 31
Brown, Sally A., 80n23
Brueggemann, Walter, 21n22, 163n30, 169
Brunner, Emil, 14, 85
Buber, Martin, 159n12
Buechner, Frederick, 54n32

calling, 51–52
Calvin, John, 62, 111, 118
Chalmers, Thomas, 18

209

Chapell, Bryan, 31–32
character, 57–59
charisma, 57–58
Charles, H. B., 69
children, 173–74, 178–79, 180, 183–84
Childs, Brevard, 63
Christians, Christianity, 159–60
  examples, 47–50, 110–13
Christian sermons, 6–7, 13–14, 35–40
church, 26, 56–57
  congregational ethnography, 94–96
  gospel proclamation, 14, 16, 22, 53
  local context, 77–78, 80–81, 85–87, 94–96, 98–99, 166–67
church fathers, 68, 110–11, 160
Church of the Brethren, 49
Cicero, 77nn11–12
Clance, Pauline Rose, 59
clarity, 7, 101–2
  academic language, 97, 112, 115–16, 117–18, 119, 120
  accessible language, 110–13, 115–20
  biblical examples, 109–10
  brevity, 123–28
  Christian examples, 110–13
  concise exegesis, 103–15
  editing, 126–28
  information trap, 125–27
  main idea, 120–23, 125–28
  precision, 121, 124–25, 128, 166–67
  relational and colloquial language, 119–20
  sophisticated simplicity, 105–10, 112–13, 122, 123, 128–29
  verbosity, 125–27
collaboration, 93, 97, 160–61, 174
commentaries, 36, 113–14, 125
Committee of Racial Equality (CORE), 41
community, 64–65
complacency and indifference, 7, 17, 20, 38

Concord Baptist Church of Christ, Brooklyn, New York, 47
concreteness, 7, 131–34
  abstraction, 7, 15n8, 26n35, 30n43, 105, 116, 131–33, 137–38, 153
  application, 149–53
  details, 133–34, 139–42
  examples, 135–36
  foundations, 137–38
  illustrations, 142–48
  ladder of abstraction, 136–37, 142–48, 152–53
  specificity, 134–36, 137–38
confidence, 46–47, 53–54
context, 73–74, 119–20, 149–52
  air metaphor, 79–81, 91, 96
  contemporary, 81–82
  definition, 74–75, 77–81
  global, 78–79, 80–81
  local church, 77–78, 80–81, 85–87, 94–96, 98–99, 166–67
  Scripture, 75–77, 139–40
contextualization, 7, 73–75, 81–85
  balance, 87–88
  congregational ethnography, 94–96
  critical, 81–83, 89
  cultural blind spots, 91–94
  definition, 85–86, 88
  feedback, listening, 82, 96–98
  hospitality, 88–89
  love, 89–91, 96
  over-contextualization, 74, 82n26, 87–88
  popular culture, 84–85
  translation, 86–87
  under-contextualization, 74, 87–88
conviction, 7, 46–47, 53–54, 70–71
  biblical examples, 44–47
  calling, 51–52
  Christian examples, 47–50
  definition, 43–44, 46
  faithfulness, 55, 56–57
  resolutions, 50–51
  stewardship, 54–56
Cornelius, 77n12

Costas, Orlando E., 91, 114
Craddock, Fred, 31, 74, 90
creativity, 7–8, 155–58
  artists, 158–59, 160–63, 164, 171–72, 183–84
  of children, 173–74, 178–79, 180, 183–84
  chronic distraction, 173–75, 177
  collaboration, 177–78
  definition, 157–58
  diversity, 177–78
  environmental obstacles, 175–77
  and faithfulness to the text, 172–73, 177
  Greek, 158–59, 161n21, 172–73
  imagination, 155, 157, 158–59, 160, 161–63
  Judeo-Christian, 159–60
  lack of, 171–72
  lived experience (la vida cotidiana), 180–81
  lone genius myth, 161–62, 163n27, 172, 178
  modern, 161–63
  research on, 161–63, 182–83
  thinking, 181–82
critical engagement, 75–76
Csikszentmihalyi, Mihaly, 160n16, 162n25, 171
culture, 16–17, 32, 74–75, 77–78
  blind spots, 91–94
  cross-cultural ministry, 76n6, 87–88, 93
  intercultural competence, 80–81, 94
  local, 85–86, 90
  popular, 61, 84–85
  values, 91–92
Czech Republic, 50

Daniel (prophet), 84
David, King, 27, 32, 44, 109
Davis, H. Grady, 120
Deadly Be's, 31–32
Dean, Kenda Creasy, 23–24, 25
Deissmann, Adolf, 110
deliberate practice, 5–6, 189–92

deliverance, 33n53
demographic shifts, 78, 93n60, 95, 96, 143–44
Denton, Melissa Lindquist, 23–24, 25
Desmond, Paul, 3
Dickens, Charles, 181
disciples, 45, 139–40
discipleship, 18, 23, 38, 91
disorientation, 8
distraction, 173–75, 177
diversity, 6, 77–78, 98, 124, 143–44, 151, 177–78, 191
Docter, Pete, 122–13
Douthat, Ross, 23n23
Dryden, John, 161n21
Duarte, Nancy, 125, 126–27
Duckworth, Angela, 183n78
Dweck, Carol S., 7n12

ear, preaching for the, 116–20
Easter, 16, 20, 165
Eastern Orthodox Christianity, 160
editing, 126–28
Edwards, J. Kent, 66
Edwards, Jonathan, 50
Einstein, Albert, 124, 175–76, 181
Elaw, Zilpha, 49
Elijah (prophet), 44
Eliot, T. S., 174
Elisha (prophet), 140–42
Elliot, Jim, 145
England, Great Britain, 50, 64–65, 128–29
entertainment, 173–75
environmental obstacles, 175–77
Ericsson, K. Anders, 5, 192
eschatology, 21–22, 29, 169–70
Eslinger, Richard, 163n30
Esther (queen), 32, 44, 89, 165
eternal life, 21–22
Everett, Edward, 102–3, 124
example, 58–59
exegesis, 63, 67, 69, 81, 142
    concise, 113–15
    details, 139–42
    original languages, 69, 115, 118–19
expectations, 57, 69, 124

experience, lived (la vida cotidiana), 180–81
eye, preaching for the, 76, 110, 116–17, 166–67
Ezra (prophet), 109–10

facts, 143–44
failure, 28
faithfulness, faith, 55, 56–57, 86, 168, 172–73, 177
Farmer, James, Jr., 41–43
fasting, 66
fear, anxiety, 55–57, 140, 172–73
Fee, Gordon D., 63n54, 67
feedback, listening, 5, 69, 96–98, 178, 182, 190
Five Cs, deliberate practices, 7–8, 13, 44, 73–75, 101–2, 131–34, 155–58, 191. See also clarity; concreteness; contextualization; conviction; and creativity
Flemming, Dean, 76–77nn6–8, 77, 89n48
Florence, Anna Carter, 131
Foote, Julia A., 49
forgiveness, 145–47
France, 50
freedom, 33, 176
Freedom Rides, 41–43, 70
Fullman, Peggy, 170

Gettysburg Address, 101–3
Gilbert, Kenyatta, 168n45
Gilbert, Robert Lewis, 59
glorification, 18
God, 35
    creation, 159, 169
    involvement, immanence of, 25, 134–35
    love of, 149–50, 170
    and mission, 25–26, 33
    and preaching outcomes, 4–5, 14–15, 53–54, 56–57, 63, 120, 191
    promises, 20–22
    reality, vision of, 167–69
    relationship with, 65–66, 128, 138
Gomes, Peter J., 19
Gore, Charles, 61

gospel
    covenant relationship, 15–17, 20
    definition, 14–17
    description, 17–22
    explanation, 36–37
    as good news, 15–17, 36–38
    proclamation, 36–37, 53–54, 114–15
    stewardship, 54–56
Gospels, 76
grace, 16–17, 35, 54, 133
    discipleship and, 30–35
Graham, Billy, 47
Graham, Martha, 183n78, 187, 188–89
Greeks, ancient, 158–59, 161n21, 172–73
Gregory, Joel C., 36, 178
Griffiths, Thomas Sharp, 13
Grometstein, Alan A., 175n63
Guibert of Nogent, 111, 126
Guilford, J. P., 162–63

habits, 57, 59–60
    negative, 60–63
    positive, 63–70
Hagar, 109, 165
Haiti, 50
Hamman, Jaco J., 64n55
Han, Kyung-Chik, 48
happiness, 23–25
Hauser, Arnold, 160n16
Hayakawa, S. I., 136–37, 153
health, 28–30, 66, 181
heart, 57, 91
Heath, Chip, 137–38
Heath, Dan, 137–38
Heidegger, Martin, 79n19
Hemingway, Ernest, 127
Herod, King, 27
Hiebert, Paul G., 81–82
High, Reginald, 27n37
Hilkert, Mary Catherine, 163n30
Hofstede, Geert H., 93
holiness, 58–59
Holmes, Oliver Wendell, 105
Holy Spirit, 16–17, 160
    preaching and, 53–54, 67, 115, 118n39
hope, 19–20, 27, 37, 47, 169

Hopewell Old School Baptist
    Meeting House, Hopewell,
    New Jersey, 11–13
hospitality, 88–89, 151
Hubbard, David Allan, 88n45
Hughes, Richard T., 27n38
Hulst, Mary S., 73
humility, 61, 96, 141–42
Hus, Jan, 50
hyper-connection, 173–74

iconography, 160
identification, identity, 76–
    77n8, 89, 92–93
idols, idolatry, 19, 28, 82, 88,
    96, 168
illustrations, 142–48
    analogies, 147–48
    facts, 143–44
    quotations, 144–45
    stories, 145–47
images, 76, 110, 116–17,
    166–67, 179–80
imagination, 155, 157, 158–
    59, 160, 161–63
    biblical, 164–66
    pastoral, 170–71
    poetic, 166–67
    prophetic, 169–70
    theological, 167–68
incarnation, 134–35
indifference, 7, 17, 20, 38
individualism, 93–94, 163n27
information trap, 125–27
Inge, William Ralph, 85
intercultural competence,
    80–81
Irenaeus, 50
Irigaray, Luce, 79n19
Isasi-Díaz, Ada María, 180n72
Israel, Israelites, 89, 165
    Babylonian exile, 75–76
Israel, Oshea, 145–47

jazz, 1–3
Jeremiah (prophet), 44
Jesus Christ, 35, 44, 46–47,
    135, 165
    clarity, 109, 110
    discipleship, 18, 23, 143
    gospel and, 15–16, 19–20
    incarnation, 134–35

Lord's Prayer, 145–47, 168
    parables, 38, 54–55, 56, 110,
        145, 149–50, 152
    preaching, teaching, 135, 143
    Sea of Galilee, 139–40
    stewardship, 54–55, 56
    Zacchaeus, 150
Jeter, Joseph R., 52, 83n32
Job, 169
Jobes, Karen H., 44n5
John (apostle), 46
John Chrysostom, 50, 53, 110,
    111n17
Johnson, Mary, 145–47
Johnstone, Keith, 179
John the Baptist, 27, 45
Jones, Jo, 2–3
Julius Caesar, 77n12
justice, 21, 26, 32, 47–48, 133,
    168
    doing, 151–52, 169
justification, 18, 30

Kagawa, Toyohiko, 48
Karr, Mary, 11
Kaufman, James C., 157n3,
    162n22, 162nn24–25,
    182–83
Kaveny, Cathleen, 20–21
Kearney, Richard, 158–
    59nn5–6, 159n7, 160n14,
    161nn17–18
Kierkegaard, Søren, 181
Kim, Matthew D., 93, 94
king, desire for, 27–28
King, Martin Luther, Jr., 41,
    47, 112–13, 134, 145
kingdom of heaven, 17, 26–28
Knox, John, 50
Koyama, Kosuke, 18
Kozbelt, Aaron, 162n25

lament, 37
language, 119–20, 166–67
    academic, 97, 112, 115–16,
        117–18, 119, 120
    accessible, 110–13, 115–20
    images, creating, 76, 110,
        116–17, 166–67
    prophetic voice, 26n35, 27,
        37, 81–82
Larson, Thomas, 1

LaRue, Cleophus J., 167
Latin America, 48, 91
Latina/o (Latinx) Americans,
    83–84, 143–44, 180n72
Lee, Jarena, 48–49, 52
legalism, legalistic preaching,
    22, 30–33
Le Goff, Jacques, 159n9
Leonardo da Vinci, 105–9,
    128
Lewis, C. S., 17, 24–25, 35, 74,
    86n37, 118
Lincoln, Abraham, 101–3, 124
Lischer, Richard, 164
listening, feedback, 5, 69, 82,
    96–98, 178, 182, 190
Livermore, Harriet, 49n15
Lloyd-Jones, Martin, 87
Lombroso, Cesare, 161
lone genius myth, 161–62,
    163n27, 172, 178
loneliness, 64–65
Long, Thomas G., 15, 36
Lord's Prayer, 145–47, 168
love, 20, 57, 89–91, 96, 133, 142
    of God, 149–50, 170
Lovelace, Richard, 30n43
Lowry, Eugene L., 31
Lubart, Todd, 163n27
Luchetti, Lenny, 54, 115n34
Luther, Martin, 31, 50,
    110n15, 111, 116
Luwum, Janani, 48

MacGregor, George, 63
MacKenzie, Warren, 185–87,
    188, 190
MacMullin, Jackie, 187–88
main idea, 120–23, 125–28
Mandela, Nelson, 70–71,
    169–70
Manetsch, Scott, 118
Martha, 109
Martínez, Juan Francisco,
    83–84n33
Martyn, J. Louis, 32–33
Mary, Queen of Scots, 49
Massey, James Earl, 51, 52
Maxwell, Jaclyn L., 111n17
Mbewe, Conrad, 48
Mbiti, John S., 92, 99–100
McCheyne, Robert Murray, 59

McClure, John S., 97
McShann, Jay, 3
memory, remembering, 38
Mergal, Angel, 167
metaphors, 79–81, 91, 96, 148, 167
Mexico, 83
Meyer, Jason C., 54n34
Miller, Calvin, 68
Miller, Michelle, 138
mindsets, 7n12
mission, 17, 35, 88
    cross-cultural, 87–88
    of God, 25–26, 33
mission drift, 12–13
Monsters, Inc., 122
Montesinos, Antonio, 50
Montgomery bus boycott, 112
Montoya, Alex, 164
moralism, moralistic preaching, 22, 30–33, 169
Moralistic Therapeutic Deism, 23–26
Morgan, G. Campbell, 63n53
Moses, 89, 165
Mother Teresa, 131
Mottesi, Osvaldo L., 125, 165–66, 180n73
movie popcorn, 131–33

narrative context, 38–39
Nathan (prophet), 27, 44
national ideology, 26–28
New, Geoff, 163n30
Newbigin, Lesslie, 16, 88, 90n51
New Jersey
    Hopewell, 11–13
    Princeton, 124–25
niceness, 23–25
Nicholas, Adrien, 108–9
Niebuhr, H. Richard, 35
Nieman, James R., 87n41
Northcutt, Kay L., 65–66
novelty, 157

obedience, 22, 30–33, 143
O'Brien, Brandon J., 92
offense of gospel, 18–19, 82n26
oral communication, 116–17
original languages, 69, 115, 118–19

Orleck, Annelise, 112
over-contextualization, 74, 82n26, 87–88

Padilla, C. René, 26
Palau, Luis, 48
Palmer, Earl F., 142
parables, 110, 145, 152
    prodigal son, 38, 149–50
    talents, 54–55, 56
Parker, Charlie, 1–3, 4, 171, 190, 192
Parker, T. H. L., 111
pastoral imagination, 170–71
Paul (apostle), 4, 32, 33n51, 53, 67, 89
    conviction, 45–46, 128
    preaching, 51, 55, 58, 76, 113, 151
Pauling, Linus, 182
Perkins, William, 118n38
Peter (apostle), 46
Picasso, Pablo, 184
Pitt-Watson, Ian, 62n47, 73, 81, 87, 120n42
Pixar Animation Studios, 122–23, 178
Plantinga, Cornelius, 168n45
Plato, 158–59, 172–73
poetic imagination, 166–67
political ideology, 26–28
Ponticus, Evagrius, 41, 68
Pool, Robert, 5
Pope, Rob, 162n23
Pope-Levison, Priscilla, 111
Porter, Stanley E., 16n10
positive thinking, 28–29
Postman, Neil, 174n57
poverty, 28–30
power, 61–62, 80, 93–94
Powery, Luke A., 41, 63
practices, 2–5, 63–64
    active, 65–66
    community, 64–65
    congregational ethnography, 94–96
    deliberate, 5–6, 189–92
    feedback, listening, 96–98, 178
    Five Cs, 7–8, 13, 44, 73–75, 101–2, 131–34, 155–58, 191
    interrogating cultural blind spots, 91–94

prayer, 67–70, 71
    receptive, 65–66
    silence and solitude, 64–65, 66
    study, 67–70, 71, 139–42
    woodshedding, 2–3, 4, 190, 192
prayer, 67–70, 71, 81, 146
    Lord's Prayer, 145–47, 168
prayerlessness, 62–63
precision, 121, 124–25, 128, 166–67, 188
Princeton, New Jersey, 124
Proctor, Samuel D., 51, 81, 120, 155
prodigal son, 38, 149–50
prophecy, prophets, 20–21, 88
prophetic imagination, 169–70
prophetic voice, 26n35, 27, 37, 81–82
prosperity gospel, 28–30, 142
Protestantism, 35
pseudo-gospel preaching, 6, 11, 22–23, 34, 39–40
    discipleship without grace, 30–33
    grace without discipleship, 33–35
    moralistic therapeutic deism, 23–26
    national or political ideology, 26–28
    prosperity gospel, 28–30, 142

quality, 127n50, 157
    quantity and, 182–83, 186
quarantine style preaching, 84, 88
Quiller-Couch, Sir Arthur, 127n50
quotations, 144–45

racism, racial equality, 47, 49, 144
    apartheid, South African, 70–71, 169–70
    Committee of Racial Equality (CORE), 41
    Freedom Rides, 41–43, 70
    Underground Railroad, 49
Radegund, 50

Randolph, David James, 14–15
Randolph, Florence Spearing, 49
reality, 29, 30, 62
    art and, 159, 161n17
    false visions of, 167–68
    God-shaped vision of, 167–69
    gospel, 3–4, 16, 27n38, 33
    preaching and, 21n22, 89, 97, 167
reason, logic, 158–59, 160, 172–73
reconciliation, 16–17, 19, 33, 55, 168
redemption, 37
Reeves, Michael, 15n8
relevance, 84–85, 86, 88, 117, 157
repentance, 33, 86n37
repetition, 117, 118, 121
resolutions, 50–51
resurrection, 19–20, 37
Revelation, book of, 73–74
Richards, E. Randolph, 92
Ricoeur, Paul, 79n19, 148
Righter Major, Sarah, 49
risk-taking, 176–77
Robinson, Haddon W., 79, 88n46, 114, 142, 147
Robinson, Ken, 157, 172, 177, 183–84
Romero, Oscar, 11, 48
Rose, Lucy Atkinson, 97
Runco, Mark A., 159n9, 162n25
Ryle, J. C., 101, 129

Salguero, Gabriel, 78
Samaritan woman, 45
Samuel (prophet), 27
sanctification, 18, 30
Sanneh, Lamin, 84n34
saturated fat, 131–33, 136
Sawyer, R. Keith, 162n25, 163
Scherer, Paul, 39–40, 69, 82
Scotland, 50
Seneca, 161n21
sermon length, 101–4, 121, 123–24, 126–27
Shakespeare, William, 155
sickness, 28–30
silence, 64–65, 66

Silverman, Art, 131–33, 136
Simonton, Dean Keith, 161, 182
simplicity, sophisticated, 105–10, 112–13, 122, 123, 128–29
sin, 19, 32, 35, 47, 168
Smith, Christian, 23–24, 25
Smith, James K. A., 57
solitude, 64–65, 66
Solnit, Rebecca, 181
Soskice, Janet Martin, 76
South Africa, 48, 70–71, 109, 169–70
Spain, 50, 83
specificity, 134–36, 137–38
Sternberg, Robert J., 157n3
stewardship, 54–55, 56
Stewart, James S., 86
stories, 145–47
Stott, John, 82
Strauss, Valerie, 144n17
Strunk, William, Jr., 127
study, 67–70, 71, 139–42
subway social experiment, 155–57, 183
success, 56–57, 61, 122
Sunukjian, Donald R., 117
suspicion, 27–28, 29
Sweet, Leonard, 167n42
symbols, 94–96
syncretism, 82n26, 84n34, 88

Tannehill, Robert C., 150
Tanner, Kathryn, 80n20
Taylor, Barbara Brown, 155, 163n30, 166n36, 168, 169
Taylor, Gardner C., 14, 27, 47–48, 52, 79n16, 120n40, 134n2, 135, 166
Tchaikovsky, Pyotr Ilyich, 181
teenagers, 23–24
Tertullian, 68
Thomas Aquinas, 160
Throntveit, Mark A., 110n13
Tisdale, Leonora Tubbs, 86, 89–90, 94–96
transformation, 18, 26, 30, 68, 85–86, 122
    contextualized preaching, 88–89

transformational approach, 76–77n8
translation, 78, 86–87, 110, 115
Trinity, 23
Torrey, R. A., 67n65
Toy Story 2, 122
Troeger, Thomas H., 163n30
Truett, George W., 17n12, 50
Truth, Sojourner, 49, 111–12
truth telling, 19, 20–21
Tutu, Desmond, 48

under-contextualization, 74, 87–88
Up!, 122

Vanhoozer, Kevin, 168, 173
vanity, 61–62, 69
verbosity, 125–27
Villafañe, Eldin, 75
Voltaire, 101

Walton, Jonathan L., 28–29
Weingarten, Gene, 156–57, 183–84
Wesley, John, 114
White, E. B., 127
Whitehead, James D., 168n43
Widmer, Ted, 102–3
Wilder, Amos N., 164
Willard, Dallas, 64n56–57
Willimon, William H., 4
Wilson, Paul Scott, 163n30
Winfrey, Oprah, 61
Winnicott, D. W., 64
wisdom, 143
Wisdom, John, 82–83
women preachers, 45, 48–50, 111–12. See also specific individuals
woodshedding, 2–3, 4, 190, 192
workaholism, 60
Wright, N. T., 57n37
written vs. oral communication, 116–17
Wycliffe, John, 50

Yancy, Philip, 4n5

Zacchaeus, 150